CW00531359

WRITING THE WORLD
Writing as a Subject of Study

Kingston University Press,
Kingston University,
Penrhyn Road,
Kingston-upon-Thames,
Surrey KT1 2EE

Copyright © 2014 Carl Tighe
The right of Carl Tighe to be identified as the author has been asserted by him
in accordance with the Copyright, Designs and Patents Act, 1988. This workbook is distributed subject to the condition that it may not by way of trade or
otherwise, be lent, resold, hired out, copied or otherwise circulated without
prior written consent. Reasonable quotation
from the workbook should cite the author.

British Library Cataloguing in Publication Data
Tighe, Carl, 1950–
Writing the World / Carl Tighe

Library of Congress Cataloguing in Publication Data
Tighe, Carl, 1950–
Writing the World / Carl Tighe

Classification details:
1. Creative Writing – Higher Education – University –
Learning and Teaching – Techniques – Theory – History and Origins
2. Literary Studies – Literature – Creative Writing –
Literature – Literary Criticism – Literary History
3. Media Studies – Cultural Studies – Cultural Anthropology
4. Humanities – Study and Teaching

ISBN 978-1-899999-53-8

Cover image 'Ogmios' Celtic god of poets, seers, writers, healers and bards,
Albrecht Durer (1471–1528) © Trustees of the British Museum
Cover design by Dorin Rufer
Typeset by Dorin Rufer

All rights reserved. No part of this book may be reprinted or reproduced or
utilized in any form or by any electronic, mechanical, or any other means, now
known or hereafter invented, including photocopying and recording,
or in any information storage or retrieval system,
without written permission.

ACKNOWLEDGEMENTS

Parts of this book have previously appeared as seminar papers at the ESSE conferences in Turin (2010) and Istanbul (2012), the PASE conferences in Wrocław (2010) and Kraków (2012); as articles in: Writing in Education; PASE Papers 2008 – Studies in Culture and Literature and in Postscripts – The Journal of Sacred Texts and Contemporary Worlds.

This book is based on the work of many other writers and teachers. It is a work of scholarship, conducted over many years. I have tried to acknowledge all my sources and reading, but there may be someone I have left out. If so, I would be delighted to amend any future edition: please accept my apologies and feel free to contact me.

I would like to thank: the International Writers' and Translators' Centre of Rhodes for their gift of peace and quiet; the staffs of the Jüdisches Museum Berlin, the Pergamon Museum Berlin, Creswell Crags Visitors' Centre, the Weston Park Museum Sheffield, Derby City Museum and Art Gallery, the British Museum, the British Library, the Ashmolean Museum, the Pitt Rivers Museum, the Knights' Castle Museum in Rhodes, the Archaeological Museum in Rhodes, the Turin Museo Antichità Egizio, the Turin Museo Antchità, the Copenhagen Nationalmuseet and the Istanbul Arkeoloji Müzeleri; A. C. Cowie, Jack Windsor Lewis and Loreto Todd of Leeds University; John Worthen, John Turner, David Sims, David Parry, Wynn Thomas and Ian Robinson of University College Swansea; my colleagues at Derby University: Moy McCrory, Simon Heywood, Jerry Hope, Adrian Buckner, Raymond Greenoaken, Matt Clegg, Neil Campbell, Sam Kasule, Christine Berberich and Bob Hudson; my friends: Cathie and Tony Gard, Mary Niesłuchowska, Brian Wasileski, Linda Pawłowska, Shirley Franklin, Yvonne Lyon, Stevie Davies, Nigel Jenkins, Maggie Kajiyama, Cliff Holden and Otto Douer. As always my thanks go to Madeleine and Luke Rose.

ABOUT CARL TIGHE

Carl Tighe won the City Life Writer of the Year 2000 Award for his short story collection Pax: Variations and was awarded the Authors' Club Prize (2002) for his first novel Burning Worm. His short stories and radio plays have been broadcast by BBC Radio Wales, Radio Telefis Eiren, BBC Radio 4 and Radio Limerick; his fiction, poetry and essays have appeared in a wide range of magazines and have been published in Germany, Ireland, Hungary, Poland, Holland, Luxembourg, Canada and Turkey.

More information about him can be found at:
www.Carltighe.co.uk.

Also by Carl Tighe

FICTION
Rejoice! & Other Stories
KsssssS
Burning Worm
Pax: Variations
Druids Hill

NON-FICTION
Gdansk: National Identity in the Polish-German Borderlands
The Politics of Literature: Polish Writers & Communism
Writing & Responsibility
Creative Writing @ University: Frequently Asked Questions

WORKS CITED

Sonny's Lettah' (120-121pp) is reproduced with kind permission of the author, Linton Kwesi Johnson, © LKJ Music Publishers Ltd. The work appears in Selected Poems, Linton Kwesi Johnson published by Penguin (2006).

CONTENTS

1
INTRODUCTION: WHAT DOES IT MEAN TO STUDY WRITING?

This introductory chapter outlines the concerns of the book,
opening up connections within the main areas of debate about
the nature of representation in writing, the history, theory and
philosophy behind writing, and its roots as the original subject of
study from which other subjects grew. These themes are taken up
and expanded in different ways later in the book:

- Representation in Writing
- Misrepresentation

It has never been possible to 'just write' because there is much more to
writing than simply putting words on paper ...

Creative Writing has now established itself as part of academic life.
But what does it mean to study Writing? The fundamental problems
are -- and always have been -- those centred on the nature of language,
the issue of truth in writing, the limits of language and the nature of
representation in writing. And underlying any attempt to address
these issues has to address three complex and intertwined underlying
issues. Firstly there is the subject's relationship to the ancient past, to the
idea of 'the Classics' and the issues the ancients uncovered when they
started to write. Secondly there is the 'great labour' of uncovering and
recovering the various 'traditions' that make up the idea of studying
to write, including the training involved in the oral traditions that
preceded writing. Thirdly there is the relationship of contemporary
writing to the established canon of national literature, to the work of
university literature departments and to the idea of the University study.

But underlying the following discussion is the assumption that Creative Writing is not the newest subject to arrive in universities, but rather the first subject of study, the original and originating subject behind all university study, the subject underpinning the idea of the university.

Representation in Writing

The development of our species is partly the history of the development of a brain that is self-aware and capable of doing more than mapping and processing geography for the essential elements of survival. As Clive Finlayson (b.1955) has written:

> Awareness of self would seem to be a natural consequence of awareness of objects in space and time including other members of one's own species. Having got it, whether because it carried some unknown advantage or more likely a side-effect of developing a large complex brain, self-awareness was added to our complex and intricate system of information transfer and communication. It produced an animal capable of situating itself in space and time, an animal that became aware of the consequences of its own behavior and mortality...[1]

Part of this self-awareness in humans is the development of spoken language and beyond that the idea of making a mark and leaving a record in writing.

Our species has been resident in Europe for only about 30,000 years, from when the retreat of the glaciers allowed permanent settlement. From earliest times, mainly from after 18,000 BC, in Africa and in Europe humans made their mark in cave paintings and portable artworks, showing a willingness to communicate by means other than speech.[2] Cave paintings, along with notched antlers and carvings in stone and bone, are a record of sorts -- they are probably the only surviving examples of a much wider range of artwork on wood, bone and skin.

---

1 C. Finlayson, *The Humans Who Went Extinct* (Oxford: OUP, 2010), p.217.
2 A. Lamming, *Lascaux: Paintings and Engravings* (Penguin: Harmondsworth, 1959); P. G. Bahn, Journey *Through the Ice Age* (Weidenfeld & Nicholson: London: 1997); P. A. Saura Ramos, *The Cave of Altamira* (Harry M. Abrams: New York, 1999); N. Aujoulat, *The Splendour of Lascaux* (Thames & Hudson: London, 2005); C. B. M. McBurney, *The Stone Age of Northern Africa* (Penguin: Harmondsworth, 1960); S. Cole, *The Prehistory of East Africa* (Penguin: Harmondsworth, 1954); J. Cook, *Ice Age Art: Arrival of the Modern Mind* (London: British Museum, 2013).

But they are very difficult to interpret, and while they are clearly signs, they are not writing.

Writing is probably the most amazing of all the human inventions. It has brought about a revolution in the life of the entire human species and it has had the most far reaching and profound influence on all aspects of human life. It brought about a revolution that was decisive for the development of the human mind and the development of human societies. Writing is not just an aid to memory or a way of recording something for the future. It is, in its very nature, a complex technology, demanding specialized areas of the brain to work at it, and as such it needs study and practice.[3] Writing is also in its very nature, creative and enabling of creativity. With writing we can behave in a whole range of ways -- good and bad -- not open to animals or to people without writing.

What I am doing in this book is looking again at writing as a subject of study, but also as something we take very much for granted. As the philosopher Hegel said:

> What is 'familiarly known' is not properly known, just for the reason that it is 'familiar'. When engaged in the process of knowing, it is the commonest form of self-deception and a deception of other people as well, to assume something to be familiar, and let it pass on that account.[4]

Writing is an incredibly flexible tool for all kinds of communication ranging though the utterly trivial, the noble, the intellectually serious and challengingly creative, the flippant and even the kind of thing that changes the course of history. We can offer advice, guidance and information, set down a record of our origins and ancestry, make a record of the laws for all to see and understand, tell each other jokes and stories, create scripts for other people to recite or enact, describe moral and religious beliefs, satirise human conduct, direct armies, build complicated constructions like cities and space rockets, write poetry in which our deepest feelings are given expression, make a shopping list, gossip, stay in touch with family and friends in other continents,

---

3 J. Jaynes, *The Origin of Consciousness in the Breakdown of the Bicameral Mind* (Houghton Mifflin: Boston, 1976).
4 G. W. Hegel, *The Phenomenology of Mind* (Harper: New York, 1970), p. 35.

write smutty novels, limericks, rude messages on toilet walls, or 'tag' a building with graffiti. We can also do damage, disguise our motives, mislead readers, produce propaganda, forge documents, fake identities, pass on secret information, smear ex-boyfriends, girlfriends, husbands, wives and lovers, perjure ourselves, change our past, rewrite history, cheat, cover our shame, gain advantage, undermine colleagues, start wars, tell untruths, 'half-truths' and bare-faced lies.

Civilization and writing are intimately connected. While the early signs and seals made by humans were concerned with food stocks, phases of the sun and moon, charting the year and menstrual cycles, writing soon moved beyond that to become a record of taxes and accounting, to set down knowledge in science and observation in nature, and then on again to record the inner life, dreams, stories, aspirations, orders and plans. Writing became the essential element in developing civilization -- in the building and regulation of cities, in developing countries, states and empires, moving armies, conquering territory, teaching languages, developing government, making laws and regulations, passing on knowledge about food production and animal husbandry, in recording genealogies for ruling families, recording transactions and land ownership, inculcating identity and citizenship, for making all kinds of communications including propaganda. It was not possible to undertake the major building projects of the ancient world, often with a labour force of thousands, unless scribes wrote the plans, regulated, fed, paid and monitored the workforce, supplied the materials, arranged deliveries, fixed the rations, clothing and supplies for the slaves and other workers. It is no accident that the development of writing and the emergence of the first great empires of the ancient world happened at the same time and in the same places.

Writing, the ancients soon realized, is essential for any kind of complex thought where arguments and evidence need to be displayed for analysis and debate. Writing, they discovered, helped to create forms of knowledge, helped to record and analyse experience, helped to shape and develop complex thoughts about the world, helped to develop plans for the future and it soon affected the ways in which humans ordered their thoughts about themselves. The ancients also realized that *writing* something is very different from *saying* something: writing allowed return -- repeated inspection, analysis, interrogation, debate. And writing, it soon emerged, was not just speech written down. Writing is a form of speech, but a speech that is silent; it knows but does not necessarily tell everything, though in time it often reveals more than at first we understood -- it says and does not say, and what it says is open to interpretation, misunderstanding and abuse. Writing is an ambiguous creation: it is morally neutral. And with this came the realization that while writing is a human invention and a conscious human act, it is deeply problematic simply because language and writing have their own inner life: they have a kind of logic all their own and there is much about them that is not quite under human control. The act of writing things down shapes and changes them -- but often in ways we do not at first perceive. Writing something not only makes a permanent record of the thing that is said, but it often, sometimes simply by leaving things out or ignoring the context in which things are written, changes that which is written.

Conversely, writing also often reveals other, previously unnoticed aspects of that which is written. Writing is not only a record of the things we consciously set out to record. It is a record of other things too, things of which we are often barely aware. Also while writing is a part of language and in part an extension of spoken language, it is not in itself language and yet, at the same time, it is a language all of its own.[5]

There is much about writing -- its history, theory, psychological and philosophical aspects -- that we still need to explore. Because writing links private emotion and opinion with public expression and intervention, and because as writers we are never exactly sure about the importance or reception of what we are writing, writing carries with it a complex 'representational burden' that other artistic media do not.[6] That is, the act of writing -- of trying to represent thoughts and feelings in writing, of trying to show a character or create dialogue for that character to speak -- demands not only the functional ability to write, but an awareness of the nature of language, the nature of writing, the possibilities of interpretation, and an awareness of the context in which we write.

The writer's search for an appropriate word, style or a literary form that allows them to capture some recognizable aspect of the 'real' world is not just a discussion about the nature of the 'real world', about

---

5 R. Harris, *The Origin of Writing* (La Salle: Illinois, 1986).
6 Rachel Cusk, 'Author, Author', *The Guardian* (30 January 2010), p.15.

'realism' or any other style, but must take into account a wide range of considerations, all connected to the nature of writing. And to a certain extent most people who write are not fully aware of these problems or they have learned to live with them.

In many ways language and writing create and reflect reality, create and shape meaning, credit events and observations with significance. Dale Spender (b.1943) put this very precisely when she wrote:

> One of the tantalizing questions which has confronted everyone from philosophers to politicians is the extent to which human beings can 'grasp things as they really are'; yet in many ways this is an absurd question that could only arise in a mono-dimensional reality which subscribed to the concept of there being only *one* way that 'things' can be. Even if there is only one way, it is unlikely that as human beings we would be able to grasp that 'pure', 'objective' form, for all we have available is symbols, which have their own inherent limitations, and these symbols and representations are already circumscribed by the limitations of our own language.[7]

The brain can neither see nor hear; it has to interpret the signs and symbols conveyed to it by bio-electrical impulses along the nerves. It can never know or experience the 'real thing', so our understanding of the processes by which we interpret the world is not just a problem of linguistics, but strays into the realms of human psychology, anatomy and physiology. The nature of humans is part of the problem. The human ability to manipulate symbols in words as part of the interpretation of 'reality' and the 'real world' is highly complex. As Ernst Casirer (1874–1945) put it, 'language is the resolution of an inner tension, the representation of subjective impulses and excitations in definitive forms and figures.'[8]

Writing is unlike the other arts -- music, painting, sculpture, even origami -- in that we have to learn to interpret the signs before we can begin to understand it. Before we can write we have to learn what the various signs are, what sounds they represent, what meaning they carry, how they might combine: in effect we have to read the signs before we can begin to manipulate them. In order to write effectively we have to

---

7 D. Spender, *Man Made Language* (Routledge: London, 1980), p.72.
8 E. Casirer, 'Language and Myth' (1923) in P. Maranda (ed.), *Mythology* (Penguin: Harmondsworth, 1973), p.26.

become very proficient at interpreting the signs. And unlike the other arts, what is not said is included in this learning, what is hinted at, not said, left out, taken for granted. The context and the referents can be important as the signs themselves. What is actually written down is only part of the message. When we represent something in writing we are often supplying a great deal more than what is written. And to read and write we have to be very adept at following, perhaps even supplying, what the author is trying to say. Unlike the other arts which all go straight to the brain via the eye or the ear, with writing we have to learn to interpret the system of signs by which we seek to represent things. It is this element of interpretation that makes writing so different from the other arts.

Though it sounds a little convoluted, and perhaps even contradictory, before we can begin to write effectively we have to develop our conscious understanding of what it means to write. That is, we have to develop an understanding of what it means to represent things (stories, characters, our past, our ideas, our plans, our perceptions of 'the world') in writing, an understanding of what can be represented effectively in writing and some idea of the limitations of writing. This understanding and the ability to manipulate verbal and written symbols are not talents we are born with -- though we do, it seems, have an innate capacity -- they have to be acquired and developed. As Raymond Williams (1921–88) put it:

Each of us has *to learn to see*. The growth of every human being is a slow process of learning the 'rules of seeing', without which we could not in any ordinary sense see the world around us. There is no reality of familiar shapes, colours and sounds to which we merely open our eyes. The information we receive from the material world around us has to be interpreted according to certain human rules, before what we ordinarily call 'reality' forms.[9]

*

The origins of the debate about the nature of writing can be seen in the ancient world, when the effects and complications of writing were just beginning to be noticed. Writing in ancient Greece, for example, took a

---

9 R. Williams, *The Long Revolution* (Penguin: Harmondsworth, 1973), p.33.

while to spread. The Phoenician alphabet was adopted and adapted by Greek culture c. 1800–700BC, and at first writing had very little impact: then somewhere c. 740–550BC writing began to appear on gravestones, on pottery, on stone tablets and plaques: the oral compositions *The Iliad* and *The Odyssey* were set down in writing. With this, Greece is in transition from an oral to a written culture and within a short space of time we can see this process in the lives of individuals. By the time of the great 'classical' philosophers writing was well established: there were schools and gymnasiums, schools of rhetoric, public and private libraries, and there were professional teachers: there were also professional letter writers and readers for hire in the market place. And we can see this transition in action in the lives and careers of famous Greeks of the time. Socrates (469–399BC) wrote nothing but relied on talking and listening; his near contemporary, the historian Herodotus (c. 484–425BC) read his manuscripts aloud in the marketplace, just like a traditional oral storyteller. But by the following generation things were different: Plato (427–347BC), who had been a student of Socrates, wrote down Socrates' dialogues and offered criticism of Athenian writers. And in the following generation things changed again: Aristotle (384–322BC), who had studied under Plato, wrote his teaching down in books in which he theorised about writing. The ancient world, it seems, went from almost no writing to a little writing and then to literary criticism and theory in little more than three or four generations.

Writing had clearly become essential to the running of complex societies -- its invention had become a necessity. At the same time society began to acknowledge the shift from rural, feudal, tribal forms to city dwelling, democracy and early forms of capitalism: the traditional public modes of literary address through oral storytellers and poets declaiming their work at festivals and parties or in the marketplace persisted, but were steadily replaced by written records, literary works and by private reading. Writing, issues of what was written, who could write, debate about what they wrote, rapidly became political matters: the ability to write opened up politics for discussion and it was in itself a democratising pressure. In Greece the change from an oral to a literate culture was marked by increasing tension between the conservative oligarchs of traditional oral style and the aggressive democrats of the new written style: in some ways we can see this clash in the long Peloponnesian War between the empire of progressive, aggressive democratic Athens and the conservative, traditionalist empire of Sparta (431–404BC); but this change is also visible in the life and work of three writers mentioned above -- Socrates, Plato and Aristotle.

All three thinkers condemned the Athenian democracy whose freedoms they made use of. Socrates, while he read books and treasured the wisdom to be found there, was very much of the embodiment of the old style, questioning everything but writing nothing. Plato, a natural conservative, in his *Protagoras*, *Phaedrus* and in the *Seventh Letter*, defended the style and authority of orality and what he saw as 'the traditional establishment' in his writings. He clearly distrusted writing and the rising class of democratic politicians along with the increasingly powerful traders and businessmen and their populist entertainments (poetry and theatre) which turned writing into a commodity. Although he wrote a great deal, he saw writing as simple minded and inflexible. In Plato's *Phaedrus*, for example, the Egyptian god Thoth shows the king of Egypt his latest invention -- writing. The king agrees that Thoth's previous inventions have all been very useful, but when Thoth tries to explain writing as an aid to memory and a record of wisdom, the king will have none of it. He says Thoth is very much mistaken: writing, far from being an aid to memory, will simply produce forgetfulness. And rather than record wisdom, it will help people to find information without actually knowing anything. It will, says the king, allow people to remain ignorant: 'You offer an elixir of reminding, not of memory; you offer the appearance of wisdom, not true wisdom ...' Plato considered orality to be the natural condition of humanity and the more effective transmitter of tradition. Writing, Plato warned, changes everything by opening up new ways of thinking and proceeding. Nevertheless, Plato was no mindless nostalgic enemy of writing: his own written work -- *The Republic* in particular -- is highly organized and demonstrates superb literary 'finish'.

Aristotle, though he wanted to exclude all manual workers from citizenship of his ideal state, was much more a part of, and in tune with, Athenian popular culture; he took care to distinguish between the art of Rhetoric -- broadly defined as public speaking for the marketplace, courts and government -- and Poetics, which he saw as a private emotional response to the works of a writer. He clearly viewed Rhetoric and Poetics as parts of both the political life and the inner life, products of the human mind, and saw both as part of the developing business of words and writing, of placing private thoughts in the public domain. Aristotle saw the possibility of logic and rationality in writing: in literacy he saw a chance of understanding and ordering knowledge of the elements of the universe and understanding the nature of creation. Writing was the key to understanding and to knowledge, and by the time of his death most of his categories of knowledge, now used in philosophy, natural science, language and literature, had been established.[10]

As writing spread in the ancient world so ideas about the difficulties and consequences of writing also developed. In an effort to describe how writing worked the ancient Greeks used the word *mimesis* (μίμησις). For the Greeks this word applied to dance, music, painting, sculpture, poetry, dialogue and drama. However, it is in how this word applies to writing, and what writing tries to do, that some of the difficulties of writing and representation revealed themselves to the Greeks. The word *mimesis* had a wide range of meanings including: imitation, depiction, representation, mimicry, similarity, the act of resembling, the act of expression, the presentation of the self, 'doing what another has done' or 'making something like something else'.

For Plato *mimesis* was not a positive concept and when he used the term there was always a slightly pejorative and satirical edge to his thought. He felt that was a distorted refection of the real world and he developed the idea that *mimesis*, in fiction and theatre but particularly in poetry, was a secondary reality, an unintelligent imitation. Worse, he said, in book X of *The Republic*, this was often an imitation of things that were bad for society. *Mimesis* pretended to be an imitation of something, when in fact that something either did not exist or it was something that society should not imitate. For Plato this was dangerous because imaginative or creative writing often undermined and weakened the intellectual strength and judgement of society, did nothing to reveal the dilemmas of the real world and did not help to build rational decision making or to promote active citizenship simply because it was not part

10 C. Caudwell, *Illusion and Reality* (Lawrence & Wishart: London, 1977), pp.54-64; P. Anderson, *Passages from Antiquity to Feudalism* (Verso: London, 1974); J. Goody & I. Watt, 'The Consequences of Literacy', in J. Goody (ed.), *The Power of the Written Tradition*, (Cambridge University Press: Cambridge, 1968), pp.49-55.

of, and did not deal with, the 'real world'.[11] Plato's ideas are those of a political reactionary: he was trying to undermine the power of writers in order to keep the rapidly developing Greek literary culture out of the hands of the masses: he did not particularly like the emerging Greek democracy and would probably have been happier in a society run by an oligarchy where the undifferentiated populace toiled away, just slightly better off than their slaves, and at the weekends enjoyed traditional oral forms of entertainment.

Aristotle was far more in tune with democracy and its commercial tastes. When he wrote of *mimesis* he quietly took argument with his teacher. He used *mimesis* to mean something rather different and less judgemental than Plato. Aristotle believed that imitation of all kinds was basic to humanity, that it came naturally to humans and that much of the process of learning in children was achieved through imitation. This, he thought was why people delighted in seeing well-made images and in reading well-made literary representations, since through them people came to understand the nature of things and 'work out what each thing is'. Aristotle differentiated between the role of Rhetoric and the role of Poetics; he understood rhetoric as an attempt to move people to a particular course of action through public speaking, and saw Poetics as an attempt to release emotion -- *catharsis* -- something more internal, personal and even private. Where Plato had been concerned with the function of poetry in society, Aristotle was more concerned with the manipulation of language and the creation and appreciation of literature as function of conscious human nature.

Aristotle used the word *mimesis* to mean that writing of all kinds (but particularly stories, poetry and theatre) did not simply represent or imitate something that actually existed; he was clear that writing fabricated, built a construct, made an artificial creation. Writing, he insisted, was not reality or even an imitation of reality; it had a relationship to the world, but was not the world; writing represented the world in its own way, but writing was a separate entity: writing was writing.[12] *Mimesis*, he said, was what distinguished Rhetoric from Literature; the aim of *mimesis* was *catharsis*, and in his book *Poetics* he elucidated the rules for producing successful mimetic effects. In saying this, even at this early

---

11 Plato, *The Republic* (Penguin: Harmondsworth, 1968), p.370.
12 Aristotle, *Poetics* (Penguin: Harmondsworth, 1996), pp.6-7.

date, Aristotle marked out language, writing and issues of representation as a legitimate area of intellectual interest and subject of study.

Interest in *mimesis* in writing may have begun with the earliest writing in ancient Greece, but it has been with us ever since. Sir Philip Sydney (1554-86) referred to Aristotle's idea of *mimesis* as 'a representation, counterfeiting or figuring forth -- to speak metaphorically, a speaking picture -- with this end, to teach and delight'.[13] In writers of the Renaissance period it is quite common to see a connection being made to imitation and the notion of 'counterfeiting' or falsity of some kind. Shelley too, in his *A Defence of Poetry* (written 1820, published posthumously 1840), pointed out that 'all things exist as they are perceived', and went on to say that 'language is arbitrarily produced by the imagination and has relation to thoughts alone'.[14] In modern times the Swiss linguist Ferdinand de Saussure (1857–1913) took up Aristotle's ideas to develop the notion of language and the way it is used by individuals, and the idea that words could be seen as a system of linguistic signs and referents which could be analysed as 'the signifier' and 'the signified'.[15] Writers and philosophers like Ludwig Wittgenstein (1889–1951), Arthur Koestler (1905–83), Marshall McLuhan (1911–80), Roland Barthes (1915–80), Paul de Mann (1919–83) and Jacques Derrida (1930–2004) have extended the debate about mimesis and representation in writing, and out of their analyses came semiotics and semiology (the study of sign systems) and post-modern 'deconstruction' theory.[16] In one way or another, *mimesis* is the dominant trend, the underlying theme and main tradition of all Western art -- visual and literary -- and the driving force behind the idea of writing.[17]

In English we do not use the word *mimesis* very often. We prefer

---

13 P. Sydney, *A Defence of Poetry*, ed., J. A. Van Dorsten, (1595: Oxford University Press: Oxford, 1997), p. 25.

14 D. H. Reiman & S. B. Powers (eds.), *Shelley's Poetry and Prose*, (Norton: New York, 1977), p.505.

15 F. de Saussure, *Course in General Linguistics* (1916: Fontana/Collins: Glasgow, 1977).

16 L. Wittgenstein *Philosophical Remarks* (Blackwell: London, 1975); A. Koestler, *The Act of Creation* (Pan: London, 1964); P. de Mann, *Aesthetic Ideology* (University of Minnesota Press: Minnesota, 1996); J. Derrida, *Of Grammatology* (Johns Hopkins University Press: Baltimore, 1976); M. McLuhan, *The Medium is the Massage: An Inventory of Effects*, (Penguin: Harmondsworth, 1967); R. Barthes, *Elements of Semiology* (Hill and Wang: New York, 1968).

17 E. Auerbach, *Mimesis: The Representation of Reality in Western Literature* (Princeton University Press: Princeton, 1953).

the word imitation; but in reference to art and writing we often use *representation*. In Latin this word was a compound of re (again) + *presentare*; to represent meant to show, show again, or show repeatedly -- literally re-present; or it indicated an image or symbol that stood in for something else which was not itself present. From this root we can see how signs might stand for or represent sounds and words, and how words might stand for or represent things or ideas.

Representation is very similar to *mimesis* and just as complex: it has a long and varied presence in philosophy, art, art history, historiography, media studies, theatre, film, cinema, computer systems, political theory, linguistics, semiotics, psychology, psychoanalysis, political theory, literary theory, and in the history of writing.[18] In addition there are English words that cover specific aspects of the idea: 'emulation, mimicry, dissimulation, doubling, theatricality, realism, identification, correspondence, depiction, verisimilitude, resemblance'.[19] The Oxford English Dictionary (OED) has shown that representation also has a wide range of connected and related meanings: to call up by description, portrayal or imagination: to place a likeness of something before the mind or senses: to serve as an image, likeness or reproduction of something: to describe, depict, symbolize or act as the embodiment of something: to stand for something; to correspond to something: to be a specimen of something: to fill the place of or be a substitute for someone or something: an appearance or impression, especially of a work of art portraying something: the act of expressing or denoting something by means of a symbol, image, act or exhibition: in the theatre the act of denoting a character, action or set of events by performance on the stage: the act of placing a fact etc. before another by means of discourse: a statement or account, especially one intended to convey a particular view or impression in order to influence an opinion or action.

The more we know about writing, the more we realize just how complex the mental processes involved in using this aspect of the mind and its revolutionary technology really are. Writing and language not only enable us to represent the world in words, allowing us to get ideas

18 C. J. Brodsky, *The Imposition of Form: Studies in Narrative Representation and Knowledge* (Princeton University Press: Princeton, 1987); M. Krieger, (ed.), *The Aims of Representation: Subject, Text, History* (Columbia University Press: New York, 1987); R. Williams, *The Long Revolution* (Penguin: Harmondsworth, 1973).
19 M. Potolsky, *Mimesis* (Routledge: London, 2006), p.1.

out of one head and into another, but language also shapes and defines our ideas for us. And these topics -- writing and representation -- are so closely connected to the roots of the subject and its nature that it is hardly possible to consider the one without engaging with the other. For a writer, issues about the nature of writing and the problems of representation are intimately connected to their struggle not only to find the right word or the right formula of words, but to find the right literary form and the most effective method of presentation for the particular thing they are trying to say. Writing is like taking a verbal snapshot of a continually changing inner personal landscape as it responds to the continually changing external cultural context, using a medium that is itself constantly changing, shifting and evolving. And for the writer these problems don't go away: they keep coming back in different ways and they are with a writer all their working, thinking life. We have little choice but to acknowledge the ability of language and writing to create, challenge, compromise and transmit ideas and values, and to consider these as complex aspects and products of the human mind. In all these areas of meaning language is central to social and individual human experience: without language human society cannot exist and without society human language cannot survive: without language a person is barely human.

Misrepresentation

Contemporary writers -- like the writers of the ancient world -- face many problems and issues in understanding and practising their craft; but if language and writing allow us to get ideas out of one head into another, to represent our thoughts about the world around us, they also allow us to lie, cheat and misrepresent the world and each other. Plato was sure that all writers were liars of one kind or another and because they were a bad influence -- particularly on young people, and mainly in undermining what he thought of as 'good citizenship' -- he wanted them banned from Athens until they could prove themselves otherwise. Certainly writing, as a morally neutral activity, can be made to represent and misrepresent the world. In the Thesaurus the word 'misrepresent' brings up some interesting synonyms including: distort, misinterpret, satirise, misteach, falsehood and untruth. But misrepresentation is not the opposite of representation: it is shorthand for a whole range of other 'takes' on what writing can do. Down the ages there have been a great variety of important and often inspired fakes, frauds, forgeries, counterfeits, imitations, copies and plagiarisms. In 1999 it was estimated that in the Far East, China and the countries of the former Soviet bloc something like 90 per cent of publishing was concerned with pirated texts, losing £200,000,000 a year to British publishers and authors.[20]

But perhaps to use the word 'misrepresentation' may be to prejudice the case. Since the mid-twentieth century we have had to develop a flexible attitude to ideas of 'truth' and literary creativity: in literary theory one man's outrageous fake or forgery is another man's equally authentic, creative and complex 'othering', a work of literary genius. The borderline between fiction and an outright lie has become increasingly blurry.

For example, Thomas Chatterton (1752–70) invented the fifteenth-century Bristol poet 'Thomas Rowley', and his faked Spencerian poems with an archaic vocabulary were collected after Chatterton's suicide and taken by many to be authentic. Even when the poems were revealed as fake, the Romantic poets were not offended -- indeed Wordsworth and Keats saw only what they took to be the work of a genuinely talented poet expressed in an unusual way. Wordsworth called Chatterton a 'marvellous boy'.

William Henry Ireland (1777–1835) is mainly remembered as the man who plugged into the growing cult of bardolatry to forge Shakespeare's plays, deeds and signatures using Elizabethan parchments he found at his work in a lawyer's chambers. He fabricated two Shakespeare plays -- *Vortigern and Rowena* and *Henry II* -- and so successful was his work that he succeeded in fooling several experts of the day. The playwright Sheridan actually produced *Vortigern* at Drury Lane in 1796. However, after this disastrous production the press and critics openly mocked him and Ireland, who knew he could not keep up the pretence of finding documents in an old chest, was forced to admit his activities. Later Ireland went on to write a volume of *Confessions* in which he openly confessed his fraud. He said he had fabricated the documents in order to please his father, William Ireland, and speak to him through the medium of the 'rare' documents. His father, it seems, was fascinated by antiquarian

20 B. Turner (ed.), *The Writer's Handbook* (Macmillan: London, 1999), pp.240-41.

matters but had no interest in his son. When the son confessed to the fraud the father simply refused to believe it.

In the late eighteenth century James McPherson (1736–96) conned money from various sources to translate a Gaelic poem by a poet he called Ossian into English. The poems appeared in 1762 and 1763 and were collected in 1765. They were enormously influential, and their popularity spread far beyond Britain where they were popular with Napoleon, Goethe and Herder. The wild and romantic emphasis on Celtic mythology and an 'untamed' past fed into the Gothic Revival, the poetry of Romanticism and also helped fuel the novels of Sir Walter Scott. McPherson went on to publish a great many other scholarly historical works and to become an MP. However, his failure to produce the original manuscripts for the poems did cause some to suspect that they were not authentic, and after his death a Committee of Inquiry concluded that he had made free with his translations of other Gaelic work to produce poems which, though clearly works of enormous labour and poetic talent, displayed scant knowledge of Gaelic, were not 'authentic' and most definitely not the work of a poet called Ossian.

McPherson was not the only Celt to feel their cultural and political standing was impaired by the poor reputation of their national literature. In Wales Iolo Morganwg (better known as antiquarian Edward Williams) started a Celtic revival by 'discovering' the literary culture of the bards in certain and ancient poems he claimed to have found, but which he had in fact written, and by instituting the Eisteddfod.[21] A similar feeling was growing in mainland Europe too. In Finland, Elias Lönnrot crafted *The Kalevala* (1835), a 22,000-line national epic poem based on traditional oral songs and performances from Karelia. Unlike MacPherson's efforts, however, the poem was created from genuine research on seven long field trips to eastern Finland in the years 1828–42. These songs helped forge a modern Finnish national consciousness, awareness and identity: but Lönnrot was quite clear he was not the 'original' author and he did not pretend that this was a long-lost national masterpiece that he had discovered and 'translated'. He was simply a collector, editor and interpreter of original materials.[22]

---

21 The main annual national Welsh language festival of literature, music and performance.

22 E. Lönnrot, (translated by Francis Peabody Magoun jnr.) *The Kalevala: or Poems of the Kalevala District* (Cambridge, Mass.: Harvard University Press, 1963).

The fashion for faking evidence to support national identity was particularly useful in Eastern Europe, where national identity tended to be hotly, and often violently, contested. The drive to bolster the powerful national identities of the Russian, Prussian and Austrian Empires and their right to rule, and the struggle of the 'smaller' national identities to get out from under the control of these empires throughout the eighteenth, nineteenth and twentieth centuries, led some scholars to forge evidence to support their claims. In general though, manufactured 'evidence' tended to be archeological rather than literary. In Mecklenburg, for example, in the 1760s, a goldsmith called Sponholz forged a series of clay statuettes known as 'the Prillwitz Idols' to support the idea of Slav claims to large areas of the Elbe and Baltic. These idols became very popular, and bedeviled real archeological work, towards the end of the nineteenth century as Poles struggled to revive their partitioned homeland. Later, German Nationalists began to use archaeology as a means of underpinning their claim to be the bringers of culture in the East. On that basis, the Nazis claimed 'Lebensraum' in the east and around Lublin Gruppenführer Odilio Globocnik, a passionate amateur archaeologist and an equally passionate Nazi, was charged with destroying any and all evidence that contradicted Nazi claims. In 1942 Globocnik, claimed he had discovered an ancient Germanic settlement at Zamość and obtained permission from Himmler to 'restore' the place to its true 'Nordic' character. To do this he expelled 110,000 Poles.[23]

Perhaps the most damaging and long lasting literary fraud of the nineteenth century was that of the *Protocols of the Elders of Zion*. The document first surfaced in St Petersburg in 1903, and it purported to be a secret record of a Jewish plan to take over the world by infiltrating the major financial, legal and media organizations.[24] Almost certainly the *Protocols* was written by a Tsarist secret policeman called Pyotr Ivanovich Rachovsky and it was aimed at a modernizing national finance minister called Sergei Witte in a clash between the reformers and the traditionalists that prefigured the Russian Revolutions of 1905 and 1917. But outside its immediate historical context Hitler referred to it in *Mein Kampf* and it has proved very important to anti-Semites, Nazis, neo-Nazis and anti-

---

23 K. Sklenář, *Archaeology in Central Europe: the First 500 Years* (St Martin's Press: New York, 1983).
24 N. Cohn, *Warrant for Genocide: The Myth of World Conspiracy and the Protocols of the Elders of Zion* (Penguin: Harmondsworth, 1970).

Zionists who take it to be an authentic statement of 'Jewish ambition' to rule the world. Nowadays it is still popular in Poland, Syria, Saudi Arabia and Iran.[25]

Australia, perhaps because it suffered from a literary inferiority complex clearly connected to the same kind of nationalist desire and opinion that helped Ossian do his work to support the idea of Scotland, has also seen a considerable literary hoax which reverberates to this day. In October 1943 the poetry editor Max Harris received a package of seventeen poems from Ethel Malley, the sister of a recently deceased young poet called Ern Malley. Harris was convinced that Australia had finally got a poet of genius and printed the work, called *The Darkening Ecliptic* in a special issue of his magazine *Angry Penguins*. The poems had a considerable impact. Only gradually and painfully did it emerge that all the poems had been written in a single afternoon by two bored but very talented young poets on military service. Since then a great many talented writers have emerged from Australia, and it is difficult now to fully comprehend the impact of this revelation on a colonial Australia which at that time was made to feel inferior to 'the home country' and had very little to offer of high culture and even less of a literature of its own.[26]

However, the late twentieth century also saw a massive proliferation of hoaxes and frauds in which the Third Reich, the Holocaust and Hitler, along with a massive trade in Nazi memorabilia, figure largely. In the early 1980s rumours began to circulate that Hitler's diaries had been found and were being offered for sale. Among many people drawn into this tale, and later embarrassed by it, the historian Hugh Trevor-Roper was asked to fly to Zurich to examine documents which lay in a sealed Handelsbank vault with a view to authenticating them. The German newspaper *Stern* was offering to sell foreign publication rights, Rupert Murdoch and *The Times* were bidding. Roper knew that Hitler hated writing anything and there was no record of him ever keeping a diary, but when Roper arrived in Zurich he was confronted by fifty-eight volumes of diaries -- 'a whole coherent archive covering 35 years' -- and reports from three handwriting experts authenticating the documents.

---

25 M. Katsoulis, *Telling Tales: A History of Literary Hoaxes* (Constable: London, 2009), pp.47-53.
26 M. Heyward, *The Ern Malley Affair* (Faber: London, 1993); P. Carey, *My Life as a Fake* (Faber: London, 2004).

Stern auctioned the rights for a massive sum -- said to be over \$3.5-4 million. However, almost as soon as the diaries began to appear they were proved to be fake by analysis of the paper, ink and binding glue. The East German secret service was suspected of planting the materials to embarrass the West, but it turned out that they were the work of a talented painter and forger called Konrad Kujau.[27]

The blurring of boundaries between fiction and autobiography, while it provided grist to the mill for academics and boosted an interest in literary theory, also provided a series of literary frauds. James Frey's *A Million Little Pieces* (2003), Margaret B. Jones's *Love and Consequences: a Memoir of Hope and Survival* (1997) and Misha Defonseca's *Misha: a Memoire of the Holocaust* (1997), though they were at first accepted and even sold well, were all revealed as fakes of one kind or another.[28] Perhaps the most complex and scandalous of these fakes and misrepresentations was Binjamin Wilkomirski's *Fragments: Memoirs of a Childhood 1939–1948* (1996). It was first published in German in 1995 and caused an immediate stir: its author claimed to have survived both Majdanek and Auschwitz and it purported to be one of the very rare testimonials of a Jewish child from Latvia who had survived Nazi genocide. Among many enthusiastic reviews it was hailed as 'one of the great works about the Holocaust', and ranked alongside works by Elie Wiesel, Anne Frank, Paul Celan and Claude Lanzmann. It won the National Jewish Book Award in the US, the *Jewish Quarterly* Literary Prize in the UK, and Le Prix de Memoire de la Shoah in France. It was translated into sixteen languages. Wilkomirski was invited to tour the world relating his story, and he gave moving, tearful interviews, readings and performances, often to Holocaust survivors along with lectures on his experience, and several appearances on TV in documentary films. He also helped set up counselling for Holocaust survivors.

However, almost from the first there were those who doubted the book's authenticity. In February 1995 a Swiss journalist called Hanno Helbling contacted the German publishers to say that the author of the book was not Binjamin Wilkomirski, a Holocaust survivor. In August 1998 Swiss-Jewish writer Daniel Ganzfried, writing in *Die Weltwoche*, also began to voice doubts about the author and the book. Liepman

---

27 R. Harris, *Selling Hitler: The Story of the Hitler Diaries* (Faber: London, 1986).
28 Donna Lee Brian, 'Non-Fiction Writing Research' in J. Kroll & G. Harper, *Research Methods in Creative Writing* (Palgrave: London, 2013).

AG, Wilkomirski's literary agents in Switzerland, engaged Dr Stefan Maechler to look into his credentials and investigate the authenticity of the book.[29] On the basis of Maechler's findings and her own research, Elena Lappin, editor of the *Jewish Quarterly*, wrote a long article in which she voiced serious doubts about the reliability of the author.[30]

According to the best evidence available Wilkomirski was neither Jewish nor Latvian and he had never been a concentration camp inmate. Indeed he had visited the camps only as an adult tourist. He was in fact Swiss musician Bruno Grosjean, born on 12 February 1941, several years later than he claimed. His mother Yvonne had been injured in a road accident: after the accident she gave birth, but was forced to give up her son for adoption. Records show that Bruno, aged three, was first fostered by Frau Aeberhard in a village near Nidau, where he had been kept short of food and starved of affection. Later he had been taken to an orphanage in Adelboden and then in the autumn of 1945 he had been adopted by Dr and Mrs Dossekke, a childless couple in late middle-age. Bruno lived with them in the prosperous bourgeois district of Zurichberg in Zurich. Their relationship to Bruno seems to have been emotionally cool and physically distant, but in every sense supportive, responsible and caring.

As a result of their investigations the German publishers announced at the 1999 Frankfurt book fair that they had withdrawn *Fragments*. The Spanish and Swedish editions were cancelled. The English-language edition of the book, available in the USA, Canada, the UK and the Commonwealth, had sold 32,800 copies and was quietly allowed to go out of print. Most of those who once honored Wilkomirski have now withdrawn their awards. In Zurich a magistrate even investigated whether charges of fraud should be brought against the author.

While the media fuss about the book has now died down, there is a general question as to why so many people were willing to believe the book and the author, and why so few realized it was a fake. And there is a lingering and very awkward question as to what the fact of its fakeness means.

Fragments appeared against a backdrop of political developments and intellectual difficulties where the Second World War and the Holocaust were in the public domain in a way they had never been before. This

---

29 S. Maechler *The Wilkomirski Affair: A Study in Biographical Truth*, (Picador: London, 2001).
30 E. Lappin, 'The Man With Two Heads', Granta, no.66 (Summer, 1999), pp.7-65.

included reaction to the collapse of communism, a move to the right in political opinion throughout Europe, a resurgence of extreme right-wing opinion and a rise in neo-Nazi political activity, and a steady resurgence of intolerance, xenophobia and anti-Semitism. Paul de Man's influential post-modernist literary theories were discovered to have their roots in his silence about his complicity with Nazism in wartime Belgium; David Irving was suing Deborah Lipstadt for daring to call him a Holocaust denier; Jewish organizations tried to remove a Catholic shrine from Auschwitz and turn the place into a purely Jewish memory; debates about the historical 'truth' of Claud Lanzmann's *Shoah*, a filmed oral record of anti-Semitism, and Steven Spielberg's *The Last Days*, a filmed oral history of the Holocaust with testimony sufficient to run continuously for fifty years, were also developing rapidly. Perhaps more importantly, Wilkomirski's book appeared as Switzerland reassessed its wartime connection with, and its post-war debt to, Nazism. It was an atmosphere in which any memoir of the Holocaust revealed to be false played into the hands of neo-Nazi Holocaust deniers.[31] For purely personal needs he has unwittingly undermined the fact of the Holocaust, and by drawing attention to his own unreliability as a 'witness' made other witnesses less credible. He had offered ammunition to Holocaust deniers.

Fragments brought into question the possibility of autobiographical and historical 'truth', and it did this at the very moment when the Holocaust itself had become a historical and philosophical 'issue'. The timing of these two things makes it difficult, but we have to wonder what the Holocaust and the Nazis have come to mean to us. The Nazis are a seemingly endless source of fascination and the basis for countless fictional books and war films. But can we now accept every fictional invention about them? Are they nothing more than a literary lightning-rod for outlandish imaginings and sadomasochistic writing?

In contrast to Wilkomirski there is the case of the 'apostle of the wilderness' known as Grey Owl. He too felt obliged to legitimate himself by creating a new personality and history to suit the things he wanted to write. Born Archibald Belaney in Hastings in 1888, Grey Owl had a rather troubled and dubious life, most of which did not emerge until

---

31 D. Lehman, *Signs of the Times* (Andre Deutsche: London, 1991); D. Lipstadt, *Denying the Holocaust: The Growing Assault on Truth and Memory* (The Free Press: New York, 1993); R. J. Evans, *In Defence of History* (Granta: London, 1997); M. Lee, *The Beast Reawakens* (Warner: London, 1997).

his death in 1938. Belaney attended Hastings Grammar School before starting work as a clerk with a lumber company. However, his boyhood trick of making bombs backfired when he set fire to the lumberyard and was sacked. His aunts moved him to Canada in 1906, to study agriculture. In Ontario he became a fur trapper. In 1910 he married and began to create a Native American identity for himself, using the name Grey Owl. In 1915 he enlisted in the Canadian Black Watch, claiming he was an unmarried trapper with no next of kin and that he had seen military service in Mexico with the US 28th Dragoons. He was sent to fight in France, where he was twice wounded. When his second wound became gangrenous he was shipped to England for treatment in 1916–17. In England he married again, without divorcing his first wife, but this marriage failed almost immediately and in the autumn of 1917 he was shipped back to Canada and honourably discharged from the army.

In 1925 he met and married a Mohawk Iroquois woman named Anahareo. She persuaded him to stop trapping animals and to become a conservationist. By 1928 he had become well enough known to feature in the National Parks Service film *Beaver People*. Writing as Grey Owl he produced a series of articles for the magazine *Canadian Forest and Outdoors* in the years 1930–35. His first book appeared in 1931. Later that year he started the work of creating a beaver sanctuary and the following year his daughter Shirley Dawn, was born. By this time Grey Owl claimed to have been born in Mexico, that his father was Scottish settler, his mother was an Apache and that they had both appeared as part of Wild Bill Hickok's Wild West Show. He also claimed to have been a scout in the Indian Wars of the 1870s.

In the years 1935–36 and again in 1937–38, Grey Owl toured Canada and England lecturing to promote his books, which were proving to be incredibly popular. He appeared, his skin dyed to darken it, in Native American costume. By this stage he was said to be drinking heavily and eating only onions. Apparently he had been an alcoholic for several years and the stress of touring exacerbated his condition. Back in Canada, in April 1938, he collapsed at his cabin in the woods and died from pneumonia.

In his lifetime he produced five notable books on the Canadian wilderness and the frontier life, many of which were translated into Polish, Russian, French, Spanish and Serbian: Richard Attenborough made a film called *Grey Owl* (1999) starring Pierce Brosnan. David and Richard Attenborough had seen *Grey Owl* speak at the London Palladium and clearly he influenced them both. Although Grey Owl was a fake Indian, an alcoholic and a bigamist, this is not necessarily what he is remembered for. Now he is celebrated as one of the very first eco-warriors.

This brief selection of fakes and frauds shows just how complex this issue of representation and misrepresentation has become. Indeed the very notion of misrepresentation begins to seem as inexhaustible as fiction. And yet, to a certain extent, this misrepresentation is embedded in the topic of representation from its very first appearance in the discussions of Plato and Aristotle: and we have accustomed ourselves to, even absorbed, the problems. Jorge Luis Borges (1899–1986) seemed to anticipate the confusions, complications and accommodations that lay ahead for scholarship when he wrote in the late 1940s or early 1950s, only slightly tongue in cheek, of Pierre Menard as the author of *Quixote*:

> Those who have insinuated that Menard dedicated his life to writing a contemporary *Quixote* calumniate his illustrious memory.
> He did not want to compose another *Quixote* -- which is easy -- but the *Quixote itself*. Needless to say, he never contemplated a mechanical transcription of the original; he did not propose to copy it. His admirable intention was to produce a few pages which would coincide -- word for word and line for line -- with those of Miguel de Cervantes.[32]

And much in the same vein, Alasdair Gray (b.1934), in his novel *Lanark*, made play with the idea of fakery and plagiarism, by saying: 'I am prostituting my most sacred memories into the commonest possible words and sentences. When I need more striking sentences or ideas I steal them from other writers, usually twisting them to blend with my own.' He went on to define plagiarism thus:

> There are three kinds of literary theft in this book:
> BLOCK PLAGIARISM, where someone else's work is printed as a distinct typographical unit, IMBEDDED PLAGIARISM, where stolen words are concealed within the body of the narrative, and DIFFUSE PLAGIARISM, where scenery, characters, actions or

---

32 Jorge Luis Borges, *Labyrinths* (Harmondsworth: Penguin, 2000), pp.65-6.

novel ideas have been stolen without the original words describing them. To save space these will be referred to hereafter as Blockplag, Implag, and Difplag.[33]

He went on to point out that what we take to be original is made up of words that have been used and reused millions of times before. Since Gray wrote this the possibility of plagiarism and fakery has increased massively through the development of digital technology and the internet. But there fraud may not be fraud at all, the law is still unclear. In the past if a newspaper item caught your eye, you clipped it out and sent it to a friend to share. This seemed fairly harmless. But now with a few key strokes it is possible to 'cut and paste' and circulate a whole article to hundreds of contacts and Facebook friends all over the world. Using the same technology it is possible to commission an undergraduate essay, written to order, from an agency, and in order to defeat this there are organizations like 'Turnitin' devoted entirely to frustrating plagiarism, intellectual theft and cheating within universities. 'Writing' -- which when it does not mean updating Facebook or texting, increasingly means blogging -- has become a kind of cottage industry.

What is clear about most of the cases of misrepresentation outlined above is not only that they somehow jumbled up and blurred categories which might have been thought separate, or even that they were an individual response to a deep psychological need, but simply that they interrupted the flow of literary history, changed perceptions for those who wrote afterwards as to what was and was not misrepresentation in writing, changed the status of the writer and the status of the thing that is written.

Whereas earlier writers may have felt that counterfeiting, forgery, plagiarism, fakery and imitation somehow compromised the genuine worth of a work of literature, post-modern writers like Umberto Eco and Jean Baudrillard revel in the way that literature can playfully dissolve and incorporate these categories. Critics, as Terry Eagleton has made clear, refer to this casual attitude to originality and plagiarism, this literary uncertainty, with the theoretical label 'inter-textuality', but the certainty of such a label (and the possibility of a theoretical approach) could also be a kind of misrepresentation.[34] And with the advent of

---

33 A. Gray, *Lanark* (Canongate: Edinburgh, 2007), p.485
34 Terry Eagleton, 'Faking it: The Art of Literary Forgery', *The Guardian* (6 June 2002).

online 'fanfic', where fans write their own stories around established series, with characters from one programme, novel or series crossing into another -- where Dr Who has sex with Buffy the Vampire Slayer -- the situation has become even more complex. Now we are not so certain about any of these things:

> So what happens to culture when fanfic becomes the dominant economic model in publishing and the leader in cultural values -- is that even possible? Surely derivative works have to be derived from something 'original'. With *Fifty Shades of Grey* this ceases to be the case, and, as we have seen, fanfic offers many tools for recycling (AU, crossover, mashup, self-insert, Mary Sue, the 12 varieties of slash etc) which takes the recombination of texts into the exponential. It is possible that with the enchanted duplication systems of fan-based epub, we might have arrived at a point in history where we've accumulated enough cultural material from the past for fans to remix indefinitely, and as they can now sell this content to each other this becomes a boom industry where none existed before. However, the point where fans become the creators, and a derivative work becomes the new original is also the point at which the culture industries stop needing to create anything new. Fanfic begets fanfic, which then in turn becomes mainstream which then begets further fanfic and so on. When we reach that point our future will not be fifty, but fifty thousand, shades of grey. [35]

And even then, this is only at the macro end of literary production: at the micro end we have all the opportunities for misrepresentation embodied in functional literacy, poor writing and unintentional error, the vagaries of English spelling, homophony and loan words, and the massive potential for ambiguity inherent in English grammar and sentence structure.

What is certain is that the intimate connection between how an individual sees the world and then puts their perceptions into writing has become much more attenuated and difficult to get at or define: the advent of the internet has meant a massive growth in the possibility of writing badly and still getting into the public domain; and the notions of originality and authenticity in writing are under considerable pressure.

Unlike the writers of the ancient world who, for the most part,

---

35 E. Morrison, 'In the Beginning There was Fan Fiction: From the Four Gospels to Fifty Shades', *The Guardian* (13 August 2012).

inhabited tiny city-states where the alphabet was the latest bit of techno-kit and great power could accrue from mastering it, students of writing now graduate into a contradictory, multi-voiced, multi-cultural, multi-media world of playful functional literacy, where, with the advent of new technologies, the possibilities and limits of creative civic participation are as yet uncharted and where the articulate, critical and active literate citizenship of the writer, when it is not irrelevant or masked by some convenient political buzz-word, is often seen as a form of dissidence, a kind of protest, a threat. But this, for all the technological distance, brings us to our starting point -- to speech as a function of human society, to writing as a complex function of the human mind and the basis of civilization. It also brings us back to the reason the ancients saw the practical study of writing, words and language as an essential intellectual discipline, a preparation for both private and public life, and as central to citizenship.

All writing, even the *idea* of writing, has social implications and resonances for those who seek political power, for those who seek to control writers and for those who seek pleasure and enlightenment by reading what writers have written. Writers write in private, nobody controls them while they work. It is only when they have written something that wealth, control, censorship, ownership, controversy, rejection, poverty, jealousy, respect, fame, influence or neglect all become possibilities. It is precisely because writing is so difficult to control and so unpredictable in its effect that it is personal and social, private and public. Because it puts private thought in the public domain, brings the public world into private life, transfers ideas from one head into another, records our inner thoughts about the external world, and looks as if, somehow, writing really does accurately represent our world to us, that it is a liberating, unsettling, culturally specific, often highly political, troublesome and contentious act.

For writers language is raw creative material. Much as a painter -- who is involved in a different kind of representation -- carefully considers different kinds of paint (poster, water colour, oils, acrylic), and a sculptor considers carefully the differences between kinds of metal, rock or wood -- so writers are concerned with the act of writing, with questions about the nature of language, with sifting the vernacular for the current and possible meaning and content of words, the precise choice of idiom, vocabulary and register. It is possible to examine various areas of representation, but at the same time we have to see it as one of many aspects and products of the human mind. However we define the human mind, we can say with certainty that its development is bound up with language. We can see the human mind as if at an angle in the issues surrounding writing and language, since they give us a view into the life of the mind and record and express some of 'the inner life' of humans in ways that the other arts do not. We can examine how we represent things in language and some of the problems of representation in language; we can look at how we represent things in literature and at how we misrepresent them too; and we can look at the human imagination and its products, the things the human mind deems important and seeks to represent in writing and literature.[36]

Increasingly we can see writing, not simply as an imitation of the world, though it does invite us to think of it in that way, but as an independent entity, a language and message all of its own. Meaning in speech and writing is part of a series of relations or correspondences between sounds, written symbols and the world of human experience. In writing representation is the complex interplay between the mind of the writer, the theme they are working on, the world around them, the areas of the language they can access and their own talent in using it. And when we write or read, we access something represented -- a world, or at least an aspect of the world -- as seen and represented in words by our imagination. And these activities of writing and reading go far beyond ourselves to help us give meaning to the marks and dots on the page, help us to imagine things that really have very little relationship to marks on the page, and help us to understand that language and writing have their own complex interaction with the world.

To look at writing in this way is something of a balancing act. I am seeking to return to ancient sources and understanding, yet at the same time to write for the contemporary world; I am seeking to restore

---

36 J. Bronowski, *The Ascent of Man* (BBC: London, 1973); P. Lieberman, *On the Origins of Language: An Introduction to the Evolution of Human Speech* (Macmillan: New York, 1975); S. Potter, *Language in the Modern World* (Andre Deutsch: London, 1975); G. Gradol, *Language Variation and Diversity* (Open University: Milton Keynes, 1981); J. Jaynes, *The Origin of Consciousness in the Breakdown of the Bicameral Mind* (Houghton Mifflin: Boston, 1976); C. Renfrew, *Archaeology and Language* (Penguin: Harmondsworth, 1989); C. Renfrew, *Prehistory: The Making of the Human Mind* (Random House: London, 2008); D. Spender, *Man Made Language* (Routledge & Kegan Paul: London 1980).

something of the past experience of writers while questioning the assumptions of the emerging new technologies; I am engaging with how writers worked in the ancient world, but with an eye to new applications for writing in the developing technologies; I am examining issues and practices from the past while pointing out how familiar these things are still for those who write today; I want to take part (for better or worse) in a global culture and its politics but I want to do this while considering the detail of my own locale; I am negotiating between the writer as a local individual in a constantly shifting context, and the contemporary ambition to universalism; I am considering the desire for popular literature, for fame and wealth that the idea of writing seems to offer, and I am emphasizing the work, the mental processes we would like to skip; I am ignoring the temptation to substitute new technology for the elements of intellect and inner life that go into writing: I am looking at the hard-gleaned knowledge and wisdom of the ancients and wondering: where it is headed, what is its trajectory?

I am questioning, as a writer and teacher, the aspects of writing we often take for granted; I am asking broad, overlapping and fundamental questions of readers, teachers and students of writing: What is the relationship between language and writing? What is writing and where does it come from? What does writing do and what are we doing when we write? What are some of the effects (positive and negative) of writing? What are the problems of trying to represent things in writing? How do we represent and misrepresent things in writing and literature? How and why does the human mind seek to represent ideas in narratives? Are language and writing accurate and truthful? How far can we trust language or writing to tell us about the world? How are writers of today connected to writers of the past? What is the link between writing and citizenship? What can we hope to represent in writing, and can we expect to accurately represent the world in words? But I think that at this point I should return to the comment that started this chapter: it has never been possible to 'just write' because there is much more to writing than simply putting words on paper.

Directed Study

How is the idea of representation in writing connected to citizenship?

How is representation connected to the idea of the alphabet and writing?

In what way is the study of writing an intellectual preparation for anything at all, let alone for public life?

In what way is writing the original subject of study?

How is writing connected to the idea of a university?

Writing imitates something, but what?

What does it mean to say: 'For writers language is raw creative material'?

What is 'the intimate connection between how an individual sees the world and then puts their perceptions into writing'?

Why can't we 'just write'?

2
WHERE DOES LANGUAGE COME FROM? LANGUAGE IN HUMANS

This chapter looks at the development of the human mind through the development of language. It asks where language comes from and considers the growth and development of language in humans. It looks at the possibilities for language in African apes, early humans, the Neanderthals and Cro-Magnon (modern) humans. It looks at their linguistic abilities and the possibility of rivalry and interaction between the two species based in their different language abilities. This chapter also wonders how and why language is 'hard wired' into the human design, and how this talent emerged; it is concerned with the growth and development of human creative and linguistic abilities.

- Apes and Early Humans
- Neanderthals
- Cro-Magnon
- Cro-Magnon v Neanderthal

The roots of humankind go back a long way and (if we go back far enough) we share common ancestors with a great many animals. Although we share something like 98 per cent of our genes with our nearest relatives, the great apes, language and our capacity for speech are what mark us off from them. Indeed one of the most important distinctions between humans and animals is not that we smoke, drive cars, get drunk, wear hats and jewellery, marry or put on expensive underwear, but that we have a highly developed sense of language in which to represent our thoughts. Language is central to the idea of humanness, an important part of what it is to be human, a vital component in our identity as humans: language is probably the single most important product of the human mind. Compared with the communication system used by animals, human language is a much more powerful and flexible tool. The communication systems used by animals is that of basic signals -- a monkey's alarm call that says 'Snake!' cannot be modified to become: 'Snake -- oh but he's had his breakfast -- I think he's on his way home -- I judge he is no threat'. The monkey alarm call persists until the snake disappears. Human language has many additional elements that modify and underlie all its messages. We can talk about things that happened a long time ago, things that will happen in the future, things that are happening now, or things that cannot happen at all. Language is intricately interwoven with how humans think; it has become a vital instrument by which we communicate with ourselves and with each other. Our use of language is very different from that of the animals. We can move our listeners to laughter or reduce them to tears, convey great truths, hide the truth in language or simply tell atrocious lies.

The skill to produce and manipulate language is apparently innate to the species and part of what we now think of as 'the human mind'. Certainly some of our ape ancestors could speak and language certainly predated modern humans. Our nearest relatives, the great apes, share our ability only to a very limited degree: some apes -- particularly chimps -- though they cannot speak, can grasp basic elements of language. What is certain is that our survival as a species has been dependant on our ability to use and develop language and to use it to produce complex thoughts, to organize each other, to shape our environment, to gather and record useful information and to entertain ourselves. This is a rapidly developing area of scientific investigation and new discoveries are being made almost every year.

So, if language is what marks humans off from the animals, when did humans first use language, when did they first speak? These are not easy questions to answer. It is unlikely that one day apes woke up and just started to chat about the weather. Language is closely interwoven with the nature of what it is to be human, with the development of what we now call 'the human mind', and since humans evolved over a very long period of time, the answer to the problem of when humans began to speak really depends on when we think humans began. What we define as 'mind' may still be problematic, but I am using it here to indicate a range of mental activities and capacities -- including notions of psyche, intellect, reasoning, rationality, cognizance, mental capacity, conceptual ability, powers of abstract thought, perception, self-awareness and inventiveness.[37] What is certain is that humanity begins when language starts. Or as George Steiner puts it: 'Man becomes man as he enters on a linguistic stage':

> Man's passage from a natural to a cultural state -- the single major act in his history -- is at every point interwoven with his speech faculties.[38]

Apes and Early Humans

The earliest identifiable remains of our hominid ancestors, dating from 23,000,000BC, have been found in Turkey, Greece, Hungary, the Far East, India and particularly in East Africa.[39]

With the development of new techniques for analysing genes and mapping DNA, scientists have decided that the split in development between early apes and the apes that were to become human probably occurred in Africa (probably East Africa) only about 7,000,000BC. The remains of *Sahalenthropus tshadensis*, our oldest ape-human direct ancestor, were discovered in Chad, in 2005, dated from around this time.

The first of our ape ancestors to abandon the trees and walk upright was called *Orrorin Tugenensis*. Its bones, gnawed by a prehistoric leopard, were discovered about 150 miles north of Nairobi, and dated to 6,000,000BC, were found in the year 2000. Although scientists guess this ape weighed around 50 kilos and stood as high as a modern chimp, nobody is sure to what extent they could speak.

Australopithecus Afarensis, discovered in 1974 in Ethiopia, is dated to

---

37 C. Caudwell, *Illusion and Reality* (Lawrence & Wishart: London, 1977), pp.169-70.
38 G. Steiner, *Extraterritorial* (Peregrine: Harmondsworth, 1972), p.70.
39 Traditionally humans, their near relatives and ancestors were classified as Hominids. This is a very broad term meaning members of the genus *Homo*, humans and near humans, both present and past -- humans, gibbons, great apes and the extinct australopithecines. Recently a system of classification has emerged taking into account genetic discoveries and acknowledging the close relationship between humans, orangutans, gorillas and chimps, placing them together in a super-family called *Hominidae*, but dividing them by placing gorillas, orang-utan and chimps in one sub-family *Homininae* (hominines) and humans in the other sub-family *Hominini* (hominins). According to this system, *australopithecines* should now be referred to as *australopiths*. B. Wood and B. G. Richmond, 'Human Evolution: Taxonomy and Paleobiology', *Journal of Anatomy* (2000), vol. 1966, pp.19-60.

about 4,000,000 BC. This hominid walked upright, but while they could almost certainly make a variety of noises it seems unlikely they could speak in a way that we would recognize. However, their descendant, *Homo Habilis* (Handy Man), who lived 2,500,000BC, had a larger brain and a significant tool-making capacity. Fossil remains indicate social skills and, therefore, some language skills.[40] And there is evidence that the later *Australopithecus Garhi*, a hominid also discovered in Ethiopia and dated about 2,000,000BC, traded for flints outside their area of habitation, and this, almost certainly, demanded social and language skills of some kind.

Most of these early hominids did not have a highly developed Broca's speech area in the brain. This part of the brain was identified and named in 1861 by French surgeon, Pierre Paul Broca. This section of the brain, along with the Wernicke's area, discovered in 1874 by the German neurologist Carl Wernicke, were major sites for processing written and spoken language. However, while the presence of these parts of the brain in later hominids indicates that speech was a possibility, scientists conclude that the small size of the spinal cord did not give sufficient breath control to allow much speech in most of these finds, and even then the shape of the throat and mouth, the position of the tongue and larynx would not have permitted much variety or control of sound. Even so, these early hominids may well have managed a series of noises and shouts similar to those of a modern chimp.

East Africa produced new varieties of ape-humans at an incredible rate. In all varieties of *Homo erectus* (so called because it walked upright) the brain increased considerably in size, probably because this was the first meat-eating ape and the Broca's area also developed further after about 2,500,000BC. We know that by about 1,800,000BC, there were at least four major varieties of *Homo erectus* all foraging along the shores of Lake Tarkana in Kenya. These ape-humans were the first users of fire. Some of these ape-humans -- a species we now call *Homo ergaster* -- arrived in Europe via the Bosporus. Settlement sites have been found in Germany, Greece, Hungary, Czechoslovakia, Romania, Sicily and Spain. A site in Yugoslavia has been dated at c. 1,500,000BC. But these were the forerunners.

---

40 P. Lieberman, *On the Origins of Language: An Introduction to the Evolution of Human Speech* (New York, 1975).

The colonization of Europe by *Homo erectus* does not seem to have started in earnest until the interglacial period between 524,000–478,000BC, when the latest variety of East Africans again moved north out of Africa into Europe via what is now Israel and Georgia along the north shore of the Black Sea to set up home in a belt of temperate land in Southern and Eastern Europe, the Middle East, the Caucasus Mountains and beyond. By about 70,000BC there is evidence that they had reached Creswell Crags in Derbyshire.

I say 'temperate', because these people followed a zone of territory where the climate was quite amenable to their hunter-gather lifestyle, but to the north of this temperate belt the climate was incredibly harsh. At its maximum the European ice-cap extended as far south as London and was at a depth of about two miles over Birmingham. The glaciers were in retreat and greatly reduced by the time ape-humans arrived here though, but much of the world's water was still locked into them and they still dominated the landscape. Because of this the coast of Europe was on average about seventy-five miles further out from its current position, and the sea was about 300 feet lower than now. From the west coast of Ireland it would have been possible to walk dry-shod through England, across the North Sea, through Denmark and Germany all the way to Poland and on into Russia along what is now the Baltic. But north of this was a wide open treeless, grassy plain, and north of that were the glaciers and the ice cap which still covered much of Northern Europe. The climate was like that of modern Alaska with a short, hot summer, a brief spring and autumn and a long, very cold winter. And when the ice cap advanced, which it did several times, the settlers were forced to move south into what is now Spain and southern France.

Neanderthals

In Europe *Homo erectus* evolved specifically to suit this cold climate and to hunt the animals they found there. By about 200,000BC they had developed into a distinct species of human. They were short in height at about five feet (a few as tall as 5ft 4ins), with deep flared chests, they were heavily muscled, had bulbous noses and a prominent brow ridge. Scientists now call them *Homo sapiens neandertalensis* and we know them simply as Neanderthals.

The remains after which the species is named were first found in the mud floor of a cave above the river Dussel in the Neander valley (*thal*) near Wuppertal in Germany in 1856. In fact a skull from this species had been found in Gibraltar in 1848, but its significance had not been understood at the time.[41] Since then remains have also been found in Portugal, Switzerland, Silesia, Italy, Czechoslovakia, Croatia, Israel, Georgia and Heidelberg in Germany. In the UK they have been found at Clacton, Torquay, Lynford, Boxgrove, Swanscombe and at La Cotte in the Channel Islands.

Our image of them was of brute, low-browed primitives, possibly cannibal. However, recent re-interpretation of their culture indicates they had an advanced level of social organisation. They seem to have lived in small, stable family-sized groupings around male-dominated territories and practised kidnapping and trading of females. They hunted red deer, reindeer and wild cattle, all of which are dangerous, but also developed hunting strategies for dealing with very large prey like woolly mammoth and woolly rhinoceros, which were even more dangerous. Neanderthals, because of the formation of their shoulder joints, could not throw well so they had little choice but to hunt even very large animals by ambushing them and then close-in for the kill with heavy stabbing spears. Another of their standard strategies were to drive animals over a cliff top (as at La Cotte). Many of the surviving Neanderthal bones show signs of fracture, probably caused by encounters with large prey animals during hunting. But the fact that these fractures healed shows that injured Neanderthals were cared for by the family and probably for long periods.

Recently it has become apparent that the Neanderthals were a musical people. Examples of their artefacts were recently discovered near Ely and are thought to date from about 50,000BC. They made bullroarers and hollowed out bones to make flutes. Their flutes have been discovered in Slovenia, Russia and France -- some dated to 82,000–43,000BC. Until recently it was thought that the Neanderthals were not visual artists. However in December 2009 evidence was revealed that the Neanderthals used face paint and made jewellery from painted sea shells.[42]

Their hunting skills and general social sophistication seems to

---

41 J. Huxley, A. C. Haddon, A. M. Carr-Saunders, *We Europeans* (Penguin: Harmondsworth, 1939) p.44.
42 J. Zilhão et al, 'Symbolic use of marine shells and mineral pigments by Iberian Neanderthals', *Proceedings of the National Academy of Science of the United States of America* (5 December 2009).

demand some kind of language. Neanderthals had the brain capacity and vocal anatomy to speak. The discovery in 2007 of the gene called FOXP2, which both modern humans and Neanderthals share and which in modern humans helps to enable the development of speech, seems to prove that Neanderthals could speak.[43] This gene seems to have developed and spread about 2,000,000 years ago, but its presence in both species indicates that their common ancestor -- *Homo Erectus* -- also had the capacity for speech.

The Neanderthal capacity for language and humanity seem hardly different from our own, except that their brain was about 20 per cent larger than ours. It seems that, like us, they were mainly right-handed and pale-skinned. About the same percentage as in modern humans were red-haired. They seem to have had a hearing range of audible frequencies between 20–20,000 Hertz, which is the same as a modern human. But because of their anatomy, what they could say is still a matter of debate. Some claim they could produce only grunts. This seems unlikely. Some argue Neanderthals could say anything a modern human could say. And others say Neanderthal vocal tracts could only manage a limited range of vowels plus *d/b/s/z/v/f* but that they were incapable of managing */g/* or */k/*.[44] It is thought they could manage only three vowel sounds, but as the character of Inspector Clusoe in The Pink Panther films has made clear, even if a speaker mangles their vowels it is still be possible to understand something: and even a limited number of vowels need not entirely hamper meaning: *Ef e spek weth enly e smell nember ev vewells ye cen stell enderstend, me. Ne?*

The presence of the Hyoid bone in the throat -- a small 'u'-shaped bone which connects muscles to the jaw, larynx and tongue, essential to human speech and providing anatomists with a fairly accurate portrait of the vocal tract in any animal or human -- along with the angle of their head, slightly forward of our own, their very large chest, the possibilities of resonance provided by their bulbous nose and brow ridge all combine to suggest that they probably had very loud voices, rather high pitched compared to our own, but which carried well in the open air. Whatever

---

43 J. Krause et al 'The Derived FOXP2 Variant of Modern Humans was Shared with Neanderthals', Current Biology, no.17 (2007), 1980-12; R. Gray, 'Cavemen may have used language', *The Telegraph* (21 Oct 2007), www.telegraph.co.uk/news.
44 P. Phillips, *The Prehistory of Europe* (Penguin: Harmondsworth, 1980), p.61; S. R. Fischer, *The History of Language* (Reaktion Books: London, 1999), pp.49-56.

the limitations, there is no doubt that they could make themselves understood -- otherwise they would not have survived for so long in such difficult conditions.

Genetic testing of DNA from Neanderthal bodies has proved conclusively that while they were related to modern humans, they were not our direct ancestors. Our direct ancestors were still in Africa.

Cro-Magnon Humans

The record is still confused, but the fossils seem to indicate that about 250,000BC *Homo erectus* in East African began to undergo a very small but rapid mutation in a number of genes. The resulting physical changes would turn them into *Homo sapiens sapiens* -- that is, modern humans, in whom the Broca's area of the brain is clearly delineated. Their jaw shortened, so the tongue was positioned further forward and their mouth cavity opened at right angles to the throat. A crucial development was that the larynx was now lower in the throat. This enlarged the area of the voice box above it which allowed greater co-ordination and control over breath so humans became more able to modify speech sounds. As yet nobody knows why these changes occurred. However there does seem to have been a trade-off as the genetic changes also meant humans became more vulnerable to certain forms of cancer and neuro-degenerative diseases like Alzheimer's.

The new Africans were taller, slimmer, lighter boned and less muscular than Neanderthals. Also instead of the Neanderthal's prominent brow ridge and low backward sloping forehead, the forehead of the new Africans was upright and showed no trace of a brow ridge. The new Africans had a much greater ability than the Neanderthal to produce and develop a wider range of language -- and to do different things with language. Greater linguistic flexibility probably helped these people to survive, flourish and expand. Also, and perhaps crucially, unlike the Neanderthals, Cro-Magnon humans used throwing spears which could kill or disable prey at a distance.

According to remains discovered in 2007, by about 160,000-100,000BC these people were living at Herto in Ethiopia and at Jebel Irhoud in Morocco; they were also fishing the coasts and rivers of East Africa and had spread to Southern Africa.[45] About 80,000-40,000BC they began to spread northwards. They moved along the coasts and up the Great Rift Valley, up the Nile Valley to the Mediterranean, across the Sinai desert, into the Middle East, Eurasia, the Caucasus and over the Bosporus: they spread into China and then into America, they spread through the Indian subcontinent, across the Indian Ocean all the way to Java and New Guinea.[46] They reached Australia about 60,000BC, a long time before they colonized the rest of Europe.

They seem to have migrated further into Europe in two waves, during interglacial periods, 39,000–37,000BC and again 32,000–29,000BC. The first of their remains to be discovered was 'the red lady of Paviland', who was in fact a young man, whose bones stained with ochre were found in Goat's Hole Cave in Paviland on the Gower Peninsula near Swansea in 1822–23. The bones were originally dated to about 18,000 years ago, but more recent testing in 2007 suggests that they are more probably about 29,000-33,000 years old. Interestingly a Neanderthal flint tool dated to around 70,000BC was also found in the same cave, indicating there here, as elsewhere if the two species did not live side by side they favoured the same sites.[47]

However, it was not until 1868, when fossils were discovered in a cave in the Dordogne in France that these people were named Cro-Magnon, after the nearby village. Further remains were discovered at Pestera cu Oase in Romania (dated to 35,000BC), at Kent's cavern near Torquay in Exeter, England, (32–30,000BC) and at Bacho Kiro and Temnata in Bulgaria (43–40,000BC). By 40,000BC there were a great many sites occupied by these people throughout Western Europe, but it has to be said that at this time the climate was still very harsh and glaciers still covered most of northern Europe including most of Britain.

In Europe Cro-Magnon habitation seems to have centred on the Mediterranean, particularly southern France, Portugal, Spain and Croatia. Cro-Magnon also moved north to occupy the forests that sprang up as the glaciers melted and by about 8,000BC it is probable that Ireland and Scandinavia had also been colonized by them. As

45 Alok Jha, '160,000-year-old jawbone redefines origins of the species', *The Guardian* (13 March 2007), p.16.
46 C. B. M. McBurney, *The Stone Age in Northern Africa* (Penguin: Harmondsworth, 1960); C. Stringer, *Homo Britannicus* (Penguin: London, 2006), p.37.
47 N. Jenkins & D. Pearl, *Gower* (Gomer Press: Llandysul, 2009).

with the Neanderthal population, Britain was at the far end of a long migration route stretching from Africa, up through the middle-east into the Georgia and then along the Eurasian plane, and very few settlers made it that far. As a result of genetic mapping and the study of DNA, scientists estimate that the spread of about 10,000 individuals out of East Africa about 200,000–150,000BC would have been enough to start the entire present population of the world, initiate the development of our current racial groups and originate all our current languages plus a lot more that have been lost.[48]

Cro-Magnon v Neanderthal

It is possible that with the advance of the ice cap during the last great Ice Age the Neanderthal population was placed under severe pressure -- there is certainly evidence from the end of this period that Neanderthals were involved in cannibalism. If this is so it would help explain that the thinly spread groups of Neanderthal were already inbred and the species in considerable difficulty by the time the ice caps retreated and Cro-Magnon humans began to arrive in Europe. In addition, the Neanderthal gestation period of about a year was longer than that of the Cro-Magnon. It is possible that the Cro-Magnon simply bred faster than the Neanderthal. There is still considerable debate about the comparative diets of the Neanderthal and Cro-Magnon humans.[49] According to analysis of fossilized coprolites, in the northern areas of Europe 85 per cent of the Neanderthal diet was meat, which, given the limitations of the climate and the availability of game, was probably their major food source. In southern Europe, where the climate was much less harsh and a greater variety of foods was available, they seem to have eaten a wider range of foods including mussels. Cro-Magnon on the other hand seems to have eaten less meat, more fruit, nuts and vegetables and when they could not get meat they ate fish.

At best the Neanderthal population was thinly spread. There were probably no more than 100,000 people across the entire range of their settlement area, with the highest population concentration of around 3,000 individuals in Southern France and Spain. It is possible that because the Neanderthals were a 'cold-adapted species' they could not

---

48 D. Miles, *The Tribes of Britain* (Phoenix: London, 2005), p.47.
49 C. Finlayson, *The Humans Who Went Extinct*, pp.56-8, 149-52.

cope as well as the Cro-Magnon when the climate began to warm up, as the glaciers retreated and the flora and fauna changed. At the time of the earliest Neanderthal occupation Europe had been a vast open treeless plain, rather like Siberia, inhabited by very large prey which moved in from the north east -- animals like the musk-ox, woolly mammoth and woolly rhino. In time as the climate warmed large stretches of Europe developed into open woodland -- birch, alder and finally oak woodlands slowly spread north. The Neanderthals could still ambush large prey. But these changes probably made life difficult for the Neanderthals. In open plains and even in mixed woodland they could stalk and ambush large animals, but in close woodland and forest there were no large prey animals to hunt: game of all kinds was less frequent, difficult to spot or ambush and could not easily be panicked. For a long time the Neanderthals hunted successfully at the edge of the woodlands, but as Europe began to settle into the kind of place we recognise today the territory did not favour large prey like cattle and horses and this meant that the Neanderthals were steadily disadvantaged: their areas of habitation seem to have shrunk, while, when the Cro-Magnon arrived, they were better adapted to the new environment, more flexible in their diet and hunting techniques and therefore able to consistently expand their range.[50]

For us the most important question -- the one that lingers -- is whether, if the Neanderthals were still with us, we would notice them, whether we would be able to identify them on the street and whether we would regard them as equally human. Some evidence suggests that the meeting between Neanderthal and early modern humans was violent and possibly even cannibalistic, but recent discoveries at cave dwellings in Israel, Spain, Portugal, Gibraltar and in Torquay, England, indicate that Neanderthals may have been peace-loving, cave-dwelling neighbours who co-operated with other early humans in hunting. The stone tools of the two species are often indistinguishable, and where they are different are often found next to each other, showing that in the Middle East these peoples coexisted for between 10–20,000 years, before the Neanderthals died out.

It was generally thought the Neanderthal had disappeared by about 35,000BC. However, the discovery in Portugal of a child's skeleton

---

50 C. Finlayson, *The Humans Who Went Extinct* (Oxford: OUP, 2010), pp.103-20.

which appears to show physical characteristics of both Cro-Magnon and Neanderthal, dated about 33,000BC, may be evidence that some Neanderthal groups survived and interbred with Cro-Magnon.[51] While there is considerable debate about the exact nature of relations between the two species of human, work on sequencing Neanderthal DNA has shown that we share something like 99.5–99.9 per cent of our genetic make-up with them, much more than we share with the great apes, and this confirms that we share a common ancestor with the Neanderthals. Specifically, it seems that from interbreeding, up to 4 per cent of modern European DNA may have been inherited directly from Neanderthals.[52]

The Cro-Magnon lived in hunter-gatherer groups of twenty to twenty-five people. They shared a world with animals now extinct: brown bears three meters tall, lions that had no manes, and wolves. They hunted red deer, horse, lemming, wild ass, musk ox, ibex, reindeer and bison, and like the Neanderthal they hunted the woolly mammoth and woolly rhinoceros but this time they hunted them to extinction. They ate wild vetch, lentils, berries, pistachio nuts and almonds. They also fished. In the former Yugoslav village of Lepenski Vir ancient settlements show carvings of carp dated to around 7,500 years ago.

The wonderful carvings and paintings left behind by our ancestors from over 14,000 years ago can still be seen in caves at Lascaux and Chauvet in France and at Altamira in Spain. Also, dating from c. 13,000BC, scratched designs and animal decorations have recently been found at Creswell Crags on the Nottingham-Derby border. The Creswell caves had previously been occupied by Neanderthals about 45,000 years ago. The caves were about twenty miles south of the ice fields and glaciers that still covered northern Britain. They are the northernmost European example of cave art and the only example of Cro-Magnon cave art found in Britain so far. In addition to a horse rib carved with a horse's head, it was discovered in 2003 that the roof of several of the Creswell caves had been carved with bison, deer, several different kinds of birds and

---

51 *Neanderthals* BBC 2 (6 August 2001); 'New Look at Human Evolution', *Scientific American Special Edition* (2003), vol. 13, no. 2; Neanderthal (BBC1, Horizon, 11 February 2005); www.bbc.co.uk/horizon/neanderthal.
52 A. Roberts and G. McGavin, *Prehistoric Autopsy: Neanderthal*, BBC2, 22 October 2012; R. Highfield, 'Were Neanderthals our enemies or lovers?' *The Telegraph*, 31 July 2007; www.telegraph.co.uk; R. E. Green, et al., 'A Draft Sequence of the Neanderthal Genome', *Science*, Vol. 328, no. 5979, (7 May 2010), pp.710-22; Alok Jha, 'Study casts doubt on human-Neanderthal interbreeding theory', *The Guardian*, 14 August 2012.

several representations of female genitalia. One carving is of an ibex, which was not a native animal, and this suggests that the carver was familiar with the animal from seasonal travels to southern France and Spain. The carvings can only be seen when the sun enters the cave in the early morning. It is possible they took over these cave sites from earlier Neanderthals. However, shortly after these art works were made Cresswell Crags was again covered by the ice and snow of a resurgent cold period and the area was not repopulated until after the glaciers receded around 10,000 years ago.[53]

Art historians now suspect that some of Cro-Magnon artists had a sense of perspective long before the Renaissance rediscovered it.[54] And very probably, if we believe the way the caves are decorated, they were not only artists, but musicians too. Paint on stalactites and stalagmites and particular areas of rock indicate resonance points for percussion. Generally the caves chosen for decoration are those that resonate particularly well to clapping and to the male singing voice.

They may have died out, but we should not dismiss or underestimate the Neanderthals. They were in existence from long before 200,000BC up to about 35,000BC in what was for the most part an incredibly harsh and unforgiving environment. Compared to our own species, that is a very long period: we are comparative newcomers, and we have existed only in a much milder climate. If we are in existence for as long as them, and in conditions half as difficult as those they experienced, we will have done well.

Commenting on the Broca's speech-area of the brain and its relation to the development of the mind in modern humans, Jacob Bronowski wrote:

Whether you are right-handed or left-handed, speech is almost certainly on the left. There are exceptions, in the same way that there are people who have their heart on the right, but the exceptions are rare: by and large speech is in areas in the left half of the brain. And what is in the matching areas on the right? We do not exactly know, so far. We do not exactly know what the right-hand side of the brain does in those areas which are devoted to

---

53 P. Bahn, F. Munoz, P. Pettitt and S. Ripoll, 'New Discoveries of Art in Church Hole (Creswell Crags, England)', *Antiquity* vol.78, no.300, June 2004; S. Beckensall, *Circles in Stone* (Tempus: Stroud, 2006): antiquity.ac.uk/projgall/bahn/index.
54 J. Berger, 'Past Present', *The Guardian* (12 October 2002), pp.18-19.

speech on the left. But it looks as if they take the input that comes by way of the eye -- the map of a two dimensional world on the retina -- and turn it or organise it into a three-dimensional picture. If that is right, then in my view it is clear that speech is also a way of organising the world into its parts and putting them together again like movable images.[55]

Cro-Magnon humans clearly used their imaginative and creative powers, but the existence of their artwork leads us to surmise about the development of their ability to think in ways their ancestors (and perhaps also their Neanderthal relatives) did not. The development of more complex language use made possible a dramatic change in humanity's attention to themselves, the world around them and their place in that world, since language allowed humans to identify and put together all kinds of information and ideas in new combinations. The growth of the Broca's area in early humans may well have been matched by developments in the frontal cortex, where imagination and forward planning seem to take place, and on the right side of the brain in the areas processing visual images: if so, these areas would certainly have made it possible for humans to process images and visual symbols in the same way that they processed sounds for meanings. There is evidence to suggest that the areas of the brain that are responsible for speech are also involved in 'intuition', creative activities and the production of tools, which suggests that in terms of brain-power, conversation and creativity overlap, that since they come from the same parts of the human mind, speech and language are 'creative'.[56] The archaeologist Colin Renfrew identified this growth in the human mind as 'symboling ability', that is the capacity to think symbolically and metaphorically, to think of language not only as a means of basic communication but as a:

… device which allows the handling by the individual of symbolic concepts and as such it is indispensable to structured thought. If this viewpoint be followed, it is at least arguable that the development of the relevant abilities of reasoning, of conceptualising, should be

---

55 J. Bronowski, *The Ascent of Man* (BBC: London, 1973), pp.421-23; J. Jaynes, *The Origin of Consciousness in the Breakdown of the Bicameral Mind* (Houghton Mifflin: Boston, 1976).
56 D. Stout, et al, 'Neural correlates of Early Stone Age tool-making: technology language and cognition in human evolution', *Philosophical Transactions of the Royal Society, B*, vol. 363 (1499), 2008, pp.1939-40; 'The Creative Brain – How Insight Works', *Horizon*, BBC2 (14 March 2013).

reflected in human behaviour patterns. It is of course possible to study these through the material remains. Such is the perspective now widely accepted. Quite naturally it places much emphasis upon the symbolic aspects of material culture, and not least upon such early depictions as are seen in upper Palaeolithic cave art; both the paintings and the small portable objects.[57]

And the material evidence for such a change in human life is available. Steven Pinker has suggested that for the Cro-Magnon humans language was innate, an instinct.[58] They certainly seem to have thought differently and organized themselves in a way that made the Neanderthals look clumsy in comparison -- they clearly used symbols, stories, metaphors, art, music, body decoration. These people could make and use fire. They could fashion tools. They made tents out of skins supported by bones. They could count. They could carry water. They had rituals: they buried their dead very carefully, with grave-goods, as if they had a belief in an afterlife. These are examples of a generalized human intelligence, but this intelligence was propelled into other activities and ways of thinking about themselves in the world by a fully developed use of language which attributed meaning to sounds and images, which made connections between things through metaphor and 'symboling', which could plan and organize, argue rationally and which could give voice to the creations of the imagination. Cave decoration and the possibility of cave music indicate very clearly that the Cro-Magnon people understood narrative and that they made music and pictures to accompany stories. These things are attributes of what we now identify as 'the human mind'.[59] Genetically we are Cro-Magnon. We are their direct descendants. The languages we speak are descended from their languages.

---

57 C. Renfrew, *Archaeology and Language* (Penguin: Harmondsworth, 1989), pp.274-75.
58 S. Pinker, *The Language Instinct: The New Science of Language and Mind* (Penguin: Harmondsworth, 1994), p.18.
59 S. Mithen, *The Prehistory of the Mind: A Search for the Origins of Art, Religion & Science* (Phoenix: London, 1966); D. Lewis-Williams & D. Pearce, *Inside the Neolithic Mind* (Thames and Hudson: London, 2009); D. Spender, *Man Made Language* (Routledge: London, 1985); J. Jaynes, *The Origin of Consciousness in the Breakdown of the Bicameral Mind* (Houghton Mifflin: Boston, 1976); G. Gradol, *Language Variation and Diversity* (Open University: Milton Keynes, 1981); J. Bronowski, *The Ascent of Man* (BBC: London, 1973), C. Renfrew, *Archaeology and Language* (Penguin: Harmondsworth, 1989); C. Renfrew, *Prehistory: Making of the Human Mind* (Weidenfeld & Nicholson: London, 2007).

WRITING THE WORLD

The story of human development is unfolding rapidly and new discoveries in this area seem to be unveiled each year.

*

It is frustrating, but we cannot say exactly at what point in pre-history apes became ape-humans, when ape-humans became humans, or when the linguistic capacities of the human mind might have emerged. There is no fixed and determined point for any of these things. Our ape ancestors date back about 23,000,000 years, but we cannot be certain when humans first emerged, but it was probably about seven to six million years ago. Nor can we say exactly when human language began: possibly ape-humans began to speak as early as two million years ago, but some experts would argue that it was also possibly as late as 40,000 years ago. The middle point somewhere around 100-200,000 years ago seems to be more likely.[60] It is very likely that one branch of apes was communicating at a very early stage in its development, that this ability was transferred to descendants, that ape-humans were speaking long before the Neanderthals developed, and long before modern humans began to migrate out of Africa. It is clear that not only did Africa give the world humanity, it also gave the world language and the arts. Beyond this we can say only a few things with confidence:

- the basic human design, a little improved over the years, has been around for a long time, but in terms of the history of planet earth, it is also still quite recent
- we cannot say when humans first started speaking, but we can infer that from very early times our ape-human ancestors had some capacity to process speech and the potential for that capacity to expand
- language is innate or 'hard wired' into the human design
- language is a major part of what it is to be human
- language is a human and a social creation
- without human society there can be no human language

---

60 P. Lieberman, *On the Origins of Languages: an introduction to the evolution of human speech* (Macmillan: New York, 1975).

- without human language there can be no human society
- a human without language is barely human
- without society humans barely function
- humans are barely equipped to survive without the protection and co-operation of human society.

Directed Study

In what way is the idea of speech in humans linked to representation in writing?

It has been said that the history of language is a history of the human mind, a history of human thought and an indicator of creativity. What do you think?

'Language and civilisation are intimately connected. Humans live in society and need language to do so. Without language there can be no human society.' What do you understand this to mean and why might this be important to writers?

If someone said: 'I'm a writer. What has any of this caveman stuff to do with me?' what would you answer?

Why do you think it is important for writers to consider human origins, speech and the beginnings of language?

'For humans, language is a historical necessity, a cultural process and an individual skill'. What do you think?

Any definition of language, and any history of the development of language in humans, is also a history and definition of humans in the world. What do you think -- why would this be important for writers?

What words do you think would have been part of a caveman's vocabulary? Imagine you are part of a tribe in late Palaeolithic Europe: invent a small vocabulary (calls, commands and statements) for basic situations you might encounter. Provide a word list and a brief description of how these words might be used. How might this vocabulary differ from that of cousins in Africa? How might this vocabulary develop in the future? What do you think could prevent this vocabulary from developing?

3
HOW OLD IS WRITING?
A BRIEF HISTORY OF THE ALPHABET

If language is the single most important product of the human mind, writing, as a means of recording language is probably the second most important. Along with the development of agriculture, the invention of writing marks one of the great and decisive turning points in human history. Before writing we have only pre-history, where we cannot understand anything except through the educated guesswork of archaeology. With the invention of writing we gain access to the lives, motivations and thoughts of those who went before us. In the three million year history of the human species, writing is a relatively recent development, but history begins with writing. This chapter asks: how old is writing? Where does it come from? It considers writing as a very effective New Technology. It looks at the origins of writing in Ancient Tokens, at the development of cuneiform, at writing under the Sumerians and Egyptians, at the development of the Phoenician alphabet, the Greek adaptation of the new writing system, its transmission and adoption by the Romans. It also questions the way in which the alphabet represents the English language.

- The Traditional View
- How Old is Writing?
- Ancient Tokens
- Cuneiform
- Hieroglyphs
- Phoenicians and the Greek Alphabet
- English Language and the Alphabet

The Traditional View

The traditional view is that there were probably four stages in the development of writing as we know it.

1: Iconography. That is when people simply made a picture to represent the thing they wanted to refer to. Usually this seems to have been a natural object, particularly an animal, the sun, moon or stars. Part of this seems to have been a magic rite -- perhaps you drew a picture of the animal you wished to hunt, your tribal totem animal, your dream guide.

2: Ideographic Writing. That is, where pictures became conventionalised for use as a sign for a thing. The combination of picture signs, or the linking of picture signs, perhaps to convey a story or provide the background to a song, was also a possibility. Conventional pictures seem to have been used for particular purposes. For example a sign might represent a name or an idea or it might be a complete sound. A picture 'stood' for a word or an idea: e.g. a picture of the sun could signify 'a day'. However there are immediate problems of interpretation. What may be bird in one instance could be sparrow, duck, goose or swan in another. What may be a badly drawn duck to one person could signify a fat duck to another. A fat duck could mean let's go hunting or I have one of these in my larder already or even I have a pet duck: it could mean winter is coming we should stock up with a few of these. Or it could mean -- beware of ferocious eagles ahead, or even it is dangerous to your health to eat carrion birds. We do not know: writing of this kind is likely to be so flexible it is impossible to interpret without a key.

3: Analytic Writing. The Egyptians and the Sumerians seem to have been the first people to realize that they could systematize their written signs. The Egyptians started to produce a standard sign system which we call Hieroglyphics (Greek, literally sacred signs). The Sumerians also started to produce a standardized written system that would develop into cuneiform. The problem was that both of these systems were huge and took a long time to learn. They also involved a special class or caste of scribes who, because of their skills, wielded increasing political power.

4: *Phonetic Systems.* Phonetic systems are what we mainly use today; each sign has a name and attempts to record a particular sound or combination of sounds. The element of interpretation is minimal.

The main problem with this schema is that it is not at all clear how the intermediate stages were managed or how one stage developed into another.

There has been some debate as to how 'proper writing' might be defined, since in a way, any sign might qualify. Setting aside all the things that might qualify as writing, S. R. Fischer has defined what he calls 'complete writing' thus:

> Complete writing must have as its purpose communication;
> Complete writing must consist of artificial graphic marks on a durable or electronic surface;
> Complete writing must use marks that relate conventionally to articulate speech (the systematic arrangement of significant vocal sounds) or electronic programming in such a way that communication is achieved.[61]

How Old is Writing?

If the ability to speak opens up all kinds of possibilities for humans, the ability to read and write opens up huge possibilities for learning, development and creation -- not just in terms of literature, entertainment and the life of the imagination, but in the assessment and exchange of ideas, in citizenship, in health (e.g. circulation of information about TB, AIDS, flu jabs etc), in education and knowledge, in the exercise of rights, responsibilities and privileges, in the way society understands itself and its past, in the way that it interprets the knowledge it accumulates in writing. That is, not just for the individual but for particular societies and for the species as a whole, for the development of what we call civilization, writing is essential.

Look at the important role writing and reading played in the French, American, Russian and Chinese revolutions and at the role it has played in the Industrial Revolution and now in the Technological Revolution. Writing is a massively important aspect of human behaviour, but it is a relatively recent human invention. The important moment was when

---

61 S. R. Fischer, *A History of Writing* (Reaktion Books: London, 2003), p.12.

humans realized they could keep some kind of a record by making a mark. It was once fashionable to say that writing was a gift of the gods. In Christianity it was normal to credit Adam with the invention of writing. In the Bible almost the first writing we hear about is the Ten Commandments, written on stone by the finger of God and gifted to Moses. The Koran, it is said, was dictated by God, in dreams and trances, to the prophet Mohamed. Hieroglyphics, the Egyptians claimed, were literally the sacred signs of the gods.

Writing is an amazing technology. It is an incredibly flexible tool for all kinds of communication ranging from the utterly trivial to the kind of thing that changes the course of history. What is certain is that the history of early writing is not a tidy one. It is not even one history: it is several histories. It is a process of experiments, tiny advances and repeats. Writing -- keeping a written record -- was invented many times before someone invented the alphabet. The alphabet has only ever been invented once, though it has been developed and improved upon and has spread throughout the world.

In Europe, apart from the carvings in Stone Age Irish tombs *c.* 8-6000BC, the earliest known written text is probably a plaque found at Gradesnica in Bulgaria, dated *c.* 5-3000BC, and three pictographs on clay tablets from Turdas near Cluj in Romania from about the same time. But what is written in these examples is not known because we cannot decipher them.

According to Denise Schmandt-Besserat, extensive research has led her to believe that writing probably developed in the Neolithic Middle East, *c.* 8-6000BC, from a widespread system of signs and clay tokens, and carved seals used for accounting throughout the areas of modern Turkey, Syria, Lebanon, Israel, Palestine, Jordan, Iraq, Kuwait, Iran, Afghanistan and the area south-east of the Caspian Sea.[62] These tokens and seals were often unrecognized or even discarded as insignificant by early archaeologists: in fact now that we know what they are, they are often found among the rubble drawers in museums. It is only with Schmandt-Besserat's research that their real importance and significance for the development of the alphabet has begun to emerge. This was a system of representing animals or goods by the use of small clay tokens and it seems to have been so widespread and general, that it could not

---

62 D. Schmandt-Besserat, *Before Writing: vol 1: From Counting to Cuneiform* (Austin University Press: Texas, 1992).

have sprung up overnight, but probably descended from even earlier practices for recording animal stock, menstrual cycles and phases of the moon by making cuts on wood or on antlers. It is possible that some of these signs also appear among the cave paintings at Lascaux and elsewhere.

The tokens appear as small models, carved seals and as geometrical shapes, including parabolas and rhomboids, and there are a great many sub-types with incisions of various kinds and added pellets or coils of clay. Altogether some fifteen types and 250 sub-types have been identified and dated to this period. At the same time *bullae* or clay containers to hold the tokens also appear. It is thought these may have accompanied a delivery or shipment of goods, with the tokens sealed inside the *bulla* to provide a record of the transaction.

The first stage of bookkeeping and writing was, it seems, tied to specific economic items represented by clay tokens and carved seals. There was a specific token for sheep, another for wine, another for a sheep-skin or an ingot of metal or a beehive or a day's work, etc. To record three sheep and two jugs of wine, the ancient bookkeeper would create the token for sheep three times and the token for wine twice. It is distinctly possible that many of the tokens simply represented the transfer of land or animals from one owner to another.

At first these tokens were kept in a sealed container, probably made of cloth, leather, horn or clay. The signs were copied onto the outside or impressed into the clay lid of the container, so that the owner knew what was inside. Later, it seems, the idea of keeping actual tokens in a pot was abandoned, but the idea of making marks or signs to keep a 'proto-literate' record was retained in the use of clay tablets with impressed signs. Many of these tablets were found at Uruk dated to *c.* 3,500BC and there is evidence to suggest that these tablets eventually gave rise to the cuneiform script of ancient Sumer and Akkadia in Mesopotamia.

Although this idea provides us with a nice neat historical and theoretical framework on which to hang the history of the alphabet, in reality even if Schmandt-Besserat is correct and writing developed from tokens, the intermediate stages are still far from clear. However it happened, the development of writing from these signs was probably not a simple and speedy process, nor is it likely that these things proceeded in an orderly fashion from one stage to the next. It is possible that the development actually happened very differently: we simply do not know for certain. But there is evidence of a great many experiments in writing and writing systems which have not stood the test of time. Some, like the Linear A system from Crete or the Indus Valley script, are still a mystery to us. Others, like Linear B from Crete, have been deciphered. Some early systems grew and developed over time and are still with us today -- like Chinese characters. Some writing systems, like Cuneiform and Hieroglyphic, lasted for a very long time and then died out because they were replaced by something more flexible.

Cuneiform

The Sumerians seem to have been the first people to realize that it was possible to produce a *system* of signs. Out of the system of signs and pictures in clay used for trade and record they produced cuneiform -- as early as 5000BC the Sumerians began to develop a system of wedge-shaped marks in wet clay. Cuneiform offered a sign instead of a token and was probably the first attempt to systematize signs. The development of cuneiform -- the first writing system in the world -- took place in Mesopotamia, in cities like Babylon between the Tigris and Euphrates rivers, in what is now Iraq.

However, Sumerian writing went through a long history of development before it became what we now recognise as cuneiform. Around 3000BC, as the city-states of the area grew in size, an increasingly complex social structure called for more sophisticated accounting techniques to record stores and business transactions. The recording of economic activities pushed the scribes to develop the script further. Tokens and tablets were replaced by pictographs drawn in wet clay using a reed stylus. At about this time scribes also realized they could record quantities and items separately. They no longer used the token for sheep three times in order to represent three sheep, but rather they began to write the pictographic symbol for sheep alongside the symbol denoting the number three.

This was revolutionary. In addition to the recording of concrete pictograph items, like sheep and flour, the script also began to record more abstract items such as the names of gods, kings and humans and spoken words. One of the most important developments of cuneiform was the idea that particular signs could be used to represent consonants.

The written script developed rapidly so that cuneiform could begin to record stories. However, it is important to note that Sumerian writing was developed initially not by writers and storytellers, but by accountants and administrators. They did not begin with poetry or stories, but with records of business transactions for the great Empires of Mesopotamia.

Cuneiform began by making use of established ideograms and pictograms, but also began to formalise the signs as abstract symbols designed not to represent an animal or an idea, but to represent particular sounds. As Akkadians replaced the Sumerians to become the ruling political power in the area, cuneiform was adapted by the Akkadians, and then later by Babylonians and Assyrians, to write their own languages.

Through the long years of its development scribes began to utilize a more complex system of notation. The evidence we have for this is of written signs impressed in soft school tablets called a 'lentil' or a 'bun', designed for teaching and learning. The shaped back of these tokens fitted naturally into the palm of the hand. There were usually four rows of signs on the front of the tablet. The teacher inscribed signs in rows one and two, and the student then took the soft tablet and copied the text into rows three and four.

The great advantage of cuneiform was that within the thousands of signs that comprised the whole writing system, it also developed a phonetic alphabetic, which we still have today. This is when the signs attempt to record the sounds and the combination of sounds in a particular language: each sign has a name and represents consistently a particular sound or combination of sounds. The element of interpretation required by the reader was minimal.

Thousands of inscribed monuments and other texts written in cuneiform survive. Mostly they are concerned with the kind of thing that could not be committed to memory -- law, economics and accounting. Often they are concerned with the allocation of rations – usually payments in beer -- for the thousands of labourers engaged in the many and various state building projects. In one tablet, for example, we learn that a temple religious community in the town of Lagash included forty-eight bakers, seven slaves, thirty-one brewers, a smith, spinners and weavers and several other artisans. Most of the tablets, however, are still temple records, legal documents and land leases. However, a list of some of the cuneiform tablets discovered in the Royal Library at Nineveh, dating from *c.* 668-631BC (now in the British Museum) gives us some idea of the society, its beliefs and structure, but also of the many uses to which writing was being put by this time:

The story of the Flood
The story of Creation
The Birth of Sargon
Ishtar's descent to the Underworld
The Legend of Etana
A list of Synonyms
The meaning of names
The origins and meanings of Archaic Signs
Spells
Prayers
Requests for Oracles
A synchronous history of Assyria and Babylonia
A list of palace officials
A theory of Omens
Star charts
Omens derived from examination of the liver of a sheep
Fortune Telling
A magical Divination to predict a conspiracy
Rituals for the sacrifice of a scapegoat for the king
Observations of the Planet Venus
Omens to be derived from deformed births
Bath House rituals and rules
Tables for computing the hours of daylight
A Royal demand for more copies of important clay tablets
A report on copying clay tablets in the Royal Library
An inventory of tablets
A petition
A list of Court Scholars
A hymn to Ishtar
The Autobiography of King Assurbanipal
Lunar Omens (badly burned)
A medical compendium of spells and cures

A spell to be whispered into the ear of a bull about to be sacrificed
so that its skin and tendons could be used to make a temple drum
The measurements of a ziggurat
Ration lists
A map of the world
A prescription against miscarriage
Gynaecological treatments

The best known of the literary works surviving from cuneiform --
and one which pre-dates Homer by about 1,500 years -- is *The Epic of
Gilgamesh: He Who Saw the Deep*. Gilgamesh was an historical king of
Uruk (modern Warka) in Babylonia, on the River Euphrates (modern
Iraq). He lived *c.* 2700–2600BC. In the story, Gilgamesh (or Bilgamesh
as he is called in the early versions) was a young Sumerian hero-king,
two-thirds god and one-third human, the greatest king and the strongest
human in existence. He kills the great Bull of Heaven and hangs its horns
on his wall. He also oppresses his people harshly. The people call out to
the sky-god Anu to help them. In response, Anu creates Enkidu, a wild
man who lives out in the harsh wilderness that surrounds Gilgamesh's
territory. This brute, Enkidu, has the strength and speed of dozens of
wild animals and he rivals Gilgamesh.[63] Eventually Enkidu is seduced
by a harlot from the city and thus begins a process by which he is tamed.
He goes to the city and meets Gilgamesh, at first they fight, then they
become strong friends (Enkidu is sometimes called Enki by Gilgamesh),
they go on a journey to the woods, where they deceive and then kill
Humbaba, an ogre who is also titled Protector of the Forest of Cedars,
and then chop down the trees and sacred groves. In his early years in the
wild Enkidu had been friends with, Humbaba: then Enkidu, possibly as
a punishment for killing his friend, becomes ill. On his deathbed Enkidu
realizes he has lost his innocence along with his wildness, and he curses
the people who civilized him. He dies and Gilgamesh falls into the most
monumental grief, weeping for seven days before he notices that worms
have begun to eat the corpse of his friend. From this moment Gilgamesh
begins to fear his own death and tries to find out the secret of how not
to die. Gilgamesh, in one version of the tale, travels to find the original

---

63 *The Epic of Gilgamesh*, trans., A. George (Penguin: Harmondsworth, 1999); *The Epic of
Gilgamesh*, trans., N. K. Sandars (Penguin: Harmondsworth, 1975).

Noah figure who survived the flood, called Uta-napishti (He Who Saw Life), because he is thought to know the secret of life.

In *The Epic of Gilgamesh* we have the first and oldest story to come down to us, in any language, from ancient times. In it we can clearly identify the voices of the main characters, and the understanding, thoughts and feelings of readers and writers from almost 4,000 years ago. *The Epic of Gilgamesh* is an important text because it tells of the threat that nature -- the wilderness that surrounded the pockets of human civilization -- posed for the peoples of those times and of their struggle to tame it: a major part of the tale is the debate about how kings should behave and the nature of good government. There is also a great deal about religious belief, and attitudes to, and preparations for, death.[64] The story also includes the earliest version of the Biblical Flood (*Genesis* 6:5-9: 17). In one version of the tale Gilgamesh is credited with being the person who restores the temples and the correct forms of worship and dispenses knowledge of farming some five generations after the chaos of the Flood. *The Epic of Gilgamesh* also anticipates several Greek myths including the Labours of Hercules. It is also very possible that with the death of Humbaba we have the first ever murder story and, in the relationship between Gilgamesh and Enkidu it is possible we have the first ever tale of homosexual love.[65]

The Epic of Gilgamesh as we know it derived from a series of oral poems composed *c.* 2200BC. It is clear that at this time very few people knew how to write or read, but copies of these poems were made in the scribal schools of Old Babylon *c.* 1800BC. In the reign of Hammurabi (1792–1750BC), there was an attempt to standardize the various texts. Later a new Babylonian version of the stories began to emerge *c.* 1400BC and this was revised into a standard version *c.* 1000BC.

These later versions of the poems seem to have been written down in Sumerian cuneiform during the reign of King Assurbanipal 669–627BC. Assurbanipal claimed to have been trained as a scribe. He certainly promoted literary efforts of all kinds and in his reign the copying of all kinds of tablets and the creation of libraries increased enormously. Assurbanipal's efforts came to grief though, when the Medes and Babylonians sacked his territory in 612BC destroying the two royal

---

64 D. Lewis-Williams & D. Pearce, *Inside the Neolithic Mind* (Thames & Hudson: London, 2009), pp.153-60.
65 *The Epic of Gilgamesh*, trans., A. George (Penguin: London, 1999).

libraries in Nineveh, burying the 25,000 clay tablets they contained under the ruins. Assurbanipal's palace was not rediscovered until the 1850s, and not explored in detail until the end of the ninteenth century: then it was realized that among many other texts, of the surviving seventy-three versions of *Gilgamesh*, at least thirty-five copies were in the Royal libraries in Nineveh. It is from the surviving fragments found in this library that we have the most complete version of the story, but other fragments and versions of the story have been found throughout the Middle East and in Turkey.

Cuneiform did not remain static and unchanging throughout its lifetime, but given that the average Babylonian scribe had to learn something like 2,000 individual signs and about 700 pictograms -- all made up of wedge shapes, some incredibly complex and unwieldy -- it is not surprising that reading and writing was restricted to a small, learned group. Knowing how to write was already a source of considerable power: knowledge of writing was a source of privilege. Scribes in Sumer, Babylon and Assyria constituted a caste apart, sometimes perhaps more powerful, in their own way, than the often illiterate king and his courtiers.

Even though the Sumerian and Babylonian kingdoms disappeared, and the Sumerian and Akkadian languages died out, the stories written in cuneiform continued to thrive for more than a thousand years under the Assyrians and then later under the Babylonians. Cuneiform was a very successful and long-lasting invention -- it survived for about 3,000 years and was used to represent a wide variety of languages -- even the Egyptians used it in letters of diplomacy to the other political powers of the region. However, cuneiform was clumsy and time-consuming to use.

The scribes of the various libraries, schools and temples continued to copy out *Gilgamesh* and other texts right down to 100BC. Later, as Semitic peoples moved northwards from Arabia and Palestine, Aramaic became widespread and a new system of writing gradually replaced cuneiform. Even so, the last cuneiform tablets were made *c.* AD 75–100. After this, knowledge of cuneiform faded and was lost until 1835, when Henry Rawlinson, an English army officer, found some inscriptions on a cliff at Behistun in Persia. Carved in the reign of King Darius of Persia (522–486BC), they consisted of identical texts in three languages: Old Persian, Babylonian and Elamite. After translating the Persian section, Rawlinson began to decipher the others. By 1851 he could read 200 Babylonian cuneiform signs. It is because of his pioneering work that we can read cuneiform texts.

Hieroglyphs

The oldest Egyptian hieroglyphs so far discovered seem to date from
c. 3,300–3,200BC. Having a standard system of signs that all the scribes
understood was a great improvement. However, although hieroglyphs
were fine for public pronouncements, when the scribes, working to
deadlines, had to produce tax returns or crop records or storage details,
hieroglyphics were simply too slow. As the scribes wrote, they simplified
and abbreviated the standard signs to form new simplified signs of a
couple of brush strokes, particularly when they were working quickly.
And by the late period of Egyptian literacy, the scribes had simplified
many of the hundreds of hieroglyphic signs to produce twenty-four
characters that attempted to render particular sounds. This was called
hieratic. They used this for everyday writing while Hieroglyphs were
for public statements -- carvings and statues. The range of documents
written in hieratic is huge -- everything from accounts, inventories,
laundry lists and tax details to prayers, poems, spells and letters to the
living and the dead. For example in the Turin Egyptian museum there
is a hieratic text from the village of the workers building the tombs in
the Valley of the Kings in Thebes. The letter describes a dispute where
the workmen downed tools because they had not been paid for several
months. They complained they had no oil, no ointments, no food and no
clothes -- all of which were part of their wage. They asked the Pharaoh
to intervene on their behalf. The dispute carried on for several months.
Another inscription -- this time written on stone -- is a typical management
document showing the names of workers, their wages and the reasons
for non-attendance at work. A lot of hieratic writing has been found on
linen wraps wound round dead bodies. While it was very difficult to
distinguish the work of an individual scribe in the hieroglyphic signs
-- probably because the scribes, carvers and painters worked in teams
-- with hieratic documents it is possible to distinguish the handwriting
of individual scribes.

This hieratic script could have been the basis of a modern alphabet,
where each sign represented a particular sound. But the Egyptian scribes
seem to have been reluctant to abandon their old ways and move entirely
to the new way of recording language. This was probably because any
simplification would have made literacy more accessible to the masses

and would have threatened their privileged position as the scribal elite. Instead they preserved their political power and social standing by combining the old system and the new, but they kept it pretty much to themselves.

Egyptian court scribes might have invented a better system of writing, but they did not make the leap into a purely phonetic alphabet. Others did that. It seems that, according to the latest archaeological information, foreign workers in mines and settlements of the Egyptian Sinai peninsula -- perhaps mercenary soldiers, captives, slaves, merchants, migrant workers, almost certainly speakers of a Semitic language from the Palestine-Lebanon-Syria coastline -- saw alphabetic possibilities in the simplified system of twenty-four Egyptian hieroglyphic signs representing particular sounds. They took and adapted these signs and began to develop them as a system without the hieroglyphic pictures and related only to specific sounds. At about the same time very similar developments and very similar alphabets developed not only in the Sinai, but throughout the area: in Syria, Lebanon and Palestine.[66] Although the exact mechanism is still unclear, it would seem that the basic idea for this writing system spread northwards very quickly from Sinai.

One of the most important elements in this development was the idea that signs could be used to represent consonants. This was particularly important in representing the Semitic languages which are built around a root framework of consonants and do not make so much use of vowels. The important realization that the simplified Egyptian system of signs could be adapted to everyday use and to languages other than Egyptian seems to have taken place in the area where the cuneiform traditions of Mesopotamia filtered south and the hieroglyphic traditions moving north met. That is, in both writing systems it seems to have been a combination of the slimmed down approach to the traditional system that contained within it the idea of the new system -- that signs could represent individual sounds (particularly consonants and that the signs could be quite simple). The realization that something new was possible seems to have happened in the area between these two great writing cultures and it seems to have happened almost simultaneously in the scribal schools at Ugarit in Syria, the port of Byblos in Lebanon, in Palestine, and particularly and perhaps first, in the settlements around

---

66 J. Drucker, *The Alphabetic Labyrinth* (Thames and Hudson: London, 1999), pp.22-48.

the turquoise mines of Serabit el-Khadem in the Sinai Peninsula. Graffiti in this script found in 1905 has been dated to *c.* 1850–1450BC. Throughout this area several very similar writing systems are recorded at around the same time.

It is curious that virtually the only significant historical events associated with the Sinai peninsula are the wandering of the Hebrew tribes for forty years after their escape from Egypt, and Moses' descent from Mount Sinai carrying the two stone 'tablets of testimony', the Ten Commandments, 'the writing of God', written on stone by the finger of God (*Exodus* 31:18 and 32:15). These two events are a long time apart. The date for the invention of the Semitic alphabet is *c.* 1850BC, but the Hebrew Exodus from Egypt took place over 500 years later, *c.* 1230BC. Nevertheless, it is possible that the story of the Ten Commandments is a record -- a folk memory, if you like -- of the invention of the alphabet or at least the Hebrew discovery that writing existed and could be accessed by them, in this area.

There had almost certainly been literate masons and scribes among the Hebrew slaves in Egypt. However with the discovery of the more accessible and transmissible form of writing in the Sinai, as Moses descends the mountain Hebrew culture seems to take on the idea of writing for itself and is changed. At one stroke they have writing, law, authority and monotheism -- that is, centralized power and divine authority on earth in the recorded word of God. After this it is possible to say that the history of Hebrew culture is that of an obsession with the word and its interpretation; as the Jews emerge from slavery and idolatry to civilization and law they literally become people 'of the word'. It is possible to see in the history of this one culture something of the impact of the invention of writing.

In ancient times there was no difference between politics, religion, genealogy, the laws as revealed by the gods, and the right to rule. They were one and the same thing and it was embodied, eventually, in writing. Writing was employed to help legitimize and secure the power and influence of the rulers. But writing brought with it other possibilities, new ways of thinking, theoretic thought, external symbolic storage of ideas in writing for others to consider, and with it came the upsetting democratization of power and education brought about by mass literacy.

Phoenicians and the Greek Alphabet

The most important of the writing systems to develop in the Middle East was the Phoenician.[67] The Phoenicians were not a nation or even a state in the modern sense, but a group of closely related ethnic groups living in what we now call Lebanon, Palestine and Israel: their major cities were Byblos, Tyre and Sidon. Phoenician speech would have been very similar to ancient Hebrew, indeed Phoenician and Hebrew were dialects of a larger language group called Canaanite: in the Bible Hebrew-speaking Abram, for example, conversed freely with the Canaanites.[68] The Phoenician writing system was created somewhere south of the lands of the Phoenicians *c.* 2000BC, but developed by them into their own alphabet after *c.* 1000BC. It is first recorded in twenty-two wedge-shaped signs made in clay, discovered at the port of Ugarit, near Ras Shamra on the Syrian coast, and later at the North African port of Carthage. Soon after this scribes began to use parchment and ink, and these new materials allowed them to make different kinds of rounded and fluid marks. The early writing systems eventually spread to Phoenician settlements and colonies around the Mediterranean, but the final stage in the development of the alphabet came when this writing system attracted the attention of that other great trading and colonizing power of the time, the Greeks. It is clear that different dialects produced slightly different versions of the basic set of signs within this area, and there is still some debate as to when the Greeks adopted the Phoenician writing system.

In understanding the speed at which writing was adopted in Greece it is important to remember that the area of Greek culture contained several earlier writing systems before the alphabet arrived: in addition to a form of hieroglyphics there was the as yet undeciphered Linear A script, recording an unknown language, dating to *c.* 1800–1450BC which had been used by Minoan palace culture on Crete and the mainland; this was superseded by the Linear B script *c.* 1450–1100BC, which seems to have been used by Mycenean Greek settlers on Crete. However Linear B was lost with the collapse of Mycenean culture.[69] In addition, there

---

67 D. Sacks, *The Alphabet* (Hutchinson: London, 2003).
68 For the Biblical definition of Canaan, see: *Genesis* 10:19; *Genesis* 17:8; *Numbers* 12:29; *Numbers* 34:8.
69 J. Chadwick, *The Decipherment of Linear B* (Cambridge University Press: Cambridge, 1958); J. Chadwick, *Linear B and Related Scripts* (British Museum: London, 2004).

is the undeciphered script recorded on the mysterious Phaistos Disc (*c.* 1850–1400BC), also found on Crete, and possibly originally from Cyprus.[70] The important point here is that although Greece lost the tiny margin of literacy afforded by these scripts within palace culture, some slim memory of literacy remained -- perhaps at a folk memory level, as indicated by the references to writing in Homer.

It is possible that by the time the Phoenician alphabet was transformed and adapted by the Greeks they had already experienced contact with other similar systems from eastern and southern Canaan. There is also debate as to whether the transmission took place in a Greek colony in the east -- in the Beka valley, in Palestine or Canaan -- or a Phoenician colony in Greece or further to the west -- in France, Spain or North Africa. One thing is certain: it could not have happened casually, but needed an area of mixed settlement where these two peoples were in daily contact. The evidence for the transmission to have taken place in a Greek colony in the east is more substantial -- in the eastern Aegean or on the Syrian-Palestinian littoral. It is certain that long before 700BC the Greeks had substantial settlements in Asia Minor, in Mesopotamia, and traded with the ports of Egypt, Crete, Cyprus, the ports along the Levantine coast, towns along the Syrian-Turkish border, up into the Beka valley, in Tel Aviv, and had settlements in Gaza. In all these places there is evidence of the use of similar but not identical kinds of writing and the earliest Greek inscriptions, scratched onto vases, date from the end of the eighth century BC, have been found in this area.[71] On the other hand it may be said, the Phoenicians had been trading and settling across the western Mediterranean since at least 1200BC, so the transmission could have taken place in a Phoenician colony there.[72] The Greek alphabet most closely resembles the Proto-Canaanite alphabet known as the Izbet Sartah Abecedary found in the Sharan Valley in Palestine, dated to around 1100BC.[73]

According to the Greek historian Herodotus, who was working in the fifth century BC and passing on older oral traditions, writing arrived in

---

70 L. Godart, *The Phaistos Disc -- The Enigma of an Aegean Script* (Itanos Publications: Heraklion, 1995).
71 J. Boardman, *The Greeks Overseas* (Penguin: Harmondsworth, 1968), pp.100-01; F. Braudel, *Memory and the Mediterranean* (Knopf: New York, 2001), p.173.
72 D. Harden, *The Phoenicians* (Penguin: Harmondsworth, 1971), p.52-9.
73 J. Goody, *The Interface Between the Written and the Oral* (Cambridge: Cambridge University Press, 1988), 47, 61.

Greece from the eastern Mediterranean. The event is recorded in sidelong fashion in Greek mythology. According to legend, Zeus, disguised as a white bull, abducted Europa from the beach at Sidon. He swam with her on his back to Crete where he shape-shifted into the form of an eagle and ravished her in an olive grove. Europa's brother Kadmos, whose name means man of the east, (and whose younger brother was called Phoinix, as in Phoenicia) set out to search for her: it was to the island of Rhodes that he went first. There, probably at Lindos, he introduced the idea of the alphabet to the Greeks, built a temple to Poseidon and dedicated a bronze cauldron with a Phoenician inscription to Athena before moving on to the mainland to continue his search. Eventually, when he had given up the search, Kadmos founded the city of Thebes. So, while the details elude us, the myth records the folk-memory that both settlers and the invention of writing came from the eastern Mediterranean.[74] But it was almost certainly in Greece -- or at least within the Greek culture of the eastern Mediterranean -- that the alphabet underwent its next development.

Phoenician writing, like most of the early writing systems devised in this part of the world recorded only consonants. It did not record vowels. This was because the languages used in that part of the world -- Aramaic, Arabic and Hebrew -- made great use of consonants but less use of vowels. This was fine as long as the writing system was used to record these languages. Greek, however, belonged to an entirely different language group and made much greater use of vowels to distinguish words and meanings.

Try writing the sentence 'I am an ass' using only consonants. Alternatively using only consonants try writing the sequence *pack, park, parka, peek, peak, peck, pike, pick, pock, poke, puke, puck*. You will see very quickly the kind of problem that using this system without adaptation would have caused for Greek speakers. And this problem was made even worse when, unlike most words in Semitic languages, a Greek word began with a vowel or a diphthong.

There are examples cited in rabbinical studies where two possible meanings might cause theological debate. At one point the Tablets of the Law are described as *hrt* (*Exodus* 32:16). The problem is that this could

74 R. Graves, *The Greek Myths*, vol 1 (Penguin: Harmondsworth, 1971), pp.194-98; M. Bernal, *Black Athena: The Afroasiatic Roots of Classical Civilisation*, vol. 1, (Vintage: London, 1991), pp.69, 85.

mean two things in Hebrew: it could mean that the tablets are *harut* (engraved) or that they are *herut* (free). Because only the consonants are written, the word 'bed' (*Genesis* 47:31) also looks very like the word 'staff' (*Hebrews* 11:21). There is another example when we are told the prophet Elijah is 'fed by ravens' (*I Kings* 17:4-6). But in Hebrew the word 'ravens' looks the same as the word for 'Arabs'.[75] Given the kind of language they had and the greater use they made of vowel sounds, the Greeks had little option but to adapt the new writing system to represent vowels.

Some of the signs they borrowed represented sounds in Phoenician and the other languages of the area that did not occur in Greek and which were therefore 'spare'. The Greeks applied the redundant Semitic signs -- A E O Y -- to Greek vowel sounds. Also they added the letter I. The Greeks took certain letter forms --Δ E N Ξ Π P H and Σ -- from Phoenician and earlier Canaanite writing systems. And they took the signs Φ X Ψ Ω from even earlier Thamudic and Safaitic alphabets, which had been developed much further south: unusually, both of these early alphabets seem to have recorded vowel sounds. In this way the Greeks developed a system of twenty-four signs, representing the seventeen consonants and seven vowels of the Greek language: they could, if needed, combine two letters to make further signs. The new alphabet was written at first only in upper, but later was written in lower case letters: upper case was better for inscriptions carved in stone, while lower case was better for 'handwriting' on papyrus and wax tablets. In the early days the Greek alphabet was written both left to right and right to left in alternate lines -- this was called *boustrophedon*, after the ox which pulled the plough in one direction then at the end of the field turned round to plough in the reverse direction. And even when the Greeks did begin to write from left to right, they did not insert spaces between the words. (Irish monks introduced spaces between words in manuscripts in the sixth century, but this idea was not adopted elsewhere until the twelfth century.)

Although the exact date of transmission is uncertain, some Greeks had been literate in the Linear B script before the Dark Ages, and probably -- though so far there is no evidence yet to prove it -- for some time afterwards. They had known what writing did and what it was for, even if that was now only distant a folk memory. Even so, the leap

---

75 S. Cook, *An Introduction to the Bible* (Penguin: Harmondsworth, 1956), p.38; J. Goody and I. Watt, 'The Consequences of Literacy', in P. P. Giglioli (ed.), *Language and Social Context* (Penguin: Harmondsworth, 1973), p.328.

to write again, to make use of a new alphabet cannot have been totally unthinkable. Be that as it may, the earliest date for the transmission of the Phoenician–Canaanite alphabet to Greece is probably *c.* 1800BC and the latest date is *c.* 700BC. Some experts favour a transmission starting *c.* 1400BC, but others favour *c.* 1100–1050 BC.[76] However, the earliest examples of the Greek alphabet appear on vases and tiles dating from *c.* 800–750BC and they make use of Semitic letter forms dating from the late ninth or early eighth centuries BC, so this seems the more likely period for transmission.[77]

The exact route of the transmission is also unknown. The origin of the Greek alphabet is certainly Phoenician, but the fact that Greeks makes use of Phoenician signs and signs from earlier Middle Eastern writing and then seems to decide on a version of the alphabet adopted further north in Syria is confusing. However, it is likely that the different trading areas within Greece picked up different versions of the alphabet at slightly different times and in different places, and that only gradually did the different variations settle down into one accepted and fairly standard form. Some Greek traders clearly made use of the alphabet they picked up from trading with Aramaic speakers on the north Syrian coast, rather than more southerly sites, and this version seems to have been carried along the coastal trading routes via settlements and colonies in northern Syria, southern Anatolia and Cyprus. Alternatively the alphabet was transmitted along this same route, as Greek myth suggests, by the movement and settlement of people from the Eastern Mediterranean into the Aegean area.[78] After 'several twists and turns' the Ionic version of the Greek alphabet -- that is the version accepted in the Dodecanese and Ionic islands -- became the 'classical' Greek alphabet.[79]

The island of Rhodes, as indicated by Greek legend, was almost certainly one of the earliest places to make use of the new writing system and may also have been a key centre for its onward transmission to mainland Greece. There, in this pivotal ancient cultural, trade and shipping centre with its links to colonies and ports in Anatolia, Syria,

---

76 M. Bernal, *Black Athena: The Afroasiatic Roots of Classical Civilisation* vol 1, (Vintage: London, 1991), pp. 431-2, 393-99, 427-33.
77 J. Boardman, *The Greeks Overseas* (Penguin: Harmondsworth, 1968), p.100.
78 M. Bernal, *Black Athena: The Afroasiatic Roots of Classical Civilisation,* vol. 2 (Rutgers: New Brunswick, 1993), pp.501-4.
79 J. F. Healey, *The Early Alphabet* (British Museum Press: London, 1993), pp.38-9.

Lebanon, Egypt and Cyprus, one of the earliest examples of Greek writing, dating from the eighth century BC, is a small black *kylix* (wine cup). Now in the Copenhagen National Museum, this cup bears the inscription 'I am the cup of Korakos'. By the seventh and sixth centuries BC writing in the new alphabet was well established on the island of Rhodes -- and unlike the writing systems of the past, which had been confined to the ruling elite and to the palaces, this writing system rapidly came into more general use. From the towns of Kamiros, Lindos and Ialysos there is plentiful evidence of Greek writing on gravestones, urns, pots, cups, jugs, plates and even on a bronze cauldron. By the end of the sixth and start of the fifth centuries BC there are records of many distinguished writers living and working on Rhodes -- the poet Pisinous of Lindos, Pisander of Kamiros, Kleobolus of Lindos (poet-tyrant of Lindos, one of seven sages of antiquity), his daughter Kleobolina, and Timokreon of Ilaysos. After the foundation of the city of Rhodes in 450BC examples of writing abound. In the fourth century there was the comedy writer Anaxandrides of Kamiros. In the third century there was the poet Simias of Rhodes, Kallixenos, and of course Appolonius of Rhodes. The rich cultural environment produced scholars like Eudemus of Rhodes, and provided a home for visiting scholars and philosophers including Aristippus of Cyrene, a pupil of Socrates. Unfortunately for the most part we only know the names and a few quotations from their writings -- mainly from their grave markers: apart from a few surviving quotations, their works have been lost.[80]

Wherever and whenever it happened, the first works of European literature were recorded in the Greek alphabet: the great epic poems *The Iliad* and *The Odyssey*, composed orally by a figure we call Homer, were written down c. 740-550BC. However, we cannot be certain whether they were among the first things to be written down (which seems unlikely), or whether they come after a period of literacy for which the evidence is scanty (which seems more likely). Certainly these poems display a level of literacy and literary competence that cannot have been acquired overnight.

In Greek the letters of the alphabet are still called *phoinikeia grammata* (Phoenician letters) and the Phoenician-Canaanite origins of the Greek

---

80 C. Karousos, Rhodes: *History, Monuments, Art* (Esperos: Athens, 1973), p.35. C. Torr, *Rhodes in Ancient Times* (3rd Guides: Oxford, 2005), pp.142-162, provides a more detailed list of the scholars, teachers and writers of Rhodes.

alphabet are not hard to see;

- The Greek alphabet takes the running order of its letters from the running order of the Phoenician alphabet -- ABΓΔE.
- The names of the Greek letters are also taken from Phoenician. The Greek letter A, for example, had originally been, upside down, a bull's head with horns and eyes. Significantly the letter is named *aleph* in Greek. The word has no meaning in Greek, but is derived from the word *alpu* which means *bull* in several languages from the Middle East including Hebrew.
- The second letter B is called *beta* in Greek, and this word too has no meaning in Greek, but is derived from the word *beth* which, in several Semitic languages -- including modern Hebrew -- means a house or court. The name of the letter and its shape were derived from the fact that in its original form it looked like the plan of a building set in a courtyard.
- Together these two words *aleph* and *beth*, alpha and beta, form the Greek and our name for the alphabet.
- The third letter -- G in English -- Γ is *gamma* in Greek, though it is sometimes referred to as a throwing stick, is a corruption of the Semitic name of the letter, *gimmel* or camel, so named because it resembled a camel's neck and head.
- The fourth letter – Δ or D is *delta* – derives from Semitic word *daleth* or door, which was the letter for both the voiced and unvoiced *d* and *t* sounds.

This is the start of our alphabet. The Greek alphabet passed to the Etruscans, then to the Romans and finally, because the Romans occupied Britain and most of Western Europe, the alphabet came down to us in its Roman version. The alphabet (unlike cuneiform or hieroglyphics) was simple to use and quick to learn and these were prime factors in its success.

Once an alphabet -- a stable system of signs representing sounds -- had been developed and made available almost anyone could learn to read and write. It was no longer necessary for an Egyptian or Babylonian scribe to spend seven to ten years learning the essential 2–3,000 signs. As the French historian of Mediterranean cultures, Fernand Braudel wrote:

Writing is basically a technology, a way of committing things to memory and communicating them, enabling people to send orders and to carry out administration at a distance. Empires and organised societies extended over space are the children of writing, which appeared everywhere at the same time as these political units, and by a similar process.[81]

More importantly, writing was a powerful accelerator for social and political change. It was not only a tool of imperial command, but an instrument of trade, of demystification and communication. Also, once the new system of alphabetic writing had been invented, literacy could not remain the property of the scribal elite for ever, knowledge -- legal and scientific -- could not stay secret but was opened up to dispute and interpretation. The days of the powerful scribal elite, with a palace power-base backed up by the mysteries of the heavens and political privilege, were clearly numbered.

English Language and the Alphabet

Writing is not language, but a supplement to language. Although writing and the way writing is taught, both encourage us to believe that somehow writing represents language, the fact is that writing is a communication system (perhaps even a language) all of its own.

The more we know about writing and the thought processes that go into writing, the more we realize that writing is related to language and even overlaps in certain respects, but writing is certainly not just spoken language written down. In writing, all languages making use of the Latin alphabet have to make an accommodation and an approximation to the alphabet, and each language does this in its own way. Some do it with strange letters like the German ß-sign, others do it by marking certain letters of the alphabet with diacritical signs like the French accents à and é, Polish nasal vowels ą and ę, the German umlaut ö, or the Hungarian double accent -- ű. The way the English language makes use of the

---

81 F. Braudel, *Memory and the Mediterranean* (Knopf: New York, 2002), p.62.

alphabet is often curious and inconsistent.[82]

The English alphabet does not distinguish between the dark and light l. Contrast the 'dark' /l/ sound in the words *film, table, bottle* with the 'light' /l/ in the words *like, lot, lump*. Polish distinguishes by marking the 'dark' sound with a bar – ł.

English uses the same letter and makes no written distinction between the 'o' sound in *go* and the very different 'o' sound in *stop*. Greek on the other hand has two letters for the same sound: O and Ω.

Our alphabet does not indicate glottal stops, common in London and in Manchester accents: *gotta lotta bottle, get a cab, Gatwick, mutton.*

In our use of the alphabet we do not always indicate differences in meaning through pronunciation. For example in English the words *pair, pear* and *pare* are all pronounced identically but it is the spelling that tells us what exactly we are referring to.

Unlike modern Greek, English does not indicate stress and intonation with accents. Indeed, as in English stress is not constant -- for example the noun *entrance* and the English verb *entrance* are not pronounced with the same stress -- the absence of stress markers can be very confusing for foreigner learners.

We do not always indicate weak and strong forms. That is, when words have two forms -- a strong or accented form and a weak or un-accented form -- for example the book / *the* book, depending whether they are pronounced with any particular force or stress. In English, over fifty words, many expressing grammatical relationships (determiners, pronouns, auxiliary verbs, prepositions, conjunctions and particles) are particularly affected. For example: *a, and, that, his, our, some, the, your, as, but, at, for, from, of, to, he, her, him, them, us, am, are, can, do, does, had, has, have, is, was, were, must, shall, could, will, would, there, not.* These words differ when they are said in isolation (strong form) and when they are said as part of a sentence (weak form). Weak forms are normal in speech, but they are not indicated in written texts or taken into account in the alphabet. Often the context of a word is important. When, for example,

---

82 Examples from: M. D. Munro Mackenzie, *Modern English Pronunciation Practice* (Longman: London, 1967); A. S. Hornby, *Oxford Student's Dictionary of Current English* (OUP; Oxford, 1978); A. S. Hornby, *Using the Oxford Advanced Learner's Dictionary of Current English* (OUP: Oxford, 1977); *Teacher's Guide to the Longman's Dictionary of Contemporary English* (Longman: London, 1979); J. D. O'Connor, *Phonetics* (Penguin: Harmondsworth, 1973).

there is a strong adverb denoting a place, the word *there* (Look over *there*) appears in its strong form. But at the start of a sentence like *There's nothing like a cup of tea*, the word *there* appears in its weak form.

In English use, our alphabet does not show assimilation. That is when adjacent sounds influence each other and become closer or similar to each other. This is very common in rapid speech. In the phrases 'ten balloons' or 'ten bikes' the phrase is likely to become *tem balloons* or *tem bikes*. In both cases the /m/ anticipates the bilabial consonant which follows. In the phrase 'bridge score', the *dge* sound clearly influences the start of the second word and modulates the /s/ into a *sch* sound. The same thing happens with Church Street, where the sound is nearer to *schtreet*.

In some cases, sounds coalesce and fuse into a new sound segment that is neither one word nor the other. In the phrase 'won't she', the final /t/ and the initial /sh/ combine to produce something like a /tch/ sound. Another example would be the phrase: 'don't you'.

In English the alphabet does not record or indicate where we have elision, that is, where in rapid speech some sounds are left out (elided) altogether. Some examples:

Acts of Parliament (ax uv)
next day (nexday)
government (gove-ment)
mashed potatoes (mash-potatoes)
police (p'lice)
tomato (t'mato)
correct (crect)
library (libry)
particularly (particuly)
got to go (gota go)
go away (go-way)
try again (try-gen)
cup of tea (cup o tea)
lots of time (lotsa time)
lots of people (lotsa people)
going to (gonna)
want to (wanna)

There are a number of occasions when there is no /r/ in the written sentence, but an /r/ sound is added. This is called the linking or liaising /r/. The liaising /r/ is important in 'helping' the passage of certain combinations of sounds, but it is not written. For example:

The Shah of Iran
I don't have an idea in my head
The China intervention
Draw up a list
India and Pakistan
Media interest
Law and order
A flaw in the diamond

Perhaps most strange of all, the commonest sound in the English language, the /ə/ or 'schwa' sound (the unstressed *a* sound and the final sound in words like *leader, actor*), is not identified as a separate alphabetic sign at all, but instead is 'covered' by a bewildering variety of possible signs.

Clearly the alphabet is not perfectly matched to the sounds of the English language and is approximate rather than scientifically accurate. This is what Derrida means when he says that an alphabetic sign is only 'half there' and even when it is there it is often 'not that'.[83] It might have been more convenient if there was only one sound for each letter -- if *a* always sounded as in the word *same*, instead of also covering the sounds in *cat* and *charm* -- but this would also have the effect of requiring us to develop more letters to cover all the sounds of the language: probably in total we would need forty to fifty letters, rather than current 26.[84] The linguistician Roy Harris tried to imagine what a Martian arriving on earth would make of all this:

It is interesting to ask oneself what conclusions a Martian might draw if alphabetic writing were the sole source of evidence available to Martians about the languages of Earth, and if it were believed on Mars that the alphabet must be a system able to cope with all the phonetic vagaries of Earthly speech.

83 J. Derrida, *Of Grammatology* (Johns Hopkins: Baltimore, 1976), xvii.
84 H. & C. Laird, *The Tree of Language* (Faber & Faber: London, 1957), p.56.

Among the first conclusions the Martian might draw, presumably, are that stress and intonation play no role in speech. Earthlings would be envisaged as endowed with organs of phonation which were limited to producing an even, monotonous vibration, with abrupt qualitative transitions between one segment and the next (...) Martian philologists would be led to conclude erroneously that, for example, the English noun *entrance* and the English verb *entrance* were phonetically identical. More generally they would be unable to detect patterns of allophonic variation of the type which distinguishes, say, the initial consonant of English *leaf*, from the final consonant of English *feel*. They would be quite unaware that there are sounds in French which never occur in English, and vice versa. They would seriously underestimate the number of English phonemes, and would be oblivious to the fact that different varieties of spoken English utilise different phonemic contrasts. They would suppose that *pair*, *pear* and *pare* were all pronounced differently, and that cough rhymed with rough. In short their attempts to reconstruct phonological systems for the languages of earth would go far astray, and they would have scarcely any information about what speech sounded like at all.[85]

We cannot fix the exact point in time where alphabetic writing emerged, or the exact spot where it was invented. But although we don't often think of them as such, reading and writing were in themselves a remarkable new technology: but with the various tools that enable reading and writing -- chisels, quills, pencils, fountain pens, styluses, biros, typewriters, printing presses, books and computers -- that is exactly what they are. These things brought about a massive revolution in the possibilities open to the human mind. As Jaques Derrida put it, alphabetic writing 'increases the power of representation'.[86] And that revolution is far from ended. While the invention of television, telephones, the computer and home videos etc. have all meant a gradual reduction in reading as a habit, the new technologies have also made it clear that the immense human possibilities inherent in reading and writing are still far from exhausted.

In the last few years, for example, we have seen a new alphabetic sign @ -- sometimes called the strudel -- added to keyboards. And with the development of a new European currency, it is perhaps only a matter of time before we lose the pound sign £ and see the sign for the Euro -- €

---

85 R. Harris, *The Origin of Writing* (La Salle: Illinois, 1986), pp.100-01.
86 J. Derrida, *Of Grammatology* (Johns Hopkins: Baltimore, 1976), p.295.

-- added to keyboards. Or, if things go badly for the European currency, before we lose the € and revert to national currency symbols. Only time will tell. But next time you write a postcard or a note for the fridge door, or your texting thumbs start to twitch, remember that the tools we use to write, the letters and combinations of letters in our alphabet, took a long time to get to us and are the end result of thousands of years of trial and development. One way to think about this is to imagine the history of humans as a single day of twenty-four hours, where the invention of writing comes very late in the evening;

Numeracy	*c.* 8000 BC	22.50hrs
Pre-writing signs	*c.* 5300 BC	23.07
Egyptian hieroglyphs	*c.* 3200 BC	23.15
Mesopotamian cuneiform	*c.* 3100 BC	23.16
Indus script	*c.* 2500 BC	23.17
Early Semitic scripts	*c.* 2000 BC	23.19
Linear A	*c.* 1800 BC	23.20
Linear B	*c.* 1550 BC	23.29
Phoenician script	*c.* 1200 BC	23.42
Greek alphabet	*c.* 775BC	23.45
Great Library in Alexandria	*c.* 250BC	23.50
Gutenberg printing press	1450	23.55
Burt's Typewriter[87]	1829	23.58
Internet	1997	24.00

However, to put this into an even longer view, if we imagine the entire biological evolution of life on planet earth as a year of 365 days, the very first signs of life appear on 1 January; hominids appear at about 5.30 in the evening on New Year's Eve; Neanderthals arrive at about twenty minutes to midnight; modern humans show up at three minutes to midnight.[88]   On this scale we've been writing for about ten seconds.

For most of our existence, humanity has been without writing and without history. And even after writing had been invented, for a very long time most people could not read or write. It is generally thought

---

87 W. A. Beeching, *The Century of the Typewriter* (British Typewriter Museum, Bournemouth, 1990).
88 J. M. Foley, *How to Read an Oral Poem* (Illinois University Press, Chicago, 2002), pp.23-4.

that in ancient times at best 2 per cent of the population could read. Up to the Industrial Revolution, probably only about 10 per cent of the British population could read. Although literacy in Britain improved slowly throughout the eighteenth century and achieved new impetus with the 1870 Education Act, it is only with the growth of lending libraries after 1900 and with the provisions of the 1944 Education Act that we might expect everyone to be functionally literate.[89] Literacy is the key to rising living standards, improving health, technological progress and the development of civilization. Literacy is also one of the keys to democracy. Throughout most of its history writing was the possession of the ruling class. What we have with early examples of writing is an insight into the life and history of the privileged elite, the ruling class. What we have with the history of writing after the invention of the alphabet is the steady democratization and the spread of at least functional literacy: what we also have in writing, as law, science, and civic mediator, is a finer system of socialization and political control.

---

89 Q. D. Leavis, *Fiction and the Reading Public* (Chatto & Windus: London, 1939); I. Watt, *The Rise of the Novel* (Chatto & Windus: London, 1957); R. Williams, *The Long Revolution* (Penguin: Harmondsworth, 1973); R. Hoggart, *The Uses of Literacy* (Penguin: Harmondsworth, 1966); S. R. Fischer, *A History of Reading* (Reaktion Books: London, 2003).

Directed Study

In what way is the idea of the alphabet linked to the theme of Representation?

Imagine you are a herder living in the deserts of the Middle East around 4000BC. You have a herd of goats, a flock of sheep, a few cows, a tent, a couple of camels, a spinning wheel and some carpets. You are tired of the nomadic life: you want to trade in your possessions and move to the city. You leave your family and go to the city. You find someone willing to buy some of your property and another man willing to buy the rest. They plan to set out tomorrow to claim their purchases, but you want to remain in the city to buy a place for your family to live. Writing has not been invented yet. What tokens will you give each man and what marks will you make on each token, so that each gets what they paid for? How will your family in the desert know that these are your tokens and these men come from you? Invent and design the appropriate tokens and marks. Explain your decisions.

What does the alphabet do and how well does it do it? For example, how accurately does the alphabet 'represent' the speech sounds of the English language?

Is writing a kind of speech? If so what kind of speech does writing 'represent'? If the alphabet does not represent either speech or even the sounds we make, what does it do? What is its function?

'Writing and civilization are intimately connected. Humans live in human society and need language to do so. Without language there can be no human society but without writing there can be no civilization.' What do you understand this to mean?

Are you familiar with another writing system or alphabet
-- for example Russian, Greek or Japanese? If so write a brief
history of that system outlining the principles on which it
works and say how well it represents the sounds of that
language.

'Writing and reading are technological inventions.' What do
you think -- are they a kind of technology?

What does Derrida mean when he says: 'Alphabetic writing
… increases the power of representation'?

What does it mean to say, 'The alphabet was a powerful tool
for democracy'?

4
THE TRANSITION FROM ORAL TO LITERATE CULTURE: FOUNDATION TEXTS

This chapter looks at some of the earliest literary creations to make the transition from oral remembrance to written text and at some more recent survivals from the oral world. Because some early texts have survived and we know something of their history, it is possible to see how and why their origins shaped the kinds of texts that have come down to us. Many early texts carry a society's foundation myths and define tribal identity, so it is perhaps not surprising that, even though their content may have been quite random and the collection and selection difficult to rationalize, they became major religious works. This chapter considers the problems of the process of the transition from an oral to a literate culture, the difficulties of transmitting texts accurately before the invention of printing, and wonders how reliable the texts that have been handed down to us can be. In particular, it asks what it means to write down something which has previously only ever been an oral composition. It asks what might have happened to early texts as they were copied down and then copied on by generations of scribes. It considers what has come down to us, what is missing and what has been mangled.

- Characteristics of Oral Culture
- The Bible
- Homer
- Oral Culture -- Counter Culture

Characteristics of Oral Culture

What does the transition from an oral culture to a written culture mean? How did it happen? What changes might be brought about by the invention and spread of writing? What happens to things when you write them down -- how are they changed? And how can the fragmented ancient texts that have survived to come down to us possibly represent what these things were once like? One of the first things we need to establish is that oral culture depends on poetry as its main and first literary form, alongside daily speech. Prose as a literary form can only really develop with literacy. That is why most of the early literary creations, emerging from oral roots, are in verse. The other points to establish are that the transition may take place over a very long period and in this the interface between the oral and the written may be complex.[90] What I want to emphasize is:

- That an oral culture is fundamentally different from a literate culture, and there is a huge difference between oral and literary transmission
- That the oral traditions of ancient Europe and the Middle East were not much different from the contemporary oral traditions that still survive in Mali, Guinea, Dahomey, Ruanda, Burundi, Congo, South Africa, Polynesia, the Marquessa Islands, Nigeria and New Zealand
- That the structure of oral composition is different from that of written work, and just because a thing is written down, that does not mean it is in any sense 'preserved', or that what is written, and what survives to come down to us, is necessarily accurate or easily understood.
- That what has come down to us may have much to tell us about its origins and may also bear the marks of its change from an oral into a written text.

The first five books of the Bible, unusually, are written in prose, but were probably originally in verse; consequently they are very close to their oral roots and display many of the characteristics of material favoured by oral transmission.[91] To take just one example, genealogies and lists, in the *Book of Ezra* we find this passage:

---

90 J. Goody, *The Interface Between the Written and the Oral* (Cambridge University Press: Cambridge, 1987).
91 J. Vansina, *Oral Tradition* (Penguin: Harmondsworth, 1973).

Now after these things in the reign of Ataxerxes king of Persia,
Ezra, the son of Seraiah, the son of Azaria, the son of Hilkiah,
The son of Shallum, the son of Zadok, the son of Ahitub,
The son of Amariah, the son of Azariah, the son of Meraioth,
The son of Zehariah, the son of Uzzi, the son of Bukki,
The son of Abishua, the son of Phinehas, the son of Eleazar, the son
of Aaron the chief priest:
This Ezra went up from Babylon ... (Ezra 7: 1-6)

Genealogies like this -- there is a similar genealogy in *Genesis* 3:18 -- are an important part of early literature and a certain sign that the text has its origins in oral culture. For us it is staggering to think that at some point in the past someone actually memorized this list of names. However, if you think this list would be difficult to remember, look at the genealogy of the Jewish tribes descended from Adam offered in *The First Book of Chronicles* -- there the list of names covers twelve double column pages. Geza Vermes has commented on the importance of genealogies in early Jewish culture:

The Bible is full of family trees which strike most readers -- apart from addicts of genealogical research -- as far from fascinating, not to say plain boring. Yet they can be rich in meaning and in their variations reveal secret purposes. Scriptural genealogies have a threefold significance. When paraphrased they may serve as an abridged account of history, but they can also be used for two practical, legal purposes. The first of these is to demonstrate the legitimacy of kings and priests. Evidence of direct descent from the house of David was indispensable for succession to the throne, and (...) for the establishment of someone's Messianic status. It was also essential for a Jewish priest, holding a hereditary office handed down from father to son, to be able to prove that he belonged to a family which could trace its line back to Aaron in the tribe of Levi. Without such a pedigree he would lose his livelihood and would not be permitted to function in the Temple of Jerusalem. A genealogical table could also be useful in contested cases of inheritance, that is, when someone claimed entitlement to ancestral property.[92]

---

92 G. Vermes, *The Nativity* (Penguin: Harmondsworth, 2006), p.26.

And this is no different in surviving oral documents from Britain. In *The Anglo-Saxon Chronicles,* which date from the ninth century and were started by Ælfred the Great, there are genealogies for all the ruling British families up to the mid-twelfth century, and every one claims descent from the war-god Woden, for whom places like Wednesbury and the day Wednesday are named. This was at the end of the period dating from the departure of the Romans roughly to the twelfth century, known as the Dark Ages because so very few documents survived. Stephen Oppenheimer comments:

> By adding illustrious ancestors, kings may hope to enhance themselves and their origins. The motivation for such risky creativity has to be legitimacy. One purpose that all royal genealogies share is to establish legitimacy through the identification of lines of descent ... In common with many other royal trees, the Germanic king lists are indeed somewhat creative and legendary, not to say mythical, often stretching back to Biblical names such as Noah.[93]

This is why in the Bible it is claimed that Jesus' parents needed to go back to Bethlehem for a census. In reality there was no census, but the journey to Bethlehem was part of a claim that Jesus was descended from the royal line of David which had its clan origins in Bethlehem. This was essential to the claim that Jesus was a legitimate leader and prophet: without this lineage and descent from the royal line of David the Jews would not take him seriously.

These genealogies indicate their claim to be the rightful descendants of ancient rulers: they tell us what the families thought of themselves and preserve what they know of their origins. This can be very useful to historians. The fact that so many royal families from Anglo Saxon times traced their origins back to what is now southern Sweden, rather than to Saxony in northern Germany, or to Angel-land at the base of the Danish peninsula, has encouraged historians to question whether what we traditionally think of as 'the Saxon invasion' after the departure of the Romans, was Saxon at all.

But to return to our Biblical examples, in the *Book of Numbers* there is another list -- this time of places on a journey -- and again the incantation of the place names, with each place name given twice, would have

---

93 S. Oppenheimer, *The Origins of the British* (Robinson: London, 2006), p.385.

allowed the travellers to memorize them like a supplement to a mental map:

> And they departed from Rephidim, and pitched at Kibbroth-hattaavah.
> And they departed from Kibbroth-hattaavah, and encamped at Hazeroth.
> And they departed from Hazeroth, and they pitched in Rithmah.
> And they departed from Ritmah, and pitched at Rimmon-parrez
> … (*Numbers* 33:16-37)

And so on for another eighteen verses. In the desert, memorizing such a list might just save your life. However, we do not always understand the purposes of passages like these in ancient texts. That is not just a matter of history and distance in time, but a mark of how different a written culture is from an oral culture: the problem for us is that things have survived into texts which, if left in oral form, would not have been preserved at all. They may have made perfect sense in the context of that time, but once written down they live on to become deeply puzzling or like the dietary restrictions embodied in *Leviticus*, become the basis of the law and the justification for the survival of ancient practices, long after the physical conditions or needs for those restrictions have passed. In a way they become the basis not only of religious belief but of an identity.

We can see something of this process at work in the creation of the Koran. From about the second century AD there is evidence of graffiti found in caves, but for the most part Arabic culture relied on a rich tradition of complex oral poetry: literacy came to Arab society rather later than to most of the other peoples of the Middle East. Writing in Arabic script began to develop with the Koran (meaning literally 'the recitation') in the seventh century AD. The Koran is said to be the earliest and finest work of classical Arabic prose. It is also the holy book of the Muslim religion. It embodies a religious system called *al islam* (surrender or submission). The Koran, it is said, is the text given by God to the prophet Mohamed via the angel Gibreel (Gabriel) in a series of visions, dreams and ecstatic seizures, beginning in the year AD 610 and continuing until the death of the Prophet in AD 632.

The messages revealed were not written down by the Prophet Mohamed because he was unable to read or write. However, it is said that the teachings and visions of the Prophet Mohamed were repeated by him to professional scribes or committed to memory and recited by professional remembrancers. It is said that the teachings of the Koran were transmitted entirely as received and that the Koran is the unaltered word of God, the 'scripture whereof there is no doubt', the finest and most perfect representation of literary style. In the ninety-sixth *sura* (verse) it is said that the Koran is a copy of the Eternal Tablet that resides in heaven.

The earliest written records of the Koran were set down on pieces of leather, palm leaves, the shoulder bones of camels, bark and any other suitable materials that came to hand during the lifetime of the prophet -- probably as aids to memory made by the people charged with remembering them accurately.[94] Once these written texts emerged problems of interpretation began to arise, since, as the Koran itself acknowledged, some of its verses were ambiguous. After the Prophet Mohamed's death, Abu Bakr (AD 632–634), one of the first converts to Islam, the prophet's father-in-law, declared himself Kalifa (Caliph, meaning successor by family line of descent) and began to collect and copy the fragments of text. In AD 633 most of those responsible for memorizing the prophet's visions and messages were killed in battle and, as a result, Umar ibn al-Khattab urged Abu Bakr to commit everything to writing.

The canonical text of the Koran was established in AD 651–52 under the third Caliph, Uthman ibn Affan, who added several sections. Caliph Uthman then had all the collected fragments destroyed.[95] While Caliph Uthman may have done this to put an end to dispute, in fact his action led to further dispute as some Muslims claimed that the prophet's son-in-law and cousin had more or less vanished from view in the canonical text, and others found the *suras* or chapters to be counter to their view of established chronology or contrary to their idea of the logical order.

With the destruction of the original versions the texts could no longer be clarified -- an important point since at this time Arabic writing, and particularly the *kufic* script used to record these visions, contained no vowels or diacritical marks, and consequently was so very ambiguous and sketchy that it was little more than an aid to the recitation of already memorized scripts. In spite of this, the problems of oral transmission

---

94 M. Cook, *The Koran: A Very Short Introduction* (OUP: Oxford, 2000): S. R. Fischer, *A History of Writing* (Chicago University Press: Chicago, 2001).
95 . Kiernan, *The Arabs* (Abacus: London, 1980), pp.124-5.

and differing traditions became ever more apparent. When in the tenth century Ibn Mujahid began to collate different versions of the Koran, he found he had to contend with no less than seven leading traditions of recitation, mostly dating back to the eighth century. An eleventh-century Islamic scholar travelling from Morocco to Central Asia recorded fifty different traditions of recitation received from 365 teachers relating to the same 1,459 lines of text.

It is important to note that Shi'ites did not accept many Sunni traditions nor have they accepted about fifty of the standard readings in the Sunni version of the Koran. In addition to the Koran they also have other religious texts written out of a different oral tradition dating from the tenth and eleventh centuries. Although there seem to have been many variant traditions within Islam, over time only one version of these visions and teachings came to dominate. But this version is not uncontested. While variant readings of the Koran are recognized within Islam, these splits and the difficulties the destruction of the original records left behind are still with Muslim communities to this day.

The first translation of the Koran from Arabic appeared in Latin in 1141. It was translated again in Venice in 1530, but the Pope and the Spanish Inquisition suppressed it. Another printed edition appeared in Switzerland in 1541, but the Basel city authorities suppressed it until Martin Luther intervened to protest at this censorship and the edition was released the following year. In Arabic, the Koran could not be printed for many years. It was issued only in handwritten copies up until the eighteenth century and it took special permission from the Turkish Sultan for the first small printed edition to appear in 1772. Only in 1874 did the Turkish government grant permission to print the Koran. In the rest of the Muslim world the printing of the Koran was forbidden. In Egypt the first printed edition appeared in 1833, but this was almost immediately locked away. Only under Said Pasha (1854–63) was this edition finally released in limited numbers. The first generally available printed edition authorized by the Egyptian government appeared only in 1925. The oral origins of the Koran have been preserved because memorization and oral recitation are said to be part of the essence of the the message and are still considered to be essential elements of Islam and the cohesive identity of every Muslim community.

The Classics

Wikipedia defines the Classics as: 'texts written in the ancient Mediterranean world'. *The Concise Oxford Dictionary* defines the Classics as: 'outstandingly important works of acknowledged excellence or value in Latin or Greek'. These are useful starting points, but 'the Classics' has a much wider range of meaning than either of these definitions. The Classics, in addition to polished and sophisticated works in Latin and Greek, also refers to work from other ancient European cultures and from further afield, and includes texts that began life as oral compositions. Texts like the *Hymns of the Rigveda,* the Bible, the Koran, *Gilgamesh, The Iliad* and *The Odyssey, Táin Bó Cúalnge, Mabinogion* and *Beowulf* are all foundation texts of literary culture and modern civilization. They all have their roots in oral culture, and they emerge into written form as part of the long, ongoing transition from an oral to a literary culture. The literary critic Northrop Frye wrote:

> An oral culture depends on memory and consequently it also depends mainly on verse, the simplest and most memorable way of conventionalising the rhythm of speech. In oral culture mythology and literature are almost coterminous: the teachers of the myth are poets, or people with skills akin to the poetic, who survive in legend or history as bards, prophets, religious teachers, or culture-heroes of various kinds. With a writing culture, prose develops, and the continuity of prose enables philosophy to take form, as a mode of thought articulated by logic and dialectic. Similarly, history detaches itself from epic, and gradually becomes the study of what actually occurred. Further, as writing culture is usually a counting and measuring culture as well, scientific and mathematical procedures form part of the same change in mental attitude.[96]

Writers look at the foundation texts in a particular 'writerly' way, since the fundamental questions about writing are often much more clearly in focus than when asked in relation to contemporary writing.

While oral culture generally may have 'perished on the air', it left its mark on what was to come. The transition from an oral to a literate culture was not sudden -- in some parts of the world and in some parts

---

96 N. Frye, 'The Social Context of Criticism' (1970) in: E. Burns & T. Burns (eds.), *Sociology of Literature & Drama* (Penguin: Harmondsworth, 1973), p.149.

of our own society, it is still going on. Even in societies where the written word is widespread, the transition took many years during which the oral culture continued to influence and shape the written culture. In ancient Greece for example -- which made a swift transition to culture and mental habits associated with writing -- it is nevertheless clear that the historian Herodotus read his texts aloud to a public audience much in the manner of an ancient storyteller working in a village square or market place. Socrates' dialogues, though written down by Plato, owe a great deal to early unwritten popular public theatre. Equally there is evidence that once a thing was written down it acquired 'authority' and that, once texts existed, even oral practitioners consulted and referred to them.

In considering texts once based on oral transmission we have to remember that we are studying myths and stories which have somehow survived to be written down, and once written, we are looking at texts which have somehow survived or have been copied-on down several generations into the present day. Also we are often dealing with differing tribal histories or scribal traditions that contributed to different parts of these documents, and that this often allowed or helped the documents to survive, but which also contributed to confusion as to their interpretation. Sometimes the documents in their various parts reveal they are but snapshots of a historical process of development and combination, since they record competing versions, changing interpretations and reinterpretations of belief systems and each of these has affected the surviving texts at every stage of their transmission.[97] We know, for example, that even in Classical Greece, written records were relatively scarce. Greek tradition mainly preserved knowledge orally. Individual families, a community, a whole clan might have a professional remembrancer to keep the tradition of their origins and the stories of their founders in oral form. It is clear from Herodotus -- Europe's first historian -- that religious centres and sanctuaries also preserved oral traditions, with varying degrees of accuracy, and that he was able to make use of these oral sources when he came to write his histories. However, he realized that what he was writing down was not as simple as it sounded since, often, when he was gathering his evidence,

---

97 J. Z. Smith, *Drudgery Divine: On the Comparison of Early Christianities and Religions of Late Antiquity* (Routledge Curzon: London, 1990), p.107.

there was not necessarily any agreement between different traditions or versions of a particular event.[98]

Clearly the fact that these texts all emerged over a very long period of time and that a great many people were involved in writing and editing them at various periods, means that the materials we have available to us have been shaped at different times by different needs, conditions and even by different traditions. Indeed, within Hebrew tradition it is clear that the first five books of the Old Testament contain competing versions of the same events (for example the Creation), presumably from differing tribal traditions. At some point both the Bible and the Koran were collected and then at a later date edited into the texts that have come down to us.

All the major religions stress the antiquity and the divine origins of their central texts. They are usually said to have been 'given' a long, long time ago and in specific circumstances. The texts are usually said to be the 'word of God': generally, however, God did not actually write them, but dictated them to a chosen man, so they are clearly the physical product of humanity. To complicate matters, however, Moses and Mohammed, the people responsible for the texts, were both illiterate.

Oral cultures generally equate hearing 'the word' with understanding and acceptance. The pre-Socratic philosopher Heraclitus (c. 535–c475BC) used the Greek word *ksuneimi*, meaning to know, but this word had the specific connotation 'to know by hearing'. Socrates and Plato both equated listening with knowledge. Religious texts like the Bible clearly privileged aural teaching: 'And God said, "Let there be light", and there was light' (*Genesis* 1:3). In the *New Testament*, Jesus is said to be 'the word of God made flesh' (*John* 1:14) or 'the word of God' (*Revelation* 29:13). Jesus, like God, did not himself write any of his teachings. Those of his teachings that have come down to us were written by Gospellers working anything from fifty to 200 years after his death. At first, while it was still a possibility that Jesus might influence the Jews, Paul and the Gospellers, in producing what was to become the New Testament, made extensive use of the Old Testament to legitimate their writings and locate Jesus as a descendant of the royal House of David -- hence the invention of a census at the time of his birth and the necessity of a return to Bethlehem. However, as it became clear that this effort was not going

---

98 Herodotus, *The Histories* (Penguin: Harmondsworth, 1996), p. xix.

to succeed, that the Jews were not going to accept Jesus, Paul and the others emphasized the less specifically Jewish and the more open and universal aspects of Jesus's teaching in order to reach a wider, Roman and Greek, non-Jewish audience. In this we can see not only the text in an emerging tradition, but also, and virtually at the same time, being reshaped to new purposes.

All writing is intended to be read by someone. Writing is an intervention in public life -- a private act with public consequences; it is designed to take an idea from one head and put it into another -- possibly into many. Writing is a conscious activity, intricately and inseparably bound up with the development of intellect, engagement with the world, the desires to make a record and leave a mark. It is also part of the fact that humans think about themselves, their lives and their situation, in ways that animals cannot. In addressing fundamental issues about the nature of the foundation texts, we are inevitably invited to think about ourselves, about our place in the world, about what we do, and to ask: What it is to be human? What is it that humans do? Why are reading, writing and speaking unique, amazing, deeply mysterious and worthy of further study?

Writing and civilization are products of the human mind: although there have been civilizations that existed largely without writing or records as we understand them, without writing civilization could not develop or survive: and without civilization there is no writing. Without writing how could we know what we had in our winter stores, direct hunting parties to game and shelter, collect tribute or taxes, order armies to move, make laws and regulations? Writing enabled civilization and civilization enabled writing.

If the use of language in humans marks a transition from nature to culture, then the use of writing marks a transition from tribal culture to urban civilization. If making marks of some sort was originally a form of keeping accounts, and later grew into what we now call writing, and if the management of stores, palaces and cities developed into what we now call civilization, why should we imagine that a connection of responsibility so intimate, so enormous on a cultural level, so important to the species, should be anything less at a personal level? Writing and civilization: an uneasy partnership. They are responsible for each other: they are quite literally each other's measure.

How reliable are the early texts that have come down to us? What was the process by which they were written down? What happens to texts as they are copied down and then copied on? How far can we trust the versions that have survived? In what ways are the surviving texts representative of the times and the culture in which they were written? Historian Leslie Adcock, for example, lamenting the lack of original texts dating from the period of King Arthur's Britain, wrote:

> No fifth or sixth century manuscripts directly relevant to our study have survived. Instead we have to make do with later manuscripts that had been laboriously copied from the original documents of our period at a time when they were still in existence. Indeed, what we normally find is that we are dealing with copies of copies ... of copies. Thus we may have a twelfth-century copy of a tenth-century compilation which includes annals written down in the fifth-century; or a thirteenth-century copy of a poem composed orally in the sixth but not written down before the ninth-century. Over this lengthy period of transmission, in the process of repeated copying, various accidents may happen to the original text (...)[99]

The possible problems for the early manuscripts are many. Firstly there are simple scribal errors, where the copyist accidentally drops letters or words -- and in an inflected language like Polish, German, French or Latin this can be crucial in determining meaning. This is made worse where the scribe is copying someone else's copy, rather than an original text. Did the first scribe understand the language he was copying? Did the text he was copying already contain errors?

Many of the key documents from British history in the fifth and sixth centuries were made after the Norman Conquest, copied by scribes who understood little or no Welsh, so many Welsh names, place names and other terms became mangled. Even Latin terms proved to be a problem for some copyists. There is an example of this in a copy of a letter by Pope Gregory the Great in which the scribe misunderstood the Latin abbreviation *mag. mil.* (*magister militum*, a Roman military rank) and copied it as *magni l*, which made no sense, but which was then corrected by the Deacon to read *magnificus*.[100]

Whole lines or paragraphs may be lost in a copied document. This

---

99 L. Adcock, *Arthur's Britain* (Penguin: Harmondsworth, 1973), p.3.
100 P. Wolff, *The Awakening of Europe* (Penguin: Harmondsworth, 1968), p.62.

is particularly likely to happen where two lines or paragraphs begin with the same word or phrases. The scribe may not notice this and resume copying at the wrong place, omitting everything in between. Sometimes scribes try to 'improve' their text by modernizing spellings, dropping case endings, or updating language they take to be archaic. Sometimes a scribe may think he knows better than his text and decide to insert additional information and thus alter the text he is supposed to be copying. Interpolations of this kind may be responsible for some of the mysteries surrounding the figure of King Arthur. For example, it is possible that in the *British Historical Miscellany* the scribe in the *scriptorium* at St David's working in the years AD 1100–1125 at copying a document dating AD 955-970, was guilty of inserting Arthur's name into an otherwise accurate reference to the Battle of Mount Badon which had taken place in the year AD 518. If this is so then, while it may not tell us much about the historical figure of Arthur, it does tell us something about the persistence of oral history, about the creation of a legend and the growing cult of Arthur that inclined the scribe to add this information. But whether this addition was in any way historically accurate, or perhaps recorded something the scribe knew from elsewhere, is still impossible to say.[101]

And even when an oral text made the transition into a written manuscript, its future was not assured as the life of a manuscript could be exceedingly tough. The Anglo-Saxon poem *Beowulf*, perhaps the most important of all the early English texts, is a good example. It is probable that Anglo Saxons were already present in the British Isles -- along the South and East Coast -- by the time the Romans arrived. The Romans recruited Anglo Saxons as mercenaries to help keep the Scots tribes north of the border. The Roman writer Tacitus, who observed the Germanic tribes at first hand, wrote in his book *Germania* (first century AD), that they had only ancient songs as their 'remembrance and history'. In the year 440, after the departure of the Romans, the Anglo Saxon areas of settlement began to expand westwards. According to legend the Welsh speaking Romano-British resisted this expansion and fought a long rearguard action -- as the story of King Arthur testifies -- but gradually the Saxons, with long established settlements in East Anglia, Kent and

---

101 *British Historical Miscellany* is also known as 'Nennius' *History of the Britons* or BM Harleian MS 3859. L. Adcock, *Arthur's Britain* (Penguin: Harmondsworth, 1973), pp.45-55.

Northumbria spread into Mercia (the Midlands) and the West Country: Celtic society was restricted to Wales, Cornwall and Cumbria.[102]

There is some disagreement as to the oral history of *Beowulf* before it was written down. The strange structure -- three monsters, three funerals -- and the mixture of actual history with fabulous elements, along with the very patchy nature of the tale itself, indicate that it had a complicated pre-literary life and that what has come down to us is probably a poet working to weave together the various strands of a pre-Christian oral tale, and the manuscript possibly records a version of the tale made up from several different oral performances during the Christian era. *Beowulf* did not become a poem on which a religion was founded, but there are religious questions to be asked about it, since it seems to have arisen at a time when the Anglo-Saxons were in the process of becoming Christian. There is some disagreement as to whether the poem is Christian, using elements of paganism from the recent past, or whether it is simply pagan but made suitable for Christian listeners. Beowulf himself makes no reference to Christianity: all the Biblical references are to the Old Testament: Christian references in the poem are not extensive or intrinsic, amounting to a few words here and there, and could have been inserted into the manuscript of what is basically a pagan tale by a Christian scribe rather than by the poet himself.

The poem *Beowulf* is set at the king's court on Heorot, a real island between Denmark and Sweden and it concerns the ancestors of the Anglo-Saxons -- a tribe called the Geats -- and their battles with monsters. The story looks back to the heroic age of the ancestors. In many ways it is a lament for bygone times and tells of two encounters the warrior Beowulf had with terrible monsters. Beowulf seems to be the last of the great heroes, surrounded by lesser men, who are complacent and untrustworthy, far from ideal leaders. Many of the characters mentioned in the poem were historic figures. Hrothgar, king of the Danes, lived in the fifth century; Hygelac is mentioned in several other documents and is known to have raided the Frisians in the year 521; Beowulf too seems to have been a real figure.

Although set some time in the sixth century, the story of Beowulf had been brought to Britain *c.* 700, composed into its present form orally *c.*

---

102 L. Alcock, *Arthur's Britain* (Penguin: Harmondsworth, 1973).

793 and written or copied *c.* 1000.[103] Although the poem originates and is set in Scandinavia, the language is in an Anglian or West Saxon dialect, but with a great many elements from other dialects and accents, and it is thought to have been written down in Mercia, probably somewhere north of Oxford. We don't know the name of the *scop* (poet) who composed the poem, nor do we know the names of the two scribes who copied it. Although we know from internal evidence the rough date of its composition, transmission and even when it was written down, what happened to it between that date and 1563, when it appears to have been in the possession of Laurence Nowell, Dean of Lichfield, is unknown. It seems likely that for most of its life the manuscript had been in the possession of one of the great British monasteries. However, when Henry VIII dissolved the monasteries in 1536 the manuscript was probably sold off or simply looted.

In 1706 the manuscript is recorded in the library of Sir Robert Bruce Cotton. Twenty-six years later a fire broke out in the Cotton library. Over one hundred of the books were destroyed and another ninety badly damaged. *Beowulf* escaped the blaze but the book in which it was bound was badly scorched and the words at the edges of the pages crumbled away before it could be rebound. Fortunately G. J. Thorkelin, an Icelandic scholar in Danish service, had visited England in 1786 and had ordered a professional scribe to make two copies of the text. Thorkelin had then set about preparing a modern edition of the poem. He was able to supply the lost words from his copies. However his edition of the poem was lost when the British navy bombarded Copenhagen in 1807, destroying Thorkelin's house. Thorkelin nevertheless managed to save his copies of the poem and was persuaded to begin his edition for a second time. In 1815 Thorkelin published the first modern edition with a Latin translation. An English edition and translation did not appear until 1837.[104] Even then the poem was mainly regarded as of interest only to antiquarians and its literary merits were not generally recognized until 1936 when J. R. R. Tolkien published his essay 'Beowulf: the Monsters and the Critics'.[105] The manuscript is now one of the most treasured possessions of The British Museum and a foundation text for English Literature.

---

103 S. Oppenheimer, *The Origins of the British* (Robinson: London, 2007), p.448.
104 *Beowulf*, trans., D. Wright, (Penguin: Harmondsworth, 1967), pp.109-111.
105 J. R. R. Tolkien, *'Beowulf: the Monsters and the Critics' Proceedings of the British Academy* vol. xxii (British Academy: London, 1936), pp.245-95.

The Bible

The Bible is a collection of ancient texts containing early writings which became sacred to both the Jewish and Christian religions. It is thought that the earliest references in the Bible are to a period of the early Middle East Bronze Age, *c.* 2250–2000BC.[106] The standard Jewish calendar indicates that Abraham, Sarah and the Patriarchs lived *c.* 1800BC and the Exodus from Egypt took place *c.* 1290–1220BC. While oral tradition pre-dates writing, the oldest written parts of the Bible seem to date from *c.* 950–725BC. Some of Old Testament had been written by 600BC and the first five books of the Old Testament had all been written down by about 400BC, though canonical acceptance came later.[107]

Authorship of the Bible is far from simple. Among the authors of the Bible are said to be Moses, Samuel, David, Solomon and the Prophets, however, close examination of the surviving texts reveals they were not 'written' by the people to whom they are attributed since these people often lived before the Jewish tribes began to keep written records. If we are to believe that Samuel was the author of the two books attributed to him we have a problem in that he dies before the end of First Book of Samuel, leaving its authorship and that of the Second Book of Samuel as something of a mystery.

Nothing in the Old Testament suggests that Moses himself actually wrote any part of the Bible. The Ten Commandments were said to have been written on stone by the finger of God (*Exodus* 31:18) and given to Moses. This is the only time where God actually writes anything. The text seems to indicate not only that Moses inhabited a largely pre-literate world where writing was still a mystery, but almost certainly that Moses could not read or write. However, it is also clear that to affect his audience Moses was reliant on the growing power, authority and mystery of the written word in the surrounding cultures of Egypt, Sinai, Jordan, Palestine and Lebanon, enhanced by the development of an alphabetic system of writing.

The Old Testament drew on ancient Middle Eastern mythological tradition. The story of The Flood, for example, possibly recalled the

---

106 G. Steiner, 'Preface to the Hebrew Bible' (1966) in *No Passion Spent* (Faber: London, 1996), p.45.
107 T. H. Lim, *The Dead Sea Scrolls: A Very Short Introduction* (OUP: Oxford, 2000); J. Riches, *The Bible: A Very Short Introduction* (OUP: Oxford, 2000); E. W. Heaton, *The Old Testament Prophets* (Penguin: Harmondsworth, 1966).

floods that created the Black Sea *c.* 6000BC, and which also appeared in ancient Mesopotamian literature; the idea of the Garden of Eden is widespread in Middle Eastern mythology; the word and the idea of *paradise* come from ancient Persian mythology. The story of the Creation, which appears in two different versions in *Genesis*, had its roots in ancient Mesopotamian tradition, where a dragon that lived in chaos had to be slain before the universe could be ordered. Traces of this story can be seen in Biblical references to the slaying of Leviathan in *Job* and *Isaiah*. Other elements were drawn from Syrian and Egyptian tradition.[108]

Modern scholars have demonstrated that the early books of the Old Testament --*Genesis, Exodus, Leviticus, Numbers, Deuteronomy, Ecclesiastes* and *Proverbs* -- began life as oral compositions before being written down and compiled together. Genesis, for example, contains passages that may date from oral compositions and traditions of the tenth century BC, but it was probably first written down around the fifth century BC. The oldest fragment of language preserved in the Bible is thought to be the song of Deborah and Barak in *Judges* 5 which may date from the oral culture of tenth or even the eleventh century BC. It is clear in the case of the prophet Amos (*c.* 760BC), that the short structured 'oracles' that have come down to us derive from the prophet's oral preaching style, but the preserved order of the verses is probably not that of the prophet, but rather the work of a scribe. *The Song of Songs, Proverbs* and *Ecclesiastes* are usually attributed in rabbinical tradition to King Solomon, and are thought to date from oral compositions *c.* 1000BC, but were all written down much later. *Proverbs* was probably written down around 500BC, but it records a much older tradition of oral advice. According to rabbinical tradition many of the Psalms in *The Book of Psalms* were composed by King David *c.* 1000–922BC. However, other commentators doubt that King David actually composed any part of it. Some compositions, like the *Book of Lamentations,* along with a general scribal urge to collect and preserve as much written material as possible, might have developed during the exile in Babylon *c.* 587–539BC. Certainly Ezra is thought to have brought 'the book of the law of Moses' from Babylon around the year 539BC and after this religious writing seems to have become a subject of serious discussion, debate and commentary within Jewish culture. Around 458–

---

108 S. Cook, *An Introduction to the Bible* (Penguin: Harmondsworth, 1956), p.24; S. H. Hooke, *Middle Eastern Mythology* (Penguin: Harmondsworth, 1976); K. Armstrong, *The Bible: The Biography* (Atlantic Books: London, 2007).

398BC the bulk of the rewriting, editing and compiling of what was to become the Old Testament seems to have taken place.[109] The impact of writing on the documents gathered is clear and it is possible to contrast the 'old style' oral prophecy in the book of Amos with the new, more considered written style of *Ecclesiastes*.[110]

The first five books of the Bible were certainly in use and in written form by about 400BC, but in several variant forms. Modern Biblical scholars think they can distinguish at least four different authors, possibly separated by hundreds of years, at work in these first five books. At some point these variants and versions must have been compiled and edited into what has come down to us. It is also possible that depending on how tribal allegiances went, some material has been left out for political reasons and is now lost entirely. Within *Genesis*, for example, it is possible to see that whoever compiled the materials was working with at least two parallel sources and tribal narrative traditions and often felt they had to include everything they had at hand or at least to include differing versions of the same event. Having established in *Genesis* 1 how the world and humans were made, the story, slightly altered, starts again in *Genesis* 2. There are many other examples of material appearing in parallel versions. The story of the flood is given in *Genesis* 7:2-3 and 6, but again in 19:7-9 and 15. Abraham's migration is recounted in *Genesis* 12:1-4, and again in 12:4-5. Two versions of the story of God's covenant with Abraham are given, the first in *Genesis* 15 and again in 17. Different versions of the manna and quail in the wilderness are given in *Exodus* 16:2-3 and then again in 16:6-35, but also for a third time in *Numbers* 11:4-34. There are also different versions of the story of the Ten Commandments in *Exodus* 20:1-7 and 34:10-28, and *Deuteronomy* 5:6-18. The dietary rules given in Leviticus 11 are different from those given in *Deuteronomy* 14. In some accounts Mount Sinai is the mount of the Covenant, in other versions it is Mount Horeb.

Evidence suggests that at least two and possibly several different Jewish oral tribal traditions were represented in the writing of the first five books of the Old Testament. For example, up to the start of the exile in Babylon it is likely that some elements of Jewish society were still polytheistic and worshipped several ancient Canaanite gods: the main

109 H. H. Rowley, *The Growth of the Old Testament* (Hutchinson: London, 1969).
110 J. Jaynes, *The Origin of Consciousness in the Breakdown of the Bicameral Mind* (Houghton Mifflin: Boston, 1976), 295-97.

one was called *El*. After the Babylonian exile a different picture emerges and monotheism seems to be the order of the day. However, even within monotheism there is evidence of earlier practice and variant traditions: one tradition referred to God as *Elohim* (E) which is actually a plural form and probably harks back to earlier Canaanite polytheism; the other tradition refers to God as *Jaweh* (J). Both these traditions were concerned with laws, dreams and divine revelations. A third tradition, the *Priestly* (P), seems to have been incorporated later: this was mainly concerned with genealogies and dates. It is likely that the first five books (often referred to as the Pentateuch or the Hebrew Bible) were put together first out of the sources deriving from the J and E traditions, and that at a later stage the P tradition materials were fitted into this narrative framework. At about the same time the materials comprising *Deuteronomy* were added. The oral traditions that preceded the writing were much older, but it is possible to date the earliest times at which the various traditions began to be written down: J: 950BC; E: 750BC; P: 587-539BC.

Even then the history of the text is still unclear. The Hebrew Bible began to be standardised only after the return from Babylonian captivity (*c*. 587–539BC). With the Fall of Jerusalem and the Destruction of the Temple in AD 70 the idea of the Hebrew Bible as a source of authority began to take shape, but a standardized canonical text -- the Massoritic Bible -- began to emerge only around AD 90–100. Since then there has not been a time when the Bible was not being 'edited, redacted, conflated, glossed, and expurgated' and no part of it has been free from this process.[111] Indeed it seems a great deal of written material dating from the period of the Old Testament has not survived. There are occasional references to it -- for example, the lost *Book of Jashar* (*Joshua* 10:13 and 2 *Samuel* 1:18) and the lost *Book of the Wars of Yahweh* (*Numbers* 21:14).

Hebrew oral and the written traditions existed side by side for a very long period. Even before the exile in Babylon, collections of written prophecies were not unknown. Ezekiel, for example, was handed a written scroll to eat as a sign of his prophetic commission and Zechariah had a vision of an enormous flying scroll which would, he says, be a curse on the face of the earth and a judgement on the people (*Ezekiel* 2.9 and 3.3: *Zechariah* 5.1-4). *Genesis* is conscious of the fact that it is a

---

111 N. Frye, 'The Social Context of Criticism' (1970) in: E. Burns & T. Burns (eds.), *Sociology of Literature & Drama* (Penguin: Harmondsworth, 1973), p.151.

written record and refers to itself as a book, saying: 'This *is* the book of the generations of Adam' (*Genesis* 5: 1). However, we know very little about the way the works of the prophets and other contributors passed from oral teaching and preaching into written form. In the King James Bible, for example, there are roughly ninety-one references to the word 'write'; thirty-eight references to 'writing'; sixty-nine references to the word 'read' and six to 'reading', fifty-four references to the word 'scribe' and 188 references to the word 'book'. The Bible is clearly very conscious of writing and the notion of 'the book', but it tells almost nothing about the process of its own formation. For such a substantial work, seeking to establish the authority of its own written record, it gives us very little information, and even then only inadvertently, about writing, reading or the life and work of the scribes.[112]

In general in the Old Testament the scribes are *soferim*, people occupied in literary study, copying and editing scripture and interpreting the Law. However, the word *soferim* was used in different ways at various times. Originally it was used simply to mean someone who was able to write, but later it came to mean in particular those who worked as secretary for a king, judge, commander or a great man (*Judges* 5:14). In *Samuel* 2 7:20-25, *Kings* 2 19:2, and *Nehemiah* 13:13 the word referred to what we would now call a secretary of state, that is someone in charge of secular affairs, but in *Kings* 2 25:19 and *Jeremiah* 36:10-21 and 52:25, it denoted someone in charge of military matters -- particularly the mustering of troops. The *soferim* it seems had originally been in charge of the process of memorizing and transmitting the texts by oral repetition without the aid of writing. Later they were thought of as the scribes, the experts in writing, and even when they committed material to memory, there was usually a text to refer to.[113]

In *Proverbs* 25:1 we learn that Hezekiah set up a group of scribes to copy and preserve the sacred books. In *Ezra* 7:6, 21 we learn that Ezra was 'a ready scribe' in the Law of Moses, and according to *Nehemiah* 8:1 he was the most illustrious of all the scribes. From Ezra onwards scribes seem to have acquired a more ecclesiastical and legal function in that they were increasingly seen not merely as copiers drudging away at texts, but as expounders of the sacred books and keepers of the law: as

---

112 www.biblestudytools.com.
113 J. Goody, *The Power of the Written Tradition* (Smithsonian Institute Press: Washington, 2000), p.33.

time went by the chief use of the term 'scribe' came to be in relation to the Word of God, of which the scribe was the copyist, depositary, expounder and even the interpreter. Martin Jaffee has given us an imaginative reconstruction of scribal work in a Hebrew scriptorium *c*.100BC:

> Imagine, if you will, a room containing twenty-two books. All of them are composed by anonymous authors, many of whom lived centuries apart. Most of the authors, moreover, are not creative writers. Their creativity consists of compiling into coherent compositions earlier literary traditions – some transmitted in writing and others by word of mouth, some of rather recent vintage and others centuries old. The books are issued on leather scrolls ranging from a few feet to many dozen ...
>
> These copies represent a major investment of labor by tanners who produce the writing surface of the scroll and scribes who laboriously copy the text. Sometimes, by error, whole lines are skipped or miscopied. If such scribal mistakes go undetected and uncorrected, later copyists will reproduce the error and transmit it as the genuine text.
>
> Nearly all the people who see these books are governmental leaders and officials from the Ministry of Culture. While most people of the country are able to read in at least a rudimentary way, these books in particular are legible only with difficulty. In the first place, they are written in an ancient version of the national language, a version that is spoken, if at all, only by antiquarian scholars. There is also the matter of the copies themselves. The scribal handwriting is a specialised script difficult to decipher... But illegibility is not a serious problem for most people since few have looked inside any but the most famous of these scrolls.... What they know of most of the library's contents comes to them from hearing portions of some of the books read aloud by trained declaimers on national holidays, commemorative festivals, and other public occasions.[114]

Up to the return from exile in 539BC the Bible existed only in fragmentary form. Under the leadership of Ezra and Nehemiah, efforts were made to gather together the written fragments and transform the mass of disconnected materials. This would be a great labour of learning and an enormous responsibility. The problem of how to write and preserve the

---

114 M. Jaffee quoted in J. M. Foley, *How to Read an Oral Poem* (University of Illinois Press: Chicago, 2002), p.73.

accuracy of these texts, their custody and transmission was entrusted to the *Sopherim* and the *Massorites*, the scribes of the Great Synagogue. The name *Sopherim* derives from the Hebrew word *safar*, to count. These were the scribes and accountants of the Temple. The *Massorites*, whose name derives from the Hebrew word *masar*, to deliver something into the hand of another, committing it to the trust of another, were the authorized custodians of the agreed text. Together they were responsible for writing down and copying the texts from ancient Hebrew script into the new 'Chaldee' or square letter script adopted in place of the ancient Hebrew characters. In time these people became a recognized order of religion. This was probably inevitable since they were doing nothing less than rewriting and preserving the national literature and an ancient identity. The copyist, transcriber and interpreter of Hebrew scripture eventually became its keeper, reader, expositor and interpreter. In general the prophets communicated new scriptures while the scribes wrote down, guarded and elucidated the old scriptures. But by degrees the scribes assumed the office of public teachers; the priests, unless they were also scribes, took second place. By the time of the Roman occupation, the *Soferim* were no longer calligraphers, simply copying texts, but a powerful new learned class devoted to the protection of the sacred books and the interpretation of the law. The work of the *soferim* was wide in scope and gradually became wider still:

> They interpreted the biblical ordinances -- civil, domestic, economic and social -- formulating their underlying principles, classifying their details, fixing their norms, regulating their usages, and adapted the laws to changes in conditions and circumstances. They (....) sought to mitigate the apparent severity of the law, bringing it more into harmony with life, and with the fundamental human wants. Among many examples of their methods that could be adduced, may be mentioned their substitution of compensation for the Biblical law of retaliation in case of assault; and their lenient application of the Sabbath laws in comparison with the rigorism of certain sects who, guided by the strict letter of the law, abstained completely from all physical activities on the Day of Rest.[115]

---

115 I. Epstein, *Judaism: A Historical Presentation* (Penguin: Harmondsworth, 1975), pp.86-7.

Following the return from exile in Babylon, it was the scribes who transformed synagogues from simple centres of religious life into 'popular universities', extra-mural departments for the main Temple in Jerusalem.[116] Their notion of what it was to be a scribe had clear political significance and their new-found role gave them enormous social and political standing. Tension about the changing position of the scribes -- brought about by the increasing use and power of writing -- is the subject of much comment in the New Testament. For example, *Matthew* 2:4-6 tells us that after the arrival of the three wise men, Herod consulted the chief priests and scribes as to where the 'King of the Jews' would be born and they examined the sacred writings in order to answer him. *Matthew* 13:52 and 17:10 also tells us that the responsibility and dignity of their office meant that scribes were seen as symbols of faithfulness in instruction. Indeed frequent appeal was made to the scribes as doctrinal authorities. However, *Mark* 12:38-40 tells us that the scribes were often accused of abusing their calling for purposes of ostentation and extortion. In *Matthew* 23:2, 3 we are told, not without a hint of criticism, that the scribe sat in Moses's seat -- that is, he was the successor to the prophet, the keeper of his teachings. Also when the people saw that Jesus taught, but not as a scribe or a Pharisee (remembrancers and interpreters of traditional oral law), they saw him as no mere expositor of another's teaching, but as an original instructor, a new prophet. *Matthew* 7:29 and 23:2, *Mark* 1:22, and *Luke* 5:21, 5:30 and 7:30 compare the Pharisees' manner of teaching with that of Jesus. In *Matthew* 22:35 a scribe quizzes Jesus as to which of the commandments is the most important and Mark 12:28 also tells of a scribe asking Jesus a similar question. And it was to a scribe that Jesus said, with more than a shred of irony: 'You are not far from the kingdom of God'. From *Matthew* 26:3 and *Acts* 4:5 and 6:12 we learn that the scribes and Pharisees were among Jesus's bitterest enemies since he threatened their power and position.

The tradition of treating the Bible as a work of literature goes back to roughly 1678, when the orator Richard Simon (1638–1712) published his *Critical History of the Old Testament*, questioning the integrity of the Biblical texts that had been handed down by history. On the continent, Baruch Spinoza (1632–77), in his *Short Treatise on Hebrew Grammar*, which appeared posthumously in 1677, took up a similar approach. Even before

---

116 E. B. Castle, *Ancient Education and Today* (Penguin: Harmondsworth, 1961), p.166.

publication, Spinoza's criticisms got him banned from his synagogue in Amsterdam. Their criticisms turned on the problem of that they called the 'repair of the text'. They both insisted that, because of the Hebrew script in which it was written, which provided only skeletal guidance on pronunciation and punctuation, the Bible as a text was often badly flawed and open to error. Simon made the point that the Bible and its interpretation were 'authorised by custom' and handed down by scribal and rabbinical tradition, and that this over-rode the normal literary and legal 'rules of interpretation'. Their questioning grew out of the fact that there was no Hebrew version of the Bible that had been 'constant through the centuries' and the cumulative effect of their thinking about the text was to see the Bible not particularly as the word of God, but as a book set down and transmitted, often faultily, by people who were inspired by the idea of the word of God.[117]

Jeremiah is the only prophet to tell us that although he speaks in the first person he had a scribe called Baruch to write his words down. The *Book of Jeremiah* (c. 605BC) is probably a mixture of Jeremiah's recorded words and the account of his activities provided by Baruch. Jeremiah is said to have been commanded by God: 'Thus speaketh the LORD God of Israel, saying, Write thee all the words that I have spoken unto thee in a book.' (*Jeremiah* 30:3) This is the first mention in the Bible of a collection of writings made to a particular purpose. We know that this was a crucial period in Jewish history and that the military power of Babylon was on the rise -- or as Jeremiah put it: 'Out of the north an evil shall break forth upon all the inhabitants of the land.' (*Jeremiah* 1:14). Jeremiah's prophecy -- seventy years of enslavement to the Babylonians -- was intended as a warning to the people of Judah about what would happen if they did not mend their ways. Jeremiah was clear that a disaster was on the way unless the people could be warned:

> And Jeremiah commanded Baruch, saying, I am shut up: I cannot go into the house of the LORD: Therefore go thou, and read in the roll, which thou hast written from my mouth, the words of the LORD in the ears of the people in the LORD'S house upon the fasting day: and also thou shalt read them in the ears of all Judah that come out of their cities. (*Jeremiah* 36:5-6)

---

117 M. Olender, *The Language of Paradise: Race, Religion and Philology in the Nineteenth Century* (Harvard University Press: Cambridge Mass., 1992), pp.21-36.

WRITING THE WORLD

The employment of a scribe does not mean that Jeremiah could not write. Nor does it mean that all his prophecies were written down, or that all the prophecies were written down by Baruch alone. Nor does it mean that all the writing recorded under his name is in fact from Jeremiah. Nor does it mean that the prophet is changing his traditional preaching or abandoning oral teaching in favour of writing. But all these things are possible.

As Jeremiah was not allowed to go into the temple (we are never told why), the only way he could publish his ideas to the priests and officials was by writing the prophecies down and asking Baruch to take the written scroll to the temple. Jeremiah's scroll was read to the people of Judah on a fast day in December. Gemariah 'the son of Shaphan the scribe' was so impressed he invited other scribes and princes to a reading in the scribe's chamber of the king's palace. However, things did not go to plan. The scribes understood the prophet's message as preaching against the city and the king. They put his scroll in the chamber of the scribe Elishama while they went to speak to the king. Not for the first time, it seems, Jeremiah and Baruch were warned to go into hiding.

Jeremiah's scroll was read to King Jehoiakim, who was not impressed by his message. Far from mending his ways, as the scroll was read to him, the king slashed it away with a knife and threw it bit by bit onto the fire. Gemariah and the other scribes advised him against burning the scroll, but without success. Jeremiah and Baruch remained in hiding and Jeremiah, we are told, was instructed by God to write a new scroll:

> Then took Jeremiah another roll, and gave it to Baruch the scribe, the son of Neriah: who wrote therein from the mouth of Jeremiah all the words of the book which Jehoiakim king of Judah had burned in the fire: and there were added besides unto them many like words. (*Jeremiah* 36:32)

This second scroll is what we now know as the *Book of Jeremiah.* The role of the court scribes in these events indicates not only that they took an interest in prophesy for reasons of state security, but also that even before the Jews were taken into captivity in Babylon, scribes and officials were writing down, sifting and collecting texts of legends, oracles and prophecies.

According to legend Ptolemy Philadelphus of Egypt (285–246BC) assembled seventy-two Hebrew scholars in Alexandria and it took them seventy-two days to complete their translation of the Massoritic text into Greek, after which it was known as the *Septuagint*. By this time Greek military power was on the rise and by the late fourth century AD Alexander had conquered much of the Middle East: Greek became the main language of trade, government and scholarship. Consequently many Jews were functionally literate in Greek but illiterate in Hebrew and Aramaic. Even after Greek translations of the Massoritic Bible became available, the bulk of the Jewish population would still have relied on their own memory and on temple texts presented orally. The Bible as we know it began to appear in Greek translation mainly for diaspora Jews who no longer spoke Hebrew or Aramaic.

It is important to grasp that the *Septuagint* was developed as the Massoritic Hebrew canon was just begining to appear as a 'fixed' text. The *Septuagint* included several books that the Massoritic Hebrew Bible left out. Also the running order of the various books and chapters differed in Hebrew, but appeared fixed in Greek. The source of the *Septuagint* was certainly a Hebrew text -- but one of many. Inevitably there are differences between the Massoritic Bible and the *Septuagint*. The *Book of Jeremiah*, for example, is longer in Hebrew than it is in Greek, since scholars were working from source material which still had no fixed canon and with stories and texts which had several variants.

There was considerable literary activity around the time of the start of Christianity, but the Christians later excluded a great deal of written material on the grounds that it was not part of the Jewish *Pentateuch*, was not written in Hebrew, or was not doctrinally acceptable. As a result a great deal of apocryphal and apocalyptic writing fell into obscurity or was later grudgingly accorded lower status. The word 'apocrypha' means hidden or secret writing, writing which is for some reason of doubtful authenticity. At various times, among others, the books *Hebrews, Jude, James* and *Revelation* have been excluded from the canon as dubious or apocryphal. On the other hand, among others, *The Epistle of Barnabus, The Shepherd of Hermas, The Two Epistles of Clement to the Corinthians* and *The Psalms of Solomon*, which are all now excluded, were once accepted and included. Indeed some of the works now excluded from the canon were once considered very important either to the various Jewish sects, to early Christians or to the Protestant Church. There are currently fourteen books which form the *Apocrypha* -- that is, books of the Old Testament which were included in the *Septuagint* and the *Vulgate*, but which do not appear in the Hebrew Bible and which consequently do not appear in modern Bibles.[118]

In the late fourth century AD St Jerome began translating the Bible from Greek into Latin. He was very diligent and went to as many Hebrew sources as he could. His translation, known as the *Vulgate*, produced a standardized text for the western world, but it also imposed a false sense of order and orthodoxy since his sources, the Hebrew, Coptic and Orthodox Bibles, all varied considerably. However, St Jerome's translation into Latin is the basis of our own King James Bible.

*

While each prophet, historian and law-giver may have had varying difficulties in getting their oral teachings written down, the problems did not cease with the creation of a text and what has come down to us is sometimes puzzling; until recently modern Biblical scholars had to content themselves with manuscripts the earliest of which dated only from the medieval period. However, in 1947 shepherds at Qumran, in the hills of Judea above the Dead Sea, stumbled upon caves containing the remains of a library of religious texts from a small isolated Jewish sect called the Essenes. Many of the Essene texts found dated from the period AD 250BC–100 and, though damaged by time and climate, the remains of the scrolls, rolls and parchments allowed scholars to see what the many and various early Biblical texts must have been like before the canon was established. The Qumran library texts also allowed scholars to see some of the problems that had developed not as a result of ambiguous vowels but as a result of the way that documents had been handled, stored, edited and transcribed.

One of the many variant readings to emerge from the documents found at Qumran is a good example of how scribes sometimes operate to leave a text that scholars take to be accurate, historically authentic, even sacred, but which in fact makes little sense. In the *First Book of Samuel,* some of which derives from the oral teachings of the prophet Samuel, we are told that Samuel had been told by God to appoint Saul as the first

---

118 *The Apocrypha* (Oxford University Press: Oxford, 1942).

Hebew king. However, the people were reluctant to assent to this. Saul was a very unpopular choice and in *Samuel* 1 10:27 we read:

> But the children of Belial said, How shall this man save us? And they despised him and brought Him no presents. But he held his peace.

This is the last verse in the chapter. The implication is that this clash will be picked up again in the next chapter. However, when the narrative resumes in chapter 11, instead of picking up the story and resolving the issue of his kingship, verse 1 has a jarring and confusing change of direction:

> 1 Then Nahash the Ammonite came up, and encamped against Jabesh-gilead: and all the men of Jabesh said unto Nahash, make a covenant with us, and we will serve thee.
> 2 And Nahash the Ammonite answered them, On this condition will I make a covenant with you, that I may thrust out all your right eyes, and lay it for a reproach upon all Israel.
> 3 And the elders of Jabesh said unto him, Give us seven days' respite, that we may send messengers unto all the coasts of Israel: and then, if there be no man to save us, we will come out to thee.

Suddenly instead of resolving the problem of Saul's lack of popularity, and for no apparent reason, Nahash the Ammonite is busy laying siege to the Israelite town of Jabesh-gilead in Trans-Jordan.

The Roman-Jewish historian Flavius Josephus (37-c. AD 100) in his *Antiquities of the Jews* (VI, v, 3), which first appeared in AD 93-94, wrote about the siege of Jabesh-gilead but he seemed to have access to a source document that made a different and much better sense of events than the Biblical account. However, until recently scholars could only wonder what that document might have been.

Some commentators assumed that gouging out the right eye was a sign that Nahash was a barbarian; others thought it a traditional punishment for traitors, for the defeated enemy or for resisting a siege. But even so, it makes no sense for Nahash to threaten disfigurement and then agree to wait seven days while the town leaders send out for reinforcements before they decide whether they will give battle or agree to have their eyes put out. One slightly desperate commentator glossed the passage thus:

A king of Ammon, who, at the very beginning of Saul's reign, attacked Jabesh-gilead so successfully, that the inhabitants sued for peace at almost any cost, for they were willing to pay tribute and serve the Ammonites. The harsh king, not satisfied with tribute and slavery, demanded in addition that the right eye of every man should be put out, as 'a reproach upon Israel.' They were given seven days to comply with these cruel terms.[119]

It was only with the discovery of an early text of *The Book of Samuel* among the many other documents found in the caves at Qumran that the mystery of these verses, with their abrupt change of narrative direction, was clarified. In the Qumran text we can read a passage that was missed out of the version that came down to us. The passage, if fitted in between 1 *Samuel* 10 and 11, allows us access to a much more satisfactory narrative, something like the text that Flavius Josephus had access to:

But the children of Belial said, How shall this man save us? And they despised him and brought Him no presents. But he held his peace.
Now Nahash, king of the Ammonites, had been grievously oppressing the Gaddites and Reubenites. He would gouge out the right eye of each of them and would not grant Israel a deliverer. No one was left of the Israelites across the Jordan whose right eye Nahash, king of the Ammonites, had not gouged out. But there were seven thousand men who had escaped from the Ammonites and who had entered Jabesh-gilead. About a month later Nahash the Ammonite went up and besieged Jabesh-gilead (...)
Then Nahash the Ammonite came up, and encamped against Jabesh-gilead: and all the men of Jabesh said unto Nahash, make a Covenant with us, and we will serve thee. And Nahash the Ammonite answered them, On this condition will I make a covenant with you, that I may thrust out all your right eyes, and lay it for a reproach upon all Israel. And the elders of Jabesh said unto him, Give us seven days' respite, that we may send messengers unto all the coasts of Israel: and then, if there be no man to save us, we will come out to thee.

This narrative makes better sense. Now we can clearly see that the brutal Nahash was intent on breaking into Jabesh because it harboured

---

119 The International Standard Bible Encyclopedia': www.searchgodsword.org.

fugitives from his war against the people of Gad and Reuben, across the river Jordan, and he intended to punish Jabesh for sheltering them. And still, even with the inserted passage, all the questions we might ask of this story have not been answered: it is clear that the people of Jabesh do not trust that anyone down on the coast, including Saul, will come to their aid. As the rest of the story unfolds, we learn that when the town messengers reached the coast Saul hears news of the siege almost by chance, but nevertheless raises an army, beats the Ammonites and proves himself a worthy leader. Only then was he appointed king. While this helps us understand the issue of Saul's kingship, it does not explain why Nahash granted seven days for the Israelites to call for reinforcements.

This is perhaps the best known of the re-readings made available to Biblical scholars by the discovery of the Dead Sea Scrolls. In 1999 the missing paragraph was re-inserted into the *New Revised Standard Version of the Bible*. It seems very likely that these lines did not figure in the Biblical text transmitted to us simply because, before the Sopherim and the Massorites fixed on an approved canonical text, a scribe engaged in copying skipped a verse. His eye jumped from a verse paragraph beginning with the word 'Nahash' to the following verse paragraph which also began with the word 'Nahash'. The error went unchallenged, the original text was lost, and the corrupted text stood for centuries. It is only because a more complete, earlier variant script was preserved in the caves of Qumran that we know how the passage should read. Or do we? How many more puzzling passages are there in the Old Testament? What else is missing? And why? And what is missing from the thousands of fragments found in Qumran?[120]

Homer

The earliest texts to be written down in Europe were those credited to Homer. What is certain is that behind Homer there was a long continuous oral tradition that stretched back unbroken over several hundred years. Homer, we now know, stands at the end of a long line of accumulated skills and talents honed by many generations of highly accomplished, but illiterate, traditional oral poet-storytellers. We know that what we have with *The Iliad* and *The Odyssey* is but a fraction of the oral epic literature that once existed. But ancient Greece and the works of Homer

---

120 J. M. Allegro, *The Dead Sea Scrolls* (Penguin: Harmondsworth, 1956), pp.50-74.

are a good place to start thinking about the oral traditions and the exact conditions of the transition to a literate society.

For the professional Greek, oral poet composition and performance were part of the same act. Mastery of both creation and performance were required parts of their profession.[121] And what is clear is that these poets learned from older poets, over many generations. A professional poet had to know a huge range of songs and stories, a whole range of poetic techniques, to be a master of formulae, lines, phrases, genealogies, geography and improvisation. Improvisation was guided by a complex inheritance of forms and expressions and established themes. New elements could be introduced; additional improvizations could be included, developed or dropped in quite a fluid manner. The poet of *The Odyssey* in the version that has come down to us, for example, incorporated Circe, Wandering Rocks, the Sirens, Calypso, Scylla and Charybdys -- material we now recognize as part of different story cycle, that of *Argonautica*, better known to us as *Jason and the Argonauts*. However, we also know that in Classical Greece there was a professional group of performers called the *rhapsodes* whose job was not to create, but to recite the Homeric poems from memory at public events. These poets performed at public gatherings and private events -- town festivals, fairs, markets and wedding parties. It is possible that after their original creation these poems lived in the memory of the *rhapsodes* until they were written down.

I want to emphasize the accuracy with which the story has been preserved. At the end of *The Odyssey*, as Odysseus sets out to murder his rival suitors and all the female servants in the house, Theoclymenus approaches the suitors and foretells their death, saying: 'The sun has been obliterated from the sky and an unlucky darkness invades the world'. For many years this reference to an eclipse of the sun was taken to be a purely literary dramatic device. However, in the 1920s scholars began to suspect that the poet might have been referring to an actual eclipse. Marcelo Magnasco, head of mathematics at Rockefeller, along with Constantino Baikouzis, a colleague from Argentina, predicted a possible eclipse at that time and, after many years of searching the literary records for evidence of such an eclipse, found several other

---

121 M. I. Finley, *The Ancient Greeks* (Penguin: Harmondsworth, 1966); A. R. Burn, *The Pelican History of Greece* (Penguin: Harmondsworth, 1965); C. Renfrew, *Archaeology and Language* (Penguin: Harmondsworth, 1989).

literary references to just such an event over the Ionian Sea. It was the only eclipse that century, so there were no other contenders. Researchers could then match this up with the eclipse mentioned in Homer. From this we know roughly when the story was told and one of the actual events it preserved -- the date on which Odysseus set out to do murder: 16 April 1178BC.[122] This puts the date of the destruction of Troy to twenty years before this event, in the year 1198BC, which is very close to the archaeologically dated destruction of Troy VIIa at *c.* 1190BC. This dating of the eclipse also allows us to see the time-depth of the poem's oral life. *The Iliad* and *The Odyssey* are thought to have been written down *c.* 740-550BC, so they were transmitted in oral form for about 400 years. At a rough calculation, if a storyteller lived on average to the age of sixty years, then this means that the oral story was handed on through seven to ten generations before it was written down.

How could they hand on something so accurately over such a long period of time? One reason is the way the storyteller/poets worked. I want to emphasize the vital poetic element of the formulaic phrase as a way of aiding memory and oral composition. The repetition of standard phrases and formulas is a feature of oral composition. In Homer we regularly encounter phrases like: 'owl eyed Athene', 'Hector of the glancing helm', 'cloud gathering Zeus', 'Triton born Athene', 'sacred Ilios', 'godlike Achilles', 'white-armed Hera', 'long shadowed spear', 'swift footed', 'rosy fingered dawn', 'the wine dark sea', 'winged words', 'well-benched ships'. It is as if these are poetic building blocks to be moved around and used where appropriate to fill out a line or link up with an established theme.

However, these phrases have another function too, because they refer to other parts of the story and other parts of the culture from which the story they are hearing is drawn. Phrases like 'owl eyed Athene', 'much suffering Odysseus', 'Hector of the glancing helm', 'cloud gathering Zeus', 'Triton born Athene' 'sacred Ilios', 'godlike Achilles' and 'white-armed Hera' are all references to things the audience already knows about these characters, and they all refer to other stories in the cycle, in the culture, in the history. They are references to a larger context and code than that of this particular story. Odysseus will not necessarily be suffering when he is referred to, Hector may not be wearing his helm,

---

122 I. Sample, 'Celestial Clues' in *The Guardian* (25 June 2008), p.11.

and Achilles may not be acting in a particularly godlike fashion: these are references to the fuller identity of the characters within tradition and culture and stand for the 'implied whole' of that tradition.[123] As such they are other pathways down which the story might have gone. They are also a reminder that tradition and transmission, a sharing of culture and references help create a common identity, and as such are part of the public nature and social function of these stories.

This 'super function' aside, about one third of the lines in these poems include a repeated, ready-made phrase. Presumably this hoard of phrases could be expanded, adapted and pruned, according to changes in the language, fashion, poetic taste and the exact nature of the audience. By the time this material came down to Homer it had already had centuries of reshaping in a formulaic oral tradition. The formulaic padding can be easily identified:

> Now though, if you wish me to fight it out <u>and do battle</u>, make the rest of the Trojans sit down, and all the Achaians, and set me in the middle with Menelaos <u>the warlike</u> to fight together for the sake of Helen and all her possessions. That one of us who wins <u>and is proved stronger</u>, let him take the possessions fairly and the woman, and lead her homeward. But the rest of you, having cut your oaths <u>of faith</u> and friendship dwell you in Troy <u>where the soil is rich</u>, while those others return home to <u>horse-pasturing</u> Argos, and Achaia <u>the land of fair women</u>.[124]

I also want to emphasize the enormous depth of time involved and the vast quantity of material to be memorized. These poems are substantial: *The Odyssey* is 12,000 lines, *The Iliad* is 15,000 lines. Both poems are ten times longer than a poet might reasonably offer at a single sitting. In fact they would take twenty-five to thirty hours to recite, let alone sing. This suggests that Homer was not a traditional travelling storyteller working where and when he could, adapting what he knew to the needs of his current audience, but rather someone with a more particular sense of purpose and with the time, energy and resources to undertake such arduous work.

We know that there were a great many poets and performers, so it is

---

123 J. M. Foley, *How to Read an Oral Poem* (University of Illinois, Chicago, 2002), pp.113-4.
124 *The Iliad* trans., R. Latimore (Chicago UP: Chicago, 1969), pp.3: 67-75.

very likely that these great poems are the only ones to come down to us. We know from references and quotations in the work of other writers that Homer's *Iliad* and *Odyssey* are the two surviving parts of what was once a cycle of eight epic poems -- all the others by different poets. We also know that while these two poems were set out each in twenty-four books, the nearest long poem in the cycle was only eleven books and that most of them were only two to five books long.[125]

We know that writing these texts down was not an easy undertaking. The written versions may have been prepared for a specific occasion, but we don't know what that occasion was. What is certain is that any text probably took years to prepare and cost an enormous amount of money. We know that *c.* 550BC the Athenian tyrant Peisistratus produced a definitive text of both *Odyssey* and *Iliad* for recitation at the Pan-Athenian festival, and he required the *rhapsodes* to recite them, perhaps from memory but more likely from the written texts; the same stories seem to have been composed, recomposed and performed by other oral bards called *aoidoi*.[126] This suggests that there were possibly several different written and unwritten versions of these poems in circulation, some by Homer. Peisistratus's version of the poems, along with all the others, does not appear to have survived. With established classical texts like those of Homer we may feel we are on safer ground. However, in reality this is not so. There was debate as early as the sixth century BC as to what was and was not the work of Homer. It was later, in the fifth century BC, that the historian Herodotus said that Homer was the author of *The Iliad* and *The Odyssey* and not the author of several other epic poems often credited him.[127]

In the third century BC Ptolemy, the Greek king of Egypt, and a great patron of arts and sciences, ordered scholars to produce a definitive text of these works. The scholars found considerable differences between the various texts available to them, but they did the best they could and the finished work is credited to Aristarchus of Alexandria. It is from his text that our own derives. Sadly it is not directly from his edition that we have our texts, but from notes and queries and discussions written in the margins of copies made in the twelfth century AD that we get

125 *Ibid*, pp.24-8.
126 J. M. Foley, *How to Read an Oral Poem* (University of Illinois Press: Chicago, 2002), p.49.
127 Herodotus, *The Histories*, (Penguin: Harmondsworth, 1996), book II, p.126.

most of our information about Aristarchus and his work. However, basic questions remain. Why would an illiterate performer, who depended upon performance before a live audience, create something which would, in fact, take several days to perform, which required substantial financial backing to write down and which would effectively put him out of a job? If he was a performance poet, how could he create something of this size and scope? When would he ever get the chance to perform it? And if he did not perform it, then who would ever read such a text out loud?

If he delivered the performance in sections, on different days, how could he have elaborated the variations on the theme and formula, the inner structural correspondents and subtle touches that mark it off from the comparative crudity of the surviving Yugoslav epics? Did writing play a substantial part in the development of these works through successive drafts or were they the product of a scribe taking down notes from an oral performance -- or even several performances? The element of writing in the newly adapted Phoenician alphabet, which seems to have been only recently taken up by the Greeks and cannot have been very widespread, surely played a part in the process of creating. Homer, even if he was an illiterate, itinerant, blind, performance poet, certainly knew what writing was. But what role did writing play and what kind of writing could it have been?

Homer in *The Odyssey* left us only a very partial view of the poet who might have performed such poems. Towards the end of the poem we encounter Demodokus, a Phaecian bard. But there is also the Ithakan court bard Phemios. In the poem Phemios's performance comes after a customary feast to celebrate the homecoming of the warriors from the Trojan wars with the tale of a returning hero. In this case the hostess Penelope interrupts to ask him to choose a different theme since, as she is still waiting for Odysseus, it is inappropriate. Her son Telemachus however, over-rules her, and we have to assume that the choice of subject was in itself part of a ritual over in which the bard felt he had little control or choice. However, Homer makes the point that Phemios performs against his will, but at the request of the suitors who are pursuing Penelope and who are in the process of usurping Odysseus's home, wife and possessions through a kind of rowdy non-stop party -- gambling, carousing and eating his cattle. Even against such an unfavourable background Phemios succeeds in his performance, not only holding their attention, but reducing Penelope to tears. Even so, while Phemios's performance here is not an anthropological recording but an idealized poetic description by Homer, it does tell us a great deal about the power of the story, the role and social standing of the bard and the nature of the social ritual.[128]

There are very few unambiguous references to writing in ancient texts, and still fewer informative references. One reference that is relatively clear is in *The Odyssey* (book 6, lines 166–80). The story is that Proitos's wife Anteia makes advances but is turned down by Bellerophon. She reports to her husband that Bellerophon has pursued her and asks her husband to kill him. Proitos gives Bellerophon a 'folding tablet' and asks him to deliver it to the King of Lykia, Anteia's father. As a result when the message is delivered he is sent on a series of suicide missions against impossible opponents, all of whom he vanquishes. The king revises his opinion of Bellerophon and offers him the hand of his unmarried daughter.

What was written on the 'folding tablet'? Homer is vague about the message. We have to wonder why Bellerophon did not sneak a look -- could he read? We also have to ask how the king read the message. In the poem the king asks to 'see' the 'sign' rather than the writing and then 'receives' it rather than reads it. This ambiguity may be because according to tradition Homer was blind and had only a vague sense of what writing and reading were. It may also be because the poem records a story from a time when writing hardly existed -- Linear A and Linear B were perhaps then current -- and when reading and writing were even less widespread than in Homer's time. At the time the poems were set down the Greeks used animal skins, perhaps papyrus, and then later scrolls of parchment for writing. But Homer refers to writing as *semata* (signs) which is the same word used the describe omens, scars and grave markers. He also uses the word *grapsas* to indicate scratchings on a *pinax* or wax-coated folding tablet. He is probably not referring to alphabetic writing, but to a system of signs used for short messages. However while the tale might refer to an earlier time, Homer's epic stories were not written down on wax-coated tablets. As a record, tablets of this sort would not have survived for very long and the Homeric texts were far

---

128 J. M. Foley, *How to Read an Oral Poem* (Illinois University Press: Chicago, 2002), pp.8-10.

too long and too important for that. The Homeric texts may have formed part of a cycle of stories that were finally gathered together and taken down in writing, but if so they were written on something other than wax.

One possibility is that the process of recording *The Iliad* and *The Odyssey* was that of dictation rather than performance, and that it extended over several years. Particular sections could be brought out, perfected in performance, written down, edited, and slowly built towards a complete text. That text could then be edited, refined, extended, adapted and could even have had additional sections added to it. Geoffrey Kirk has suggested that the epics were the work of one supremely talented oral poet, whose work was transcribed by bards and scribes in this way, as a definitive version, then passed on through two or three generations of transmission by professional singers, reciters and performers from the guilds -- *rhapsodes* or *homeridae* -- who had no connection to the originating performance, to the original poet or scribes, and who were not necessarily poets.

In *The Iliad* there is an interesting example of what might be either a mistake by the poet or a scribal insertion, which may confirm this process and illustrate something of the problems it created. In Book 9 we are told that Agamemnon and Nestor plan to send a delegation to visit Achilles' tent to persuade him to rejoin the war. In the text that has come down to us, Nestor names Phoenix, Ajax and Odysseus as the envoys. Later in the poem we learn that Phoenix was one of Achilles' commanders and had brought Achilles up as his own son. Why, if their relationship is so close, is Phoenix not with Achilles at his tent? No explanation is offered and the ambassadors leave on their mission. However, as their mission proceeds there is something strange about the language. For the whole of the meeting between Achilles and the ambassadors, Achilles uses a particular Greek mode of dual pronoun which indicates that Achilles is speaking to two ambassadors: it is as if he were constantly saying 'You two gentlemen...' when there are three of them.

It looks as if in the original version there were only two ambassadors, and that Phoenix was added in later. Homer (or the scribe responsible) forgot Phoenix's close relationship with Achilles and put him in the wrong place, with the Greek generals rather than with Achilles, and then forgot to alter the grammar to include his presence as a messenger to

Achilles' tent. Or perhaps Homer died before the correction could be made. If the text was based on a performance it would be easy to correct the mistake in the written version. But if the correction was left until later it is obviously more complicated.

The *rhapsodes* would have been oral performers until at least a generation after Homer's death. It is hard to imagine that any one of these competent performers, who had memorized the whole of the poem, could not have made the correction. The only solution is that the text that came down to the *rhapsodes* as the authentic word of the dead Homer, was something to be revered and preserved almost as scripture, rather than corrected. If that is so it seems likely that what was transmitted was a written text prepared by Homer or based on a performance by Homer, where the slip either went unnoticed or was falsely corrected by one of the original scribes who realized Homer had made a mistake, but was not thorough in his correction. After Homer's death that text -- complete with imperfect correction -- would then be the only text which no-one was prepared to challenge or change. But this is speculation ...[129]

Much of what we suspected about Homer and the emergence of his texts has been confirmed by research into oral storytelling in the Balkans and in Africa. To a certain extent a storyteller, remembrance and oral historian can get away with minor inconsistencies in an oral context, and can even make corrections when the text is written down. But a written text is organized very differently from a spoken story. It is a different category of thing. It has a different status. It represents a different way of thinking and ordering materials. An oral story, once told, is gone. It cannot be recalled precisely and it cannot be interrogated. However, we can refer back to a text: we can read it again, we can interpret it and we can question it.

Until recently it was thought that at best only about 60 per cent of any oral text could be recalled with total accuracy by most storytellers. Or so it was thought. Oral storytelling was still a living art form and part of Yugoslav culture until at least the late 1930s when it was studied and recorded in considerable detail by A. B. Lord. What he realized was that the Yugoslav storytellers were still operating in the same tradition -- though much altered -- as the Homeric storytellers of ancient Greece. Until very recently in the Balkans, Serbo-Croat *guslari*, Muslim and

---

129 G. Kirk, *The Iliad: A Commentary* (Latimore: Chicago, 1985), p.xxv.

Christian, many of them blind, still sang epic poems of incredible size from memory to the sound of a one-string instrument called a *gusle*.[130] Lord transcribed 12,000 lines from one singer (roughly equivalent to the length of *The Odyssey*), and discovered that 25 per cent of the half-line phrases, and 50 per cent of the whole-line phrases were reused variations, verbal formulae, just like those used by the ancient Greek poets. Lord wrote:

> Had we gone beyond 12,000 lines, the number of formulas would have continued to mount, and had we included material from other singers it would have increased still further, until it became clear that almost all, if not all the lines in the sample passages were formulas (...) The formulas in oral narrative style are not limited to a comparatively few epic tags, but are in reality all pervasive. There is nothing in the poem that is not formulaic. [131]

The extent of this reliance on pre-made phrases led him to surmise that on the one hand performers, though a prodigious act of memory was involved, did not in fact memorize these stories word for word, line by line. Rather, they recreated them at every performance from pre-made phrases. They improvised along lines already well established, relying on a huge stock of memorized formulaic phrases, lines and episodes. Every time they sang a poem, it came out different in detail, but broadly the same. However, Lord also made recordings of a Yugoslav storyteller at work, on two occasions seventeen years apart, and after a detailed comparison found almost no difference between the wording of the two very lengthy performances.

More recently we have a very good example of what happens when the tales of an oral tradition start to get written down. In 1994 David Conrad went to the village of Fadama in north-eastern Guinea, West Africa. He recorded the *Sunjata Epic* of the Mande peoples, about events said to have taken place in the thirteenth century. The story was performed for him by master storyteller Djana Tassey Condé, the son of Babu Condé, said to be the last and the greatest of a long line of traditional Mande storytellers who had lived and worked during the period of the colonial occupation. The epic story is often told to the accompaniment of

---

130 M. Holton & V. D. Mihalovich, *Serbian Poetry from the Beginnings to the Present* (New Haven, 1988).
131 A. B. Lord, *The Singer of Tales* (Harvard University Press: Harvard, 2000), p.47.

flutes, a xylophone and twenty-one-stringed calabash *kora*. It is always told with the participation of a chorus of *naamu* sayers, members of the audience who respond to the storyteller's lines with encouragement and interjected comments of *naamu* -- meaning 'yes indeed' or 'I hear you', and also with shouts of 'it's true' and 'I swear'.

The recording, which is probably very like an original performance of a Homeric poem, took five day-long sessions to complete. Almost immediately the recording hit a problem. Conrad wrote:

> The first recording session with Tassey Condé at Fadama in 1994 was preceded by several hours of social formalities, explanations, and negotiations. When it was finally possible for the bard to begin his performance, he did so in an unusually abrupt fashion, without the usual Islamic blessings, introduction of family members, and genealogical references. Tassey commenced the next day's performance with all these features, thus making it possible to provide the book with a classic Mande epic beginning. I have therefore violated one of the rules of handling oral tradition and borrowed our first sixty-seven lines from the opening of the second recording session.[132]

Conrad went on to say that even after five long days of performance and explanation, it took several further sessions to be sure he had everything straight and to his surprise at each visit to Tassey Condé 'more was added in subsequent interviews'. He began to realize that in his recording he was only getting one possible performance of the epic sequence and that all storytellers made choices with their materials each time they re-told their tales, 'depending on the occasion and audience'. He also began to appreciate that Tassey Condé also knew and understood things about his material that other storytellers, handling the same materials, did not know. Tassey Condé, he said, provided 'details or even entire episodes that are not heard from other performers...' He could, for example, explain why a particular character behaved in an odd, seemingly inexplicable way, or why strange things happened for no apparent reason, offering 'reasonable motives and logical explanations', which other storytellers could not. In short Conrad realized that what he had recorded and what emerged on the page was only a tiny portion of the cultural material of the tales and their possible patterns of telling.

---

132 D. C. Conrad (ed.), *Sunjata: A West African Epic of the Mande Peoples* (Hacket: Indianapolis, 2004), p.xii.

Oral Culture – Counter Culture

All these poems come out of long oral traditions before they achieved written form. When they were finally written down, parts of the original cycle were selected, excluded, missed out, edited, mangled. As such the surviving texts all show remarkable similarities -- they all contain catalogues of names and things, genealogies, dietary codes, information about horses or pigs, how to disembark from ships, how a hero's funeral should be conducted. They had all functioned as the dominant educational resource for a society that needed to commit information to memory, and as such they were also a focal point for the identity of the group that 'kept' the tale. The recitation of these works was part theatre, part library visit, part musical concert, part tribal gathering, part religious festival and part educational event. They were also, crucially a renewal of identification.

The trained memory and the spoken word performance were much more adaptable than the word written down and studied in private. History and stories, once written, were fixed. The introduction of writing changed the nature of story-telling since it brought into play the logical sequence of events, prescribed laws, trails of evidence, cause and effect, the limitations of humanity, geography and time. Also, it must be said that by committing the best minds to preserving and memorizing these oral tales, society was preventing those minds from speculating and reflecting on what the society knew. It was only when texts were established that the best minds of these cultures could abandon the effort of memory, improvisation and preservation and begin to think and create with the texts, through the texts and around the texts.

Professional storytellers survive in sub-Saharan Africa, in places like Mali and Guinea, though the written word and the growth of formal education is slowly squeezing them out. The tension between the two traditions can be seen in the work of people like the Nigerian writer Amos Tutuola, whose work reads very much like that of an oral storyteller simply written down. Paradoxically, while our culture is predominately that of TV, mobile phones, MP3, the iPod and the internet, and there has been a dramatic decline in reading for pleasure, there has also been a move back to oral culture and there has been a huge revival of interest in storytelling. There has also been a dramatic upsurge in rap music and if you listen to rap artists improvising over a groove of bass and drums, you will hear that among all the talk of *ho's, homies, bitches, guns* and *boys in the hood,* rap artists use the same techniques oral poets have used for centuries. Like auctioneers (the other major oral practitioners) these artists make use of speed of delivery, rhythm, formulaic constructions, variations on words and stock phrases to help tell their story.

While most of us are no longer directly connected to any well-developed folk culture, oral culture and oral performance are not quite dead. Indeed folk and storytelling may well be undergoing a renaissance. Dub-poet Linton Kwesi Johnson's poem 'Sonny's Lettah (Anti-sus Poem)', which along with much of his poetry is often performed to music provided by his own band, makes use of this blending of cultures, attitudes and political awareness in a protest at injustice and race-hate.

The much hated 'Sus' law was introduced to the UK in the 1960s. Based on Sections 4 and 6 of the Vagrancy Act (1824) this law made it 'illegal for a suspected person or reputed thief to frequent or loiter in a public place with intent to commit an arrestable offence'. This effectively permitted the police to stop and search anyone they chose, purely on the basis of suspicion that they might be about to commit a criminal offence. Police misuse of these powers in harassing young black men was a major factor in sparking the Brixton Riots of 1981. These riots, and evidence of the abuse the 'Sus' laws by the Metropolitan Police, led to the abolition of the law. However, the police were reluctant to give up this power and found other areas of the law that allowed them to stop and search people on suspicion. When the Stephen Lawrence inquiry reported in 1999, young black men were still five times more likely to be stopped and searched by the police than their white counterparts. By 2005, even though the law had been amended, this disproportion had increased dramatically -- young black men were eight times more likely than young white men to be stopped and searched. Linton Kwesi Johnson wrote a spoken-word poem protesting at the 'sus laws';

*

Sonny's Lettah (Anti-sus Poem)[133]

Jeb Avenue
London, South West 2
Inglan

Dear Ma Maa,

Good Day
I hope that when these few lines reach you
they may find you in the best of health

Ma Maa I really don' know how to tell yu dis
'cause , I did meck a solemn promise
to teck care a likkle Jim and try
mi best fi look out fi 'im

Ma Maa a really did try mi best
but none de less
mi sorry fi tell yu sey
poor likkle Jim get aress'
it was de middle a de rush 'our
when everybody jus' a hustle an a bustle
fi go 'ome fi dem evenin' shower

Me and Jim stand up waiting pon a bus
  not causing no fuss
when all on a sudden a police van
      pull up
out jump 3 police man
De 'ole a dem carrying baton

Dem walk up to me and Jim
one a dem 'ole on to Jim
sey 'im teckin 'im in
Jim tell him fi leggo a 'im
fa 'im no do nuttin
an 'im naw tief, not even a button

Jim start to riggle
De police start to giggle

---

133 Linton Kwesi Johnson, *Forces of Victory* (CCD 9566, Island Records, 1979).

WRITING THE WORLD

Ma Maa, meck a tell yu weh dem do to Jim
Ma Maa , meck a tell yu we dem do to him

Dem tump 'im in 'im belly
  an' it turn to jelly
Dem lick 'im pon 'im back
  an 'im rib get pop
Dem lick 'im pon 'im head
  but it tuff like lead
Dem kick 'im in 'im seed
  an it started to bleed

Ma Maa I just couldn't just stan' up
  deh a no do nutten

So mi juck one ina 'im eye
  an 'im started to cry
Mi tump one in 'im mout
  an 'im started to shout
Mi kick one pon 'im shin
an 'im started to spin
Mi tump 'im pon 'im chin
  an 'im drop pon a bin
    an crash an dead

Ma Maa more police man come down
  an beat me to de ground

Dem charge Jim fi sus
Dem charge mi fi murder
Ma Ma! Don't fret
don't get depress an down 'earted
be of good courage

Till I hear from yu

I remain your son

Sonny

The poem clearly blends semi-literate street language with the established letter-form to create an effective hybrid of powerful protest. The revival in the UK of oral culture and storytelling, shading into hip-hop and street pop culture, is a way for some immigrant communities to assert themselves and their own identity. It is also part of an amalgam of the many different cultures that now make up multi-ethnic Britain, part of the emerging blend of British cultural identities. It is also a protest at 'institutional racism', part of a 'local' reaction against 'globalization', a reaction to the dominant commercial techno-culture and, more ambiguously, a protest at the class power vested in literacy, education, the power of the state and the status quo.

These poems are the product not only of individual talents, but of the interaction of these individuals with an audience and with a tradition -- that is with generations of storytellers and poems that preceded them. But it is from the complexities of this traditional oral root that early literature springs and early texts, just like Johnson's poem, often carry marks of their crossover from oral performance.

Directed Study

What techniques do you think the composers of the *Rigveda*, the Bible and the Koran had in common with Homer, the ancient Anglo Saxon, Irish and Welsh poets, Amos Tutuola and Linton Kwesi Johnson?

Writing killed oral storytelling; films killed the book; TV killed films; video killed TV. So what did DVDs kill? And what happens next?

Listen to a recording of Linton Kwesi Johnson's performing his poem 'Sonny's Lettah'. In what ways do you think this is part of an oral tradition? In what ways does the 'orality' of 'Sonny's Lettah' contribute to its effect? What elements of the written tradition does the poet make use of? In what ways does the poet achieve oral effects in writing? In what ways might it be said that the poet is subverting the 'dominant culture'? In what ways might it be said that the poet is also offering a mildly satirical comment on the language and style of the 'sub-culture'?

So, what difference does it make when you write a thing down, rather than just remember it and speak? Is the meaning the same now as it was when the ancient texts were first written down?

How accurate or complete are the ancient texts we now study? Can we trust or believe the accuracy of the texts we have inherited?

When the ancient texts were written down, were they in any sense 'safe' or 'preserved'? In what ways do we trust a thing more when it is written down, as opposed to when it is merely spoken and why? Is it wise?

5
THE WORLD BEFORE WRITING: DRUIDIC TRADITIONS, TRACES AND SURVIVALS

Sometimes the transition from oral to literate culture is a very long process and incomplete before the oral traditions mutate into something else. This chapter looks at the culture, practice, traditions and social role of the Druids and their rigorous training. While the Druids themselves are barely attested in surviving records, it is clear that theirs was an ancient, pre-literary tradition which survived long enough to be partially observed by the Greeks and Romans. What we can reconstruct of it gives us some insight into the world before writing and hints at an invisible cultural legacy that still lingers. The Romans tried to destroy Druid literary traditions, but while the Druids themselves disappeared some of their traditions and achievements -- changed by time and circumstance -- persist to the present day.

- Celtic Literature
- The Druids
- Training for the Celtic Literary Hierarchy
- Druid Learning and Lore
- The Assault on Druidism
- Druidic Survivals

Very little is known for sure about the Druids and even less about the early Celtic bards. The archaeological record is meagre and largely ambiguous and neither the Greeks nor the later Romans can be entirely trusted as observers of Celtic life. The Greeks were often purveyors of marvellous tales of barbarian life in the far beyond, and the Romans, anxious to denigrate the people on their borders -- particularly those with whom they were about to go to war -- often passed on Greek stories. Caesar, though he lived alongside the Celts in Gaul, prefers to repeat tales he heard from the Greeks, rather than offer his own first hand observations.

We can infer little from the other scant records remaining to us, except that the people of the past referred to as Celts were probably not ethnically uniform nor did they necessarily speak a Celtic language, and that the societies we now refer to as Celtic do not derive directly from the Celtic societies of ancient times. However, these difficulties to one side we can be certain that the Druids did once exist, that their impact was formidable and probably outlived them by many centuries. Beyond this it is difficult to pin the subject down. Whatever they once represented, the Druids and their traditions have been massively distorted by time. Modern historians are still grappling with the difficulties. J. G. Frazer, for example, though he collected a great deal of anthropological material, did little more than repeat Greek and Roman tales of human sacrifice.[134] More recently the historian Gwyn Alf Williams commented that the Druids were thought at one time to have conducted sacrifices in sacred groves and enclosures, but also that:

> ... there appear to have been among, or dependent on, the Druids not only magicians dedicated to the customary frenzy, magic and shape-shifting but shadowy orders of heraldic and remembrancer poets, givers and interpreters of the law and soothsayers, astronomers and regulators of the seasonal life rhythms who cultivated medicine and a form of science.[135]

It is not the whole of the Druidic order I am concerned with here, but the nature of their training and the power of their oral tradition from ancient times to the present, its incredible tenacity and its unexpected offshoot.

Celtic Literature

Among the literatures of Europe, Greek and then Roman are the oldest. North of the Alps, Ireland has the oldest European vernacular literature, and is particularly rich in prose narratives. The manuscript *Amra*

---

134 J. G. Frazer, *The Golden Bough: A Study in Magic and Religion* (Macmillan: London, 1967), pp.856, 860-8, 928-9.
135 G. A. Williams, *When Was Wales? A History of the Welsh* (Penguin: Harmondsworth, 1985), p.9.

Choluim Chille dates from the sixth century, and the *Wurzburg Codex*, an early collection of Irish documents, dates from about AD 700. Welsh literature is not quite so old: while the oldest examples of Welsh may go back to oral compositions of the sixth century, the earliest surviving texts compiled in *Llyfr Du Caerfyrddin* (The Black Book of Carmarthen) date to about 1250, and are based on compositions from the ninth and tenth centuries. Nevertheless, this means that Welsh is the oldest surviving continuous vernacular literature in Europe.[136]

The world of the Celts encompasses Ireland, Wales, Scotland, Brittany and the Isle of Man. At one time it also included most of the English Midlands as far east as Derby, the area west of the Pennines -- Lancashire, Cheshire and the Lake District, the east coast round Tyne Side, the West Country -- Cornwall, Devon and most of the south coast including London. Up to the departure of the Romans from Britain there were plentiful cultural and trade connections between Ireland, Wales and Brittany. It is likely that at the time of the Roman invasion in Scotland and South Wales Irish Gaelic was spoken, that Scotland, North Wales and most of western and northern England spoke either Irish Gaelic or an early form of Welsh.

On the continent, France, southern Belgium, Switzerland, northern Spain, northern Italy and Portugal were all part of the Celtic settlement area. The Celts were mainly an Atlantic coast phenomenon, but their settlements can also be traced across Europe in Paris, Berlin, Vienna, Czechoslovakia, Yugoslavia and Turkey -- St Paul, for example, corresponded with the Celts of Asia Minor in Galatia. Celtic languages were once spoken in all these places. This Celtic world was mysterious and rather threatening to non-Celts: partly this was because while the Celts were clearly an ancient and civilized people in their own way, they preserved a culture, languages, ideas and modes of behaviour that had long been abandoned or superseded by the civilizations of the Roman-Greek-Hebrew-Egyptian-Mesopotamian world.

Early religions all seem to have had an overarching Mother god and early human societies seem to have been matriarchal: kings were not hereditary rulers in their own right, but merely the consort of the female god, a sacred ritual leader, a kind of head priest. However, in the period 3–2,000BC, as farming and the mechanisms of breeding animals

---

136 D. Johnston, *The Literature of Wales* (University of Wales Press: Cardiff, 1994), p.1.

-- particularly the role of the male in propagation -- began to be better understood. Part of the consequence of this was a change in the way the world was perceived: male gods replaced females and matriarchy transformed into patriarchy. The role of the king altered too and with that the role of the priest was no longer to guide and protect the king as a religious leader, but to celebrate his power as the earthly representative of a male god.

In the Celtic world, but particularly in Ireland which remained outside the Roman Empire, the ancient religion and a very different social position for women persisted into historical times; modified rather than superseded by the ideas of religion introduced by the Romans and later modified rather than superseded a second time by Christianity.

The Druids

The Druids are first seen in Greek classical sources around the fourth century BC, but the order had probably been developing over the previous 1,000 years. The Druid belief systems seem to have been many, various, overlapping and local, rather like Hinduism. They probably represent a continuation of ideas present in Europe since at least c. 2,000BC and it is likely that the Druids -- men and women -- developed as an intellectual caste or social strata out of the pre-Celtic world as members of society who embodied the total knowledge, wisdom and collective memory of the people. Druidic training was the University of its day: they were the priests, philosophers, judges, educators, diplomats, advisers, strategists, historians, doctors, herbalists, seers, astronomers, astrologers, teachers, poets, storytellers and genealogists: they were responsible for the transmission of all history, law, identity, language and knowledge. In this they were akin to the Brahmin caste in the Hindu world.[137] The Druids are also rather like the fierce, powerful figures of the Old Testament prophets, combining several pivotal social, religious, cultural, educational and political roles as they guided earthly rulers and interpreted the will of higher powers.[138]

---

137 B. Cunliffe, *Druids: A Very Short Introduction* (OUP: Oxford, 2010), p.135; T. G. E. Powell, *The Celts* (Thames and Hudson: London, 1963), pp.158-9; J. Davies, N. Jenkins, M. Baines, P. I. Lynch (eds.), 'Druids', *The Welsh Academy Encyclopedia of Wales*, (University of Wales Press: Cardiff, 2008), pp.226; T. W. Rolleston, *Myths & Legends of the Celtic Race*, (Constable: London, 1911).
138 M. J. Green, *The World of the Druids* (Thames & Hudson: London, 2005), p.125.

Caesar referred to the Druids as *druides* and Cicero called them *druidae*. These are Latinized forms of the Celtic word *drui, druad* or *dryw* which probably derived from the Celtic word *der* (Welsh *derw*) meaning oak. There is evidence to suggest that the Druids held oak groves to be sacred symbols of deity: in Welsh der-wydd, probably meant something like 'oak-priest', 'oak-seer' 'oak-wise' or someone with 'knowledge from the oak'. This may be from the Proto-Indo-European root words *deru* 'oak' and *weid* 'to see'. It is this same root that gives us the town names Derry and Kildare -- place of the oaks and oak-church. Although we often refer to them simply as 'the Druids', they were divided into three specialized and often overlapping sections: Bards, Seers and Druids. While their training overlapped, each had its own function. Later, as the caste developed and was subject to various historic pressures, it changed and these functions became less distinct.

The Druids considered certain streams, rivers, wells and lakes as sacred. In 1954 the lake at Llyn Cerrig Bach on Anglesey yielded up a great number of late Iron Age weapons, chariot furniture, slave chains, cauldrons and fragments of bronze -- presumably these were offerings. The Druids also seem to have made offerings to the River Thames and to the River Trent. It is almost certain the practice of well-dressing, which still survives in Derby, is a leftover from Druidic practice. The Celts seem to have believed that death merely meant the transfer of the soul from one body to another. It is certain that the Druids had at one time practised human sacrifice, probably by decapitation, but it is also clear that by the time the Romans invaded Britain they had long given this up in favour of animal sacrifice. The Druids kept large herds of cattle and it seems likely that the bull was the favoured sacrificial animal. There is evidence of bull sacrifice at Stonehenge; bull skulls marked elite burials throughout Wessex and were also found at a burial at Bryn Celli Ddu on Anglesey.[139] The bull also figures prominently in the Irish tale *Táin Bó Cualnge* and appears on the Gundestrup bowl; the White Horse of Uffington (dated *c.* 1400–600BC) is more likely a bull. However, it is possible in Britain the Druids reverted to human sacrifice under pressure of the Roman invasion: Lindow Man (dated 2BC–AD 119) and other bog bodies seem to indicate that the Roman Invasion called for desperate measures.[140]

---

139 M. Rice, *The Power of the Bull* (Routledge: London, 1998), pp.231-3.
140 N. Chadwick, *The Celts* (Penguin: Harmondsworth, 1970), pp.157-159.

When Caesar invaded Celtic Gaul in 58–49BC he accused the Druids of burning colossal human statues with living victims, animals and convicted criminals inside. However, it is likely that Caesar was simply recycling propaganda tales told by earlier Greek writers rather then offering information from his own personal observation.[141] However, he noted that while the Druids were not priests themselves, they were present at religious ceremonies, regulating sacrifices, monitoring procedures and giving rulings in religious matters. He also noted that because they were held in high public esteem large numbers of young men flocked to them for instruction. They also acted as judges in all disputes between tribes and individuals, regardless of whether the issue was murder, inheritance or land boundaries, and their judgement regarding recompense was usually respected by all: where their judgement was not respected the individual was punished by banishment, or by being ostracized. Caesar wrote:

> The Druids are exempt from military service and do not pay taxes like other citizens. These important privileges are naturally attractive: many present themselves of their own accord to become students of Druidism, and others are sent by their parents or relatives. It is said that these pupils have to memorize a great number of verses -- so many, that some of them spend twenty years at their studies. The Druids believe that their religion forbids them to commit their teachings to writing though for most other purposes, such as public and private accounts, the Gauls use the Greek alphabet. But I imagine that this rule was originally established for other reasons because they did not want their doctrine to become public property, and in order to prevent pupils from relying on the written word and neglecting to train their memories; for it is usually found that when people have the help of texts, they are less diligent in learning by heart, and let their memories rust.[142]

Caesar, whose friend Divitiacus was both a ruler and Druid of the eastern Aeduan Gauls, was careful to say that his observations were based on the Druids of Gaul, but also careful to add that the order had its roots in Britain. This was certainly true. Before the arrival of Christianity,

---

141 P. V. Glob, *The Bog People* (Paladin: London, 1971); J. Joy, *Lindow Man* (The British Museum: London, 2009).
142 Julius Caesar, *The Conquest of Gaul* (Penguin: Harmondsworth, 1974), pp.31-3.

Druids, seers and poets from all over the Celtic world trained in Britain and Ireland. In Britain their ritual centre was on the island of Anglesey: in Ireland the centre of Druidism was Tara.

Training for the Celtic Literary Hierarchy

In Ireland the arch-*ollamh* ranked at the top of the hierarchy as a kind of grand vizier to the king or queen, sitting next to them at court: his ability to kill with satire made his person sacrosanct and made him a terror even to the warriors.[143] The *ollamh* (as the original Irish master poets had been called) was a kind of professor, and had survived a prolonged and intense training at a 'forest college', learning magic, healing, divination, history, music, law and poetry. The master poet trained through seven degrees, the first of which qualified him as the lowest grade of poet; a storyteller trained for seven years: a Bard was one who had not yet completed his studies. In Wales, where things were not quite so intense, the training of a poet nevertheless took nine years. In Ireland there were four grades of poet. In Wales there were three grades: Disgybl ysbâs heb radd -- unqualified apprentice, *disgybl disgyblaidd* -- qualified apprentice, *pencerdd* -- head or master poet. Each grade took at least three years of study.[144]

When the Irish poet went for his final qualifying degree he had to compose an improvised poem on any theme suggested by the judges; demonstrate his mastery of Irish history, Irish antiquities and the genealogy of all the leading Irish families.[145] Treatises on poetry identify 338 different verse forms the fully trained poet had to know.[146] We know from the *Lebor Laighneach* (The Book of Leinster, written before 1160) that in Ireland a fully trained *ollamh* (Druid professor) had to master no less than twenty-four main types of poem ranging over 350 kinds of metre. He also had to master, memorize and be prepared to deliver correctly, word perfect, at a moment's notice, 350 *prímscéla* (main epic tales -- each one a night's entertainment) and 100 *fóscéla* (subsidiary stories) in prose and also in prose and poetry, consisting of monologues, dialogues, narrative and description. For example, king Mongan, the sixth-century ruler of east Ulster, had his *filí* (storyteller), tell him a different story every night

---

143 R. Graves, *The Crowning Privilege* (Penguin: Harmondsworth, 1959), pp.17-19.
144 M. Hopwood, *Singing in Chains* (2004), p.15.
145 S. MacManus, *The Story of the Irish Race* (Devin Adair: New York, 1967), pp.179-80.
146 W. P. Ker, *The Dark Ages* (Nelson: London, 1955), p.330.

from Samhain to Beltaine (1 November – 1 May). Unfortunately very few of these tales have survived, but the repertoire of a tenth century *filí* still exists in the form of two lists of his tales.[147]

The training for Druid poets and storytellers was hard, strict and conservative: it had to be if the poet was to master all aspects of the craft. Robert Graves has given us an imaginative reconstruction based on research:

> … twenty years of hard study at the Druidical college are first called for and it is by no means every candidate who succeeds in passing through the necessary thirty-two degrees. The first twelve years are spent in being initiated in turn into all the other secret societies, in learning by heart enormous sagas of mythological poetry and in the study of law, music, and astronomy. The next three years are spent in the study of omens and magic. The tests put upon candidates for the priesthood are immensely severe. For example, there is a test of poetical composition. The candidates must lie naked all night in a coffin-like box, only his nostrils protruding above the icy water with which it is filled, and with heavy stones laid on his chest. In this position he must compose a poem of considerable length in the most difficult of the many bardic metres, on a subject which is given him as he is placed in the box. On his emergence next morning he must be able to chant this poem to a melody which he has been simultaneously composing and accompany himself on the harp. Another test is to stand before the whole body of Druids and be asked verse-riddles, also in verse. These riddles all refer to obscure incidents in the sacred poems with which the candidate is supposed to be familiar. [148]

If we can judge by the surviving fragments and allusions, the repertoire of the Irish and Welsh storytellers was huge. Examples of how they combined poetry and prose in a narrative can be found in the Welsh *Mabinogion* or in fragments that make up the Irish *Taín*. The *Mabinogion* seems to have been a collection of the basic stories an apprentice minstrel was expected to know and they date back at least to Roman times, though they were written down in their current form in *Llyfr Gwyn Rhydderch* (White Book of Rhydderch) in *c.* 1300–25 and *Llyfr Coch Hergest* (The Red Book of Hergest) in *c.* 1375–1425.

---

147 N. Chadwick, *The Celts* (Penguin: Harmondsworth, 1970), p.263.
148 R. Graves, *Claudius the God* (Penguin: Harmondsworth, 1976), pp.221-22.

The Welsh storyteller, known as *y cyfarwydd* (literally, the learned one), probably did not memorize the entire story, but rather the outline of the story and the main events, improvising the rest and leaving space for local references and flattering genealogies where necessary. The narrative was in prose, with verse restricted to praise poems, set speeches and improvised commentaries: almost certainly dramatic verse was only employed at moments of great emotional stress, and may have been accompanied by the harp. Some of Gwydion's narratives, for example, were supplemented with verse. The verse form known was usually *englyn* or *englynion*.[149] This is one of the twenty-four classical metres, and it is one of the oldest Welsh poetical forms dating back at least as far as the battle of Catraeth in 565BC. It is a complex and demanding format for a four line verse of thirty syllables in lines of ten, six, seven, and seven syllables. The sixth syllable of the first line must rhyme with the last syllable of the other three lines; the final syllable of the first line is without rhyme. And then there are the *cynghanedd*, the harmonic or poetic aspects of alliteration and rhythm. There are in total ninety rules for the Bardic *englyn* in Welsh. An example of a simplified *englyn* in English:

In flight, the butter*fly* knows utter bliss.
Sun today, soon to *die*,
Full of joy, life on the *fly*
Scales the void, the scombroid *sky*.[150]

It is quite possible that the prose narrative was improvised from basic elements and that only the complex verses were memorized. This would explain why the verses have survived in written form while only fragments of the prose narratives have been preserved.[151] The surviving *Englynion y Beddau* (Englyns of the Graves) listing the burial places of the Welsh heroes was probably a memory test for the budding storyteller.

---

149 *The Mabinogion* trans., G. Jones and T. Jones (Penguin: Harmondsworth, 2000), pp.65-6; M. Hopwood, *Singing in Chains: Listening to Welsh Verse* (Llandysul: Gomer, 2004); L. Turco, *The New Book of Forms: A Handbook of Poetics* (University Press of New England: London 1986); F. Stillman, *The Poet's Manual And Rhyming Dictionary* (Thames & Hudson: London, 2006), p.77.

150 www.noggs.dsl.pipex.com/vf/englyn. Scombroid -- Mackerel-like: modern Italian *Lanzardo* or *sgombro cavallo*.

151 A. Conran, *The Penguin Book of Welsh Verse* (Penguin: Harmondsworth, 1967), pp.83-95.

The *Mabinogion* also gives us some idea of the standing of the storyteller and their way of working. In the story of Math, Gwydion and his eleven companions disguise themselves as bards and set out to go to Rhuddlan Teifi (in modern Cardigan) to play a trick on Pryderi -- basically they want to steal his pigs. When Pryderi, failing to see through the disguise, and noticing only travelling bards, asks for a story 'from some of the young men yonder', Gwydion says it is their custom that on their first night at the home of a 'great man', the Chief Bard among them would be the first to tell a tale. From this we learn that travelling bards -- even in travelling in groups -- were not unusual, that it was normal for them to have their rules and order of precedence, that it was expected that they would offer a tale, and that it was normal that they would stay some time at the home of a 'great man'. That night Gwydion, 'the best storyteller in the world', told stories until he was praised by all, and then Pryderi took pleasure in conversation with him.[152] Unfortunately what tales he told can only be guessed at from the fragments of stories that have survived elsewhere.

Another contemporary portrait of a Druid in literature is Cathbad in *Taín Bó Cualnge*. There we see the Druid as teacher -- Cathbad is said to have a hundred pupils of omens and portents at his school in Emhain Macha -- and as a seer making prophecies at the court of king Conchobar -- he predicts that he who takes up arms on a particular day will be famous but short lived, and also that a woman will give birth to a daughter, Deirdre, who will bring ruin to Ulster. Elsewhere in the story we see Cathbad using his Druidic skills to try to protect Cú Chulainn from the magic of Queen Medb. Cú Chulainn's end is linked to Druid magic. He is approached by three Druids, each one asking for one of his three spears. He knows he cannot refuse a Druid or he will be satirized in their verse. He throws his spears at the Druids, killing two; the third spear is picked up by his enemy who throws it back and kills Cú Chulainn.

There were also female Druids. In the *Taín* Fedelma is said to be both prophet and poet, and Scáthach is said to be a seer and warrior in charge of teaching the craft and skills of war in Ulster. Both of these characters can be seen as figures with supernatural powers and origins. Fedelma, who appears clad in red under a speckled cloak -- which in itself signals

---

152 *The Mabinogion* trans., G. Jones and T. Jones (Penguin: Harmondsworth, 2000), p.51.

the supernatural -- says she studied poetry in 'Alba', which is part of Scáthach's spirit world. The name Scáthach means 'of the shadows', which perhaps links her to the Roman goddess Diana, the huntress. There are several other references to Druids and Bards in early Irish literature. The twelfth-century Irish Fenian Cycle of tales about Finn and his band of warriors, the Fianna, tell us that Finn was brought up by a female Druid and a female seer, that he was sent to the Bard, Finngas, to learn the art of poetry. Finngas fed him the Salmon of knowledge, and as a result he became wise enough to deal with the machinations of his enemy, the Black Bard.

The *Lebor Gabála Érenn* (Book of Invasions), written down *c.* 900–1200 but based on much earlier materials, says that the first colonizers of Ireland were led by Partholan who brought with him as part of his household three Druids named Fiss, Tath and Fochmarc -- whose names translate as intelligence, knowledge and enquiry. The following invaders, Tuartha Dé Danann (children of Dana), use Druidic magic to cloak themselves. The final invaders, the Gaels, find that the Druids of the Tuartha Dé Danann conjure up storms in an attempt to repel them, but the Gael Druids have magic enough of their own. However, after this final invasion, the book records, there was friction between the two groups of Druids lasting many years.

The Druidic poet seems to have been top of the Celtic literary community. In Ireland the poets were considered part of the nobility. Celtic lords in Wales had in their company, up to the time of the Roman departure, a *pencerdd* or head poet who would compose poems and songs, a *bardd teulu* or household poet, a Reciter who would sing their songs to the assembly, and musicians who would accompany the performance. At banquets poems would be sung to a harp accompaniment, and if the lord liked the result the poet, the Reciter and the musicians would be rewarded with gold, silver, horses, cattle, etc. When the lord went into battle the bards composed a new poem of praise. It seems that the poets of opposing sides would sit together to observe, comment on and record the battle, and would intervene when they judged a battle had been won or lost. Their version of events was accepted by all.

It is hard for us to appreciate the social standing and the responsibility shouldered by the Druid storytellers and poets. It is significant that at a time when most people, including the poets, were anonymous, in the sixth century we know the names of no less than five Welsh poets, including Taliesin, Llywarch Hen and Aneirin, some of whose works have survived to the present day. Norah Chadwick has written:

> The *filíd* were the poets and intellectuals, and a very ancient institution of which we hear first in ancient Gaul. They were responsible for the whole intellectual life of the people and for its transmission, first in rhythmical prose, later in prose and verse. Since all knowledge was transmitted in oral form the *filíd* had to know and teach all required knowledge; and since at that time no clear distinction existed between history, as we understand it, and tradition, all narrative of the past was part of their repertoire.[153]

Although the fashion may have changed through time and varied from place to place, the Druids always had a distinctive appearance -- the front part of the head was shaved from ear to ear in what is known as the 'Celtic tonsure'. They were entitled to wear a gold torc around their neck. Some are thought to have worn tartan while others wore a cloak speckled with gold and gold earrings. The arch-Druid is thought to have worn an oak garland surmounted by a golden tiara inset with 'snake stones'. Poets carried a small branch with tiny bells. The *ollamh* carried a golden branch or staff, while others lower down the hierarchy carried silver or bronze. We know that in the ninth century the Welsh poets and storytellers wore a long cloak the bottom half of which was decorated with white and multi-coloured bird feathers and the upper part of which was decorated with iridescent feathers from the neck and crest of a mallard.[154] Medieval Irish laws refer to *fili* being allowed to wear six different colours in their clothing as a mark of their status. Fergus, who is credited with reciting the whole of *The Taín* so that the poets might memorize it, is said to have worn a green cloak with a red embroidered hooded tunic, a gold hilted sword and bronze sandals.[155] When they attended public rites and functions Druids wore white robes. Female Druids, devotees of the Irish war goddess Morrigan or the British equivalent, Rhiannon, wore black cloaks. If we are to believe the carved stones with figures of *genii cucullati*, or 'cloaked spirits,' found at several holy sites in Britain and in Europe, the cloaks were worn with the hoods up when the Druids were working.

153 N. Chadwick, *The Celts* (Penguin: Harmondsworth, 1970), p.264.
154 M. & S. Aldhouse-Green, *The Quest for the Shaman* (Routledge: London, 2005), p.196.
155 *The Taín*, trans., T. Kinsella (OUP: Oxford, 2002), p.1.

Druid Learning and Lore

Throughout the Celtic world, apart from a few inscriptions on stone found in Italy, France and Spain, the Druids refused to write down their learning and knowledge. The subject of what exactly the Druids 'knew' is very difficult, and as the poet and scholar Robert Graves says, 'the Irish *ollamhs* had no interest in making it plain to outsiders'.[156] Without doubt the Druids had control of oracles and shrines. Apart from this, however, we cannot know for sure what other knowledge or lore the Druids were protecting, but Robert Graves conjectured, on fairly substantial evidence, some of the things they were keen to hide. The first surprise is that although the Druids did not write their secret lore down, they knew how to write -- Caesar had observed that the Gauls used 'Greek letters' for day to day business -- and it seems they knew an alphabet called Beth Luis Nion. A further surprise is that although no Druidic writing survives from before the sixth century, this alphabet was clearly an adaptation of one of the earliest alphabets, called Formello-Cervetri, dated to around the fifth century BC, and derived from Greece via Spain, rather than the later version we are now familiar with, developed by the Phoenicians, adopted by the Greeks and adapted by the Etruscans and then the Romans. Transliterated from the Irish Ogham script into their modern equivalents, the alphabet looked like this:

```
B   L   F   S   N
H   D   T   C   Q
M   G   NG  FF  R
A   O   U   E   I
```

These letters -- which consisted of nicks across the corner of a length of wood or bone - could also be signalled silently across a shin bone or table-edge with the fingers or by using the fingers, tips and joints of the hand. There is no P but there is a Q in this alphabet -- which identifies the language of the users as Q Celtic (Irish), rather than P Celtic (Welsh), but a version was developed later in Wales.

Another aspect of this secret lore was that the name of each letter was that of a tree or shrub from the sacred grove. Here it is in the later P Celtic (Welsh) version:

---

156 R. Graves, *The White Goddess* (Faber: London, 1999), p.199.

B, beth, birch	A, ailm, silver fir / elm
L, luis, rowan	O, onn, furze / broom
N, nion, ash	U, ura, heather
F, fearn, alder	E, eadha, white poplar or aspen
S, saille, willow	I, idho, yew
H, uath, hawthorn	
D, duir, oak	
T, tinne, holly / gorse	
C, coll, hazel	
M, muin, vine	
G, gort, ivy	
P, pethboc, dwarf elder	
R, ruis, elder	

The thirteen consonants provided an alphabet of trees for the thirteen months of the lunar year (each month of twenty-eight days, total 364 days = one lunar year). Another secret aspect of this alphabet was that it could be used to transmit to initiates the secret names of the gods, or later, when Christianity began to have an impact, the secret name of God.

The Druids also controlled the calendar, for farming but also for prediction of auspicious dates. In addition to various carved stones marking the entrance to religious areas, the discovery of the first century bronze Coligny calendar in 1897 offers rare confirmation of Druidic practice with an actual example of surviving material culture and proof of literacy even at this early date.[157]

The bulk of surviving Celtic inscriptions, and most of the evidence of Celtic writing, date from the Christian era. But in the oldest pre-Christian Celtic writing, the Druids of Ireland are recorded as reading and writing. The Celts -- particularly the Irish -- attributed the eloquence of all Druids, poets, seers, healers and bards to a mysterious patron god called Ogmios in Gaul, in Ireland Ogma and in Britain Ogmia. The Celts said he was the son of Dagda, father of the gods. Ogma was credited

---

157 Further evidence of early Celtic literacy came with the discovery of a leaden tablet from Larzac in France in 1983 and a bronze tablet from northern Spain in 1992. P. Beresford Ellis, *A Brief History of the Druids* (Robinson: London, 2002), pp.162-3.

with the invention of the Ogham script. He was similar in function to the Egyptian god Thoth, the god Roman Mercury (who was popular among the Celts of mainland Europe) and the Greek Hercules, who was also the son of Zeus, father of the gods. There are very few written references to the god Ogma, and the Romans don't seem to have known much about him, which probably means his name was taboo. A piece of pottery found in Richborough in Kent, England shows him with long curly hair and the rays of the sun shining from his head. The Greek writer Lucian of Samosata described a picture of Ogmios which he saw in Celtic Gaul, at Gallia Narbonensis, near modern Marseille. In this picture, he wrote, Ogmios was depicted with the bow and club normally associated with Hercules, but instead of the powerful, beautiful youth of Greek and Roman mythology, Ogmios was an old man, bald and burnt by the sun, drawing behind him a happy band of men, attached by thin gold chains linking their ears to the tip of his tongue.

The Assault on Druidism

Although the Romans conquered Gaul, Britain continually sent Druids to Gaul to stir up opposition and resistance to Roman rule. Understandably the Romans considered the Druids to be a major political nuisance and it is likely they were a major factor in the decision to invade Britain. The first Roman invasion of Britain came in 55–7BC and seems to have been little more than a reconnaissance in strength. The second invasion came in AD 43, started at Richborough and was a much more serious affair. The Romans after subduing much of southern Britain went on to attack the Druidic order in Britain in AD 60, when, under governor Suetonius Paulinus, they invaded Anglesey, the sacred centre of Druidism. There they massacred the population and cut down the sacred groves. In AD 78 the new governor, Agricola who had served in the legions during the first invasion of Anglesey in Wales, invaded the island a second time and then garrisoned it, making sure that Druidism could never again threaten Roman power.

There was also a legal assault within the Empire and various Roman emperors also passed decrees against Druidism. Emperor Augustus (27BC–AD 14) decreed it impossible to be a Druid and citizen of Rome. Emperor Tiberius (AD 14–37) introduced laws banning Druidism, native soothsayers and healers. Emperor Claudius (AD 41–54) suppressed the

Druids by banning all Druid religious practices. By the end of the first century, as Celtic society became absorbed into Romanized society, Druidism seems to have almost disappeared within the area of the Roman Empire. In the Celtic societies of Scotland and Wales it survived in a much diminished way until Christianisation in the fifth to the seventh centuries. However, there are a few references to Druids in Latin literature long after they had in theory been suppressed. In the middle of the second century the *Scriptes Historiae Augustae*, for example, twice mentions female Druids. The future Emperor Diocletian, on military service in Gaul, chided for his meanness by a female Druid, was warned by her that he would only become Emperor after he had killed the boar. This riddle hinted he would have to kill the Prefect of the Praetorian Guard, who was called *aper* (boar) to become emperor. Elsewhere a female Druid called to Emperor Severus Alexander as he rode out to war, warning him not to expect victory and not to trust his troops. The emperor was killed by his own soldiers.

In Gaul a memory of the Druids survived: the fourth century Bordeaux writer Ausonius mentions them twice in his *Commemoratorio Professorum Burdigalensium*, recalling a rhetorician friend called Delphidius who claimed descent from the Druids of the temple dedicated to the healing god Belenus at Bayeux, and he also mentions a university teacher of rhetoric who was rumoured to be descended from the Druids of Armorica. By this time it seems, some 300 years after the destruction of the Druid stronghold on Anglesey and the Romanization of Gaul, not only was there still a clear family tradition in existence, but also a clear connection between Celtic oral tradition and a profession connected to teaching, words and language, as if Druidism had somehow metamorphosed in both cases into the teaching of rhetoric. Also it was by this time clearly acceptable in Roman society to admit to having Druid ancestors.

The Celts in Asia Minor occupied an area in Anatolia (modern Turkey) known as Galatia. They were rather hard-headed and St Paul, who had spent some time with them, called them 'foolish' in his 'Epistle to The Galatians' (3:1), thought to have been written from Rome about *c*. AD 49–58. They had arrived in the area of the Pontos from Thrace around 270–78BC, probably as a large mercenary war-band seeking employment. Initially they served king Nicomedes of Bythnia, but after about twenty years in his service they moved on to conquer a large area of the Turkish central steppes. It is known they had a holy meeting place twenty miles southwest of Ancyra (modern Ankara), which the Greeks called *Drynemeton* (Gallic *daru-nemeton, holy place of oak). However, the Roman legions under Gnaeus Manlius Vulso defeated the Galatians in 189 BC, after which they begin to fade from view, absorbed into the the Roman army, where they established a fierce reputation, and into the mainly Greek speaking populace. Their language may have lived on for two more centuries. St Jerome (AD 347–420) in his *Comentarii in Epistolam ad Galatos* (2.3), composed around the year AD 387, wrote that the Galatians of Ancyra and the Gaulish Treveri of Trier (now in the Rhineland) spoke the same language. Only a few clearly Celtic place and personal names survive in the region, but it is possible that their language loaned a number of words that survive in modern Turkish.[158] However, apart from the fact that like the Celts of Western Europe they fought naked and wore torques, and a passing reference to them in the works of the Greek historian and Geographer Strabo (*c.* 64BC–*c.* AD 24), there is almost nothing in the historical record about how they organised themselves, the nature of their government, or whether they maintained Druids.[159] However, the continuance of the tradition of fighting naked and the survival of their language, suggests that other traditions, like Druidism, may have lingered on until the Galatians themselves disappeared from view.

The Romans had traded across the Irish Sea but never attempted an invasion, so there Druidism survived intact and undamaged to be observed and experienced by incoming Christian monks in the fifth to seventh centuries. Druidic culture had probably benefited from the Roman departure from Britain: it is possible that Druids had moved from Gaul and Britain under pressure of barbarian and Saxon population movements. The incoming missionaries had to contest the influence of the Druids, but they also had to tolerate it. Before the arrival of Christianity the esteem of poets and storytellers in Wales was as high as in Ireland. The Druids persisted alongside Christianity for

---

158 S. Young, *The Celtic Revolution* (Gibson Square: London, 2010): www.galloturca. com/galatians_files/galatianwords.
159 The statue known as 'The Dying Gaul', showing a warrior naked except for a torque was commissioned between 230-20 BC by Attalus I of Pergamon to celebrate his victory over the Celtic Galatians in Anatolia. The statue is currently in the Capitoline Museum in Rome. There are several copies.

a very long time. In some early Celtic Christian Latin texts the words 'Magus' and 'Druid' are used interchangeably. The Irish St Columba (also known as Colum Cille, Colum of the Cell) for example spoke of Christ as his Druid, and working in Iona, was credited with the Druidic gift of foresight. Also on visiting pagan Celts in north Britain he is said to have bested the locals at the Druidic game of 'weather magic'. On the other hand, in the ninth-century Latin text, *The Book of Armagh*, St Patrick is said to have fought a fierce battle with the Druids at Tara, the very centre of Irish Druidism. The seventh century *Life of St Brigit* also records a clash between St Patrick and the Druids and the Irish language text *The Tripartite Life of Patrick* (895–901) says that nine Druids attempted to assassinate St Patrick. But then, St Patrick is also said to have had two Druids as close friends, and a *filid* is said to have converted to Christianity after conversing with St Patrick about the Irish Laws. What is certain is that the transfer of knowledge and power away from 'the joint memory of the ancients, the transmission from one ear to another, the 'chanting of the poets', was undertaken as part of its Christianising mission by the Church. The eighth-century volume known as *Senchas Már* with its compilation of traditional Irish laws harmonized to blend with Christianity shows the process in action.

While some of the Druidic order became wandering minstrels, we have to assume that the training, ritual accomplishments and social standing of the Druids also allowed some intellectuals to transfer without too much difficulty into the Christian Church, particularly into the new Celtic Christian monasticism, where they could remain married and where their standing, social skills and love of learning could be continued. These monasteries were unlike the Benedictine monasteries of the later medieval period: they showed a clear Druidic influence in that were willing to educate male and female children of all ages and of all classes, to provide texts from their own scriptoria free of charge; a willingness to teach all seven degrees up to Sai Litra (Doctor of Letters) across a curriculum that included divinity, classical poetry, philosophy, Latin, Greek, science and literature. Indeed, in the early days, the skills of the Druids may have eased the transition to Christianity in Ireland by shaping Celtic Christianity through its monasteries and later in preserving some of the stories and texts that have come down to us.[160] For example, we know from St Columba's Convention of Drum Ceatt (560) that many Druids were brought into the Church by being offered posts in monasteries and schools as teachers of song and poetry. Some Druids may have become the new Christian clerics, supporting the church as the new intelligentsia, and some like the living Celtic goddess Bridget became the Christian Saint Bridget.

The most powerful figures in the Irish monastery movement were St Columba (531–597) and his friend St Columban (530?–615), the two great successors to St Patrick. Ultimately the descendants of these Irish monks were to found the great European monasteries, and through them the medieval Cathedral schools out of which grew the earliest universities in Europe. In the years up to 575–725 it is estimated that Irish scholar-monks founded over 150 monasteries -- Kell, Lindisfarne, Durrow, Bangor, York, Ripon, Jarrow, Yearmouth, St Gall, Echternacht, Salzburg, Bobbio, Nonantola, Luxueil, Lyon, Corbie, Autun, Tours, St Amand, St Medard de Soisson -- transplanting their love and skill with books, their Latin and Greek texts, and their copyists' skills.

However, in general, the Christian Church saw pagan powers preserved in the Druids. Druid healers and seers were characterized as witches, fortune tellers, magicians, quacks, sorcerers, tricksters and purveyors of potions. The Church did its best to displace the traditional poets and storytellers too, by forcing them to become itinerants. After the Synod of Whitby in AD 663 the Celtic church with its married clergy, distinctive version of monasticism, different date for Easter and its Celtic tonsure (previously the mark of the Druid) were legislated to the fringe of Roman Christianity and doomed to fade away. The monasteries were gradually absorbed into the Benedictine monastic system. Robert Graves has been careful to distinguish the situation before the arrival of Christianity in Wales with what happened afterwards:

> When the Welsh poets were converted to orthodox Christianity and subjected to ecclesiastical discipline (...) their tradition gradually ossified. Though a high degree of technical skill was still required of master-poets and thought the Chair of Poetry was still hotly contested in the various Courts, they were pledged to avoid

---

160 J. K. W. P. Corcoran 'Celtic Mythology' in: R. Graves (ed.), *New Larousse Encyclopedia of Mythology* (Hamlyn: London, 1968), p.238.

what the Church called 'untruth', meaning the dangerous exercise of poetic imagination in myth or allegory. Only certain epithets and metaphors were authorised; themes were similarly restricted, metres fixed, and Cynghanedd, the repetitive use of consonantal sequences with variation of vowels became a burdensome obsession. The master poets had become court-officials, their first obligation being to praise God, their second to praise the king or prince who had provided a Chair for them at his royal table.[161]

*

Irish literature is the oldest European literature north of the Alps. At some time around the start of seventh century Irish scribes began to write down the tales they heard. However, the act of writing the tales down seems to have contributed to their destruction. By the twelfth century, the date of the earliest surviving Irish manuscripts, the scribes who wrote them down were not performance artists, but clerics and copyists with little or no storytelling skills. In writing them down they rendered these stories almost unintelligible and unusable in a traditional setting. If these stories were transcribed in the banqueting halls, then it is clear that the scribes, working at speed and by poor light, grew weary of their task long before the storyteller had finished.

Perhaps the text that illustrates this history, and at the same time explains why this literature is so little known, is the *Táin Bó Cúalnge* (*The Táin*: or *The Cattle Raid of Cooley*). *Táin Bó Cúalnge* seems to have originated as a series of oral compositions possibly as early as AD 400. It was first written down in the seventh century, by which time the various narrative elements seem to have coalesced as one long story. However, although there are several texts of the tale, none of them is very satisfactory. After a promising start, almost every version of this story immediately becomes problematic: different manuscripts leave out important episodes, truncate them or simply become confused. And where the manuscript is then copied on by another scribe the confusions, mistakes and problems multiply. It is hard to imagine many listeners would come back for a second night to hear the stories as they have come down to us.

Lebor na hUidre (The Book of the Dun Cow) contains some parts of the story (sixty-seven vellum leaves from a total of 130): it was written

---

161 R. Graves, *The White Goddess* (Faber: London, 1999), p.14.

down about the year 1100 and is derived from ninth-century texts, which were in turn based on texts from the sixth or seventh centuries, but to what extent the earliest texts were based on oral versions of the story, or how many versions of the story once existed, is impossible to say. There is another version of the story in the fourteenth-century *Yellow Book of Lecan*. This seems to make makes use of the earlier *Lebor na hUidre* text, but also mangles it by including 'interpolations, re-writings, palimpsests, redundancies, repetitions, narrative contradictions and lacunae.' All of which poet Ciaran Carson takes to be evidence that it was compiled not from documents, but from an oral tradition that included variant performances.[162] A third version is found in the twelfth-century *Book of Leinster*. Here a scribe seems to have set out to compose a new and more coherent 'literary' text.

When the poet and scholar Thomas Kinsella, and after him Ciaran Carson, set out to make their modern translations of *Táin Bó Cúalnge*, they both had to stitch together the full story from several rather poor surviving manuscripts in order to reconstruct what must once have been a very powerful traditional tale.[163] In both reconstructed modern versions there is much of interest, value and charm about *The Táin*, since we are quite literally looking in on Bronze Age Ireland, and we can still sense what a wonderful entertainment and history the tale must once have been.[164]

The attitude of the Irish monks who copied the early texts was usually very severe and rather lacking in patience or sympathy. One monk, after copying a version of the *Táin Bó Cúalnge* added a traditional formulaic oral blessing: 'Amen: a blessing on everyone who will memorize the Tain faithfully in this form, and not put any other form on it.' And then he added:

I, who have copied down this story, or more accurately fantasy, do not credit the details of the story, or fantasy. Some things in it are devilish lies, and some are poetical fragments; some seem possible and others not; some are for the enjoyment of idiots.[165]

162 C. Carson, 'Introduction', *The Tain*, (Penguin: Harmondsworth, 2007), p.xiii.
163 *The Táin*, trans., T. Kinsella, (Oxford University Press: Oxford, 1970).
164 N. Chadwick, *The Celts* (Penguin: Harmondsworth, 1970), pp.266-7.
165 T. Cahill, *How the Irish Saved Civilisation* (First Anchor: London, 1995), pp.160-3.

These are clearly the words of a man who is sympathetic up to a point, but who is mainly concerned with the literate Christian world, rather than the pagan oral world. We have to assume that where the monk copyists did not maim the tales, they certainly did not labour over-long to save or improve them beyond the limits of what they thought was appropriate.

There must have been many more of the Irish tales than have come down to us. However, what the scribes did not mar, was probably destroyed by the Viking raids that plagued Ireland in the years 795–1071. It may be that much better written versions of the surviving Irish tales once existed, but much of Irish written culture was destroyed in these years, and what has come down to us is a sad remnant of a once powerful tradition.

*

In Wales it would seem that one of the advantages of training and qualifying as a bard was that, even in the less favourable circumstances of the new Christian Welsh aristocracy, under the laws of Hywel Dda, a tenth-century Welsh king who made no mention of Druids, no bard could ever be made a slave. Otherwise Hywel Dda had little use for bards. In the earliest version of his laws bards are seen as having a place at court, but in a later version of this law, called the Demetian Code, bards are denied a place at court. But in a later version, the Venedotian Code, bards are said to have a worth equivalent to six score and six cows -- that is below the value of a court porter or the queen's candle bearer.[166]

While Druidism may have been broken as a political and socially cohesive force, and the social standing of the bards undermined by the invasion, the tradition of bardic poetry had a kind of survival through the bardic hedge-poets. In Wales Llywarch ab Llewelyn (1160–1220), Filip Brydydd (1200–1250) and the *Red Book of Hergest* (c. 1375–1425) all speak of the Druids with some familiarity, as if they were still in these years a part of everyday life in Wales. However, at this time while there were itinerant poets and storytellers, for the upper classes Bardic poetry was increasingly the tame, respectable, Christian, 'official poetry' of eulogies and elegies as court poets restricted themselves: as a result their

---

166 R. Graves, *The Crowning Privilege* (Penguin: Harmondsworth, 1959), p.180.

narratives become truncated, incoherent and bare, lacking in detail, their characters are sketched in with a few epithets and descriptions are brief.

Although it is traditional to blame Welsh cultural decline on the English conquest of Wales, in terms of poetic tradition this process seems to have been well under way by the end of the tenth century -- before the Anglo-Norman conquest started. The Welsh bard was by then appointed by a king or prince who had scant respect for their poetic talent, and who cared only about their morals. The Welsh poet held his office at court because he praised God in established metres and diction, and avoided 'untruth'. As Robert Graves put it, the training had so far decayed by this time that a Welsh bard might 'praise his prince as having the might of Aegwl, the disposition of Alexander, the strength of Alun, the energy of Beli' -- without in the least knowing who these personages were.'[167] In the first half of the twelfth century, Gruffydd ap Cynan and his son Owain Gwynedd returned from exile in Ireland to recover their Welsh inheritance in the lands of Gwynedd, and imported Irish minstrels and bards in an attempt to revive Welsh bardic practice. Briefly there was a flowering of poetry by named authors who clearly regarded themselves as a kind of order or profession. Court poetry in Wales reached a peak in the 'period of the princes' -- that is in the period from the arrival of the Normans to the end of the thirteenth century.[168] The end point for this development seems to have come when stubborn Welsh tribal society clashed with the advancing power of feudalism as King Edward I embarked upon the conquest of Wales in 1282. After this, Norman castle building confined the Welsh to rural areas by excluding them from most towns and areas of 'English' settlement; the Welsh princes, on whom poets depended for patronage, were virtually eradicated.

However, after the Norman invasion of 1066, court poetry also began a strange reversal. Although the troubadours of southern France began their wandering work in the late eleventh century and the *trouvéres* of northern France developed around the end of the twelfth century, in Wales the *clêr* (low grade bards specializing in popular songs and satire), hedge-poets, minstrels and storytellers -- at the mercy of geography, politics, language and culture -- had already been on the *clera* (gigging circuit) for some considerable time. The Norman lords, many of

---

167 R. Graves, *The Crowning Privilege*, p.181.
168 K. H. Jackson (ed.), *A Celtic Miscellany* (Penguin: Harmondsworth, 1971), p.228.

whom were Celts from Brittany, did not see wandering minstrels and storytellers as vagabonds but as honoured members of society, welcome at every home. A wandering storyteller would probably prolong a performance at a nobleman's home to last over several evenings, since this would maximize pay, shelter and hospitality. After the Norman conquest of Ireland in the twelfth century, a similar pattern seems to have been established, where minstrels and storytellers were welcomed by Norman lords.[169] As Welsh and Norman families began to intermarry it became difficult to keep the wandering Welsh minstrels out of the court, and from the end of the twelfth century, through the end of fourteenth century, as the difficult, atrophied and archaic poetry of the Welsh courts was dying, the tales and sagas of the hedge poets and itinerants began to surface, suitably reworked, in Poetic Romances.[170]

By this time official Christian court bards and the ecclesiastical scribes and storytellers in Wales had long ceased their training in Ireland and as a result were regarded by the Irish as unqualified practitioners, untrained dabblers, a joke. It was only in Ireland that the master poet retained the power, expectation and freedom to create in a traditional and original manner. In Wales the popular romances of the period were told not by court bards, but by itinerant 'minstrels' -- the surviving remnant of the displaced Druidic stratum -- who were not subject to the courtly laws of composition or the strictures of the Church. These were the gleemen of popular culture, often referred to as *eirchiad* (supplicants or beggars) and they do not seem to have been entirely Christianized or tamed. These two traditions -- the courtly and the itinerant -- coexisted side by side for several hundred years, and yet there was almost no contact between them. The court bards were forbidden to compose in the minstrel style or to visit the house of any but the noble families; the itinerant minstrels, storytellers and gleemen did not perform at court and did not use the complex and increasingly atrophied literary forms of the court.

It is recorded in *Ireland's Ancient Historical Documents* that King Henry II's Norman Lords were astonished to find in their invasion of Ireland in 1172 that Abbots and Bishops all seemed capable of singing, playing

---

169 M. E. Collins, *Conquest & Colonisation* (Gill & Macmillan: Dublin, 1969), pp.10-11; R. Graves, 'The Old Black Cow' in *The Crowning Privilege* (Penguin: Harmondsworth, 1959), pp.178-183.
170 R. Graves, *The White Goddess* (Faber: London, 1999), pp.15-17.

the harp and reciting many long poems.[171] In Ireland, in spite of the clash with Christianity, many of the ancient traditions of storytelling and Bardic poetry were to remain strong and feed into the particularities of Irish Christianity until at least the sixteenth century. However, what remained in Ireland of the ancient pre-Christian, Druidic world was mortally wounded by Elizabethan adventuring and then by Cromwell's invasion. A lament from a seventeenth century Irish bard called Mahon O'Heffernan survives in which it is clear that because of damage to the social structure and economic power of Irish families brought about by the English intervention, the Bardic tradition is in difficulty:

> I ask, who will buy a poem? Its meaning is the true learning of sages. Would anyone take, does anyone want, a noble poem which would make him immortal?
>
> Though this is a poem of close-knit lore, I have walked all Munster with it, every market place from cross to cross -- and it has brought me no profit from last year to the present.
> Though a groat would be a small payment, no man nor any woman offered it; not a man spoke of the reason, but neither Irish nor English heeded me.
>
> An art like this is no profit to me, though it is hard that it should die out; it would be more dignified to go and make combs -- why should anyone take up poetry?
>
> Corc of Cashel lives no more, nor Cian, who did not hoard up cattle nor the price of them, men who were generous in rewarding poets -- alas, it is good-bye to the race of Éibhear.
>
> The prize for generosity was never taken from them, until Cobhthach died, and Tál; I spare to mention the many kindreds for whom I might have continued to make poetry.
>
> I am like a trading ship that has lost its freight, after the FitzGeralds who deserve renown. I hear no offers – how that torments me! It is a vain quest about which I ask.[172]

Ireland was to endure another 400 years of English occupation with all its anti-educational policies, steady dispossession and cultural demolition, by the end of which the ancient traditions were barely a folk memory. Without the support of Gaelic rulers and a Gaelic-speaking community, poetic training was impossible, and it became harder and harder to make

---

171 J. O'Curry, (ed.), *Ireland's Ancient Historical Documents* (Dublin, 1868).
172 K. H. Jackson (ed.), *A Celtic Miscellany* (Penguin: Harmondsworth, 1971), pp.241-2.

a living by keeping to the profession. With their patrons gone the poets gradually fell silent. Poets like Daidhidh O Bruadair and later Aodhagán O Rathaille, displayed pride in their craft while bitterly lamented the passing of the old way of life, but there was nothing they could do. A few Gaelic-speaking families managed to retain land, but to do so they often had to change their religion, and within a generation many -- like the Luttrells of Dublin, the Bronwes of Westport, the MacDonnells of Antrim, the O'Neils of Clandeboye, the McCarthy's, O'Sullivans and O'Reillys -- had become thoroughly Anglicized. Increasingly the wandering poets and scholars of Ireland could not continue in their vocation and, along with the rest of the population, had no choice but to turn to farming, teaching and hedge schools but also increasingly to military service or emigration.[173]

Unlike Ireland, Welsh culture did not engage in a fierce defence of itself against the power of English, but rather accommodated itself to a long 'wasting sickness' and slow decline. Sir Phillip Sidney (1554–87) who was connected to Wales though his sister's marriage to the Earl of Pembroke, thought that in spite of the Romans, Saxons, Danes and Normans 'who did seek to ruin all memory of learning among them', Welsh bards had nevertheless survived 'even to this day'.[174] However, towards the end of his life the poet Owen Grufydd (1643–1730) believed the Bardic line to be dead in Wales; when he wrote 'The Men that Once Were' he found himself 'betrayed to wander the world in search of aid' and kept 'his poets' trade hidden in despair'.[175] Mahon O'Heffernan and Owen Grufydd may have been correct in identifying the end to the long tradition of Druidic Bardism, but this did not mean the fragments of Druidic lore had been entirely lost or forgotten. By this time they had already transformed themselves into something else entirely.

Druidic Survivals
In France (except for Brittany), Italy, Spain and Turkey the Celtic identity disappeared altogether leaving only place names to mark its territory. The Druids faded from view, while their 'old ways' were either absorbed into

---

173 M. E. Collins, *Conquest & Colonisation* (Gill and Macmillan: Dublin, 1969), p.159.
174 Sir Phillip Sidney, *A Defence of Poetry* (1595/98: Oxford University Press: Oxford, 1997), pp.20-1.
175 A. Conran, *The Penguin Book of Welsh Verse* (Penguin: Harmondsworth, 1967), pp.65, 205.

Christianity or became obscure and fragmented folk practices. However, Arthurian poems and stories preserve in a truncated, telegraphic and decayed form the last vestiges of pre-Christian Druidic belief, knowledge, lore and memory, if transformed into Christian Romance.

The earliest references to Arthur appear in the *Annales Cambriae*, dated from AD 518 and AD 539, where he is identified as a Christian Briton with the cross on his shield, probably living in the years AD 367–490, fighting off Saxon, Pictish and Irish invaders, and is said to have perished at the battle of Camlan.[176] William of Malmesbury refers to Arthur in his *Deeds of the King* in 1125, and in 1129 Henry of Huntingdon also referred to Arthur. However, while literary and historical references are rare, by the mid-twelfth century popular oral tales of Arthur abounded, and significantly it is in the twelfth century that the bones of Arthur were 'discovered' at Glastonbury.

Matthew Arnold in *On the Study of Celtic Literature* (1867) hinted that while the Druids and Druidic Bards may have 'subsisted' under the Romans, their traditions and habits of mind 'were not likely to be so speedily extinguished' and in his opinion these things survive as 'traces' in documents dating up to the twelfth century and in the work of the 'bards and rhapsodists' mentioned by Geraldus Cambrensis.[177] However, the Reverend Evan Evans, in correspondence with Bishop Thomas Percy in the 1760s, may have been the first to make a connection between the tales of King Arthur and the Druids.[178] Jessie L. Weston, in her famous and influential book *From Ritual to Romance*, was the first to assert that the legend of Arthur and the Quest for the Holy Grail represented the transformation of the memories of the figure of Arthur and surviving bits of Druidic lore into Christian Romance.[179] Since Weston made this claim others have taken it up and found considerable evidence to support the idea. Weston identified a Welshman called Bleheris or Bledri (*c.* 1070–1150), an obscure historical figure, who lived near Manorbeer in Dyfed, as both a possible repository of Druidic knowledge and the probable original Grail author. She says he was noted as a storyteller and on very good terms with the Normans. But while almost nothing is known for

176 L. Alcock, *Arthur's Britain* (Penguin: Harmondsworth, 1973), pp.45-88.
177 M. Arnold, *On the Study of Celtic Literature* (NuVision: Sioux Falls, South Dakota, 2008), pp.35-6.
178 M. A. Morse, *How the Celts came to Britain* (Tempus: Stroud, 2005), pp.42-3.
179 J. L. Weston, *From Ritual to Romance* (Doubleday-Anchor: New York, 1957).

certain about Bleheris, it can be said that if he was not the exact person who performed this task -- gathering materials and moulding stories -- it was somebody very like him. More likely it was probably not one person, but several, working over generations to pass on stories and traditions.

The transmission and its details are hard to pin down, but the main agents are most likely to have been the Breton lords among the Normans who flooded into Wales in the eleventh century -- particularly the Breton poets, storytellers and conteurs among their retinues. Since the Breton and Welsh languages were very close, Breton speakers would have been able to understand Welsh tales. The Breton poets and storytellers had contact with their own surviving Celtic myths, and access to Welsh and Irish Bards: the Welsh poets and storytellers visited Norman lords in Ireland, England and Wales, and they travelled throughout France and beyond. The Bretons seem to have recognised in the tales of the Welsh minstrels better versions of the stories they had heard told at home, or at least materials they could reuse in tales for their Norman lords. It is probable that at first they acted as translators for the Welsh artists, and then, such is the nature of storytelling, in time they 'acquired' the stories, cut out the Welsh storytellers, and made the tales their own. The Normans understandably favoured tales of Celtic warriors over those of Anglo-Saxons.

After the Norman Conquest, as the Bretons operated as *contacteurs* between the Welsh, Irish, Normans and French, the fragments of pre-Christian Druidic lore seem to have combined with ease around the figure of Arthur to create a literature of and about a marginalized, subject people. Whatever oral life these stories had in the intervening years we cannot know for sure, but even if the basic tales had become stale for the Welsh bards, during the Norman period, with the accession of Henry II of the French Plantagenet line (and his wife Eleanor of Aquitaine) in 1154, these tales acquired a new gloss and cross-channel life. In particular Geoffrey of Monmouth (c. 1100–c. 1155), a Breton whose family had arrived with the Norman conquest and been awarded lands in Gwent, probably used Nennius, Bede, lost Welsh language materials from Bleheris, and the eleventh-century tale of *Culhwch and Olwen* to produce fanciful but incredibly popular tales of Arthur in his *Historia Regum Britanniae* (History of the Kings of Britain) c.1138. He shows King Arthur as a British leader resisting the power of Rome, rather than as a Welsh leader resisting the Anglo Saxons, as he was later to become. In 1155 the manuscript was translated into Norman French by Wace -- who also added in the invention of the Round Table -- after which, the tales proved enormously popular. Over 200 copies have survived -- an incredible number given the labour of copying by hand and their generally poor rate of survival. So taken with these tales were the continental aristocracy that Geoffrey Plantagenet, to help fulfil the prophecy of Arthur's return and cement a claim to Britain, named his first son Arthur.[180]

Doubtless the cross-channel traffic occasioned by the arrival of the Plantagenets on the English throne fed into and was supplemented by that of the Crusades, which began at around this time (First Crusade 1096–99; Second Crusade 1144–55; Third Crusade 1187–92). Together these two developments brought a great many knights, bards and minstrels with tales from Wales into the courts of France, Germany, Provence and Italy, creating a considerable cultural exchange. The minstrels of France took up what they began to call 'le matiére de Bretagne', the matter of Britain. So widespread was the power and influence of these stories that the hope of 'delivery' by the prophecy of Arthur's return was to become known as 'the Breton Folly'. [181]

The interest in Arthur and his knights may have begun to grow in Norman Britain, but it was in France and Germany that interest really took flight. The first of the elevated French Arthurian courtly romances was written by Chretien de Troyes. He served Marie of France in the years 1160–72 and produced several Arthurian tales, including *Yvain -- the Knight of the Lion* (c. 1177–81), *Lancelot -- the Knight of the Cart* (c. 1177–81) and *Perceval -- the Story of the Grail* (c. 1181–90).[182] Though it has not been found, Chretien De Troyes and the authors of *The Mabinogion* were probably working from an earlier common source.[183] Although Chretien de Troyes does not seem to have had access to *The Dream of Rhonabwy* and *Kilhwch and Olwen,* he seems to have used French versions of *The Lady of the Fountain, Geraint* and *Peredur* to produce his own *Iwain, Erec* and the *Conte du Graal*. De Troyes was open about his sources and complained in

180 R. S. Loomis, *The Grail: From Celtic Myth to Christian Symbol* (Princeton University Press: Princeton, 1991).
181 W. P. Kerr, *Medieval English Literature* (Oxford University Press: Oxford, 1962), p.86.
182 *Chretien de Troyes: Arthurian Romances* (Penguin: London, 1991); C. Muscatine, *Chaucer and the French Tradition* (University of California Press: Berkeley, 1969).
183 *The Mabinogion*, G. Jones and T. Jones, trans., (Penguin: Harmondsworth, 2000); W. P. Ker, *The Dark Ages* (Nelson: London, 1955), p.337.

his prefaces that he intended to straighten out the oral tales he had heard mangled by *jongleurs*. But he did more than a little straightening of plot lines. It was Chretien de Troyes who created the tale of Lancelot's affair with Guinevere and invented the name of Camelot. He, or one of those who continued his tales after his death, also turned the Celtic Cauldron of Plenty into the Holy Grail -- variously, the dish that carries the sacred host or the chalice that caught Christ's blood at the crucifixion.[184]

The stories of Arthur were also taken up by a woman known simply as Marie de France (late twelfth century). She seems to have been a member of the court of Henry II and Eleanor of Aquitaine; possibly she was the natural daughter of Geoffrey Plantagenet and hence half-sister to Henry II: she produced Breton lais (short rhymed tales of love, chivalry, the supernatural and fairy-world of Celtic motifs) on the theme of Arthur and Tristram and is thought to have lived and done most of her writing in England. Later the Grail theme was taken up by the German authors Wolfram von Eschenbach (*c.* 1170–1220), Gottfried von Strassburg (died *c.* 1210) and Hartman von Aue (*c.* 1170–*c.* 1210).

Later, as these tales became increasingly fashionable, there was a significant recognition of their geographical origin. Though many of the romances were anonymous, *The Death of Arthur* (1215–1230), part of the major thirteenth-century French Arthurian romance cycle, was credited to a Welshman called Walter Map (1140–*c.* 1210). The real author is unknown, but Map, from Herefordshire, had been a storyteller and on good terms with Gerald of Wales and other 'Welsh compatriots', though he was probably dead by the time this story was created: Map seems to have written an Arthurian romance -- not the one that has come down to us with his name on it -- which had been translated into Dutch by a poet from Brabant, then taken up in France. Crediting him with *The Death of Arthur* may have been some sort of compliment.[185]

In time, after their success in France and Germany, these stories re-emerged in Britain, this time in English Arthurian romances, the most famous of which are *Sir Gawain and the Green Knight* (*c.* 1400) and Sir

---

184 R. S. Loomis, *The Grail: From Celtic Myth to Christian Symbol* (Princeton University Press: Princeton, 1991); L. Alcock, *Arthur's Britain* (Penguin: Harmondsworth, 1973), p.163.
185 *The Quest of the Holy Grail*, P. Matarasso, trans., (Penguin: Harmondsworth, 1969); *The Death of King Arthur*, J. Cable, trans., (Penguin: Harmondsworth, 1971). G. A. Williams, *When Was Wales? A History of the Welsh* (Penguin: Harmondsworth, 1985).

Thomas Mallory's *Morte Darthur* (completed in 1469, printed in 1485 just as the Tudors sought to justify their ascent to the throne by their connections to Wales and to Arthur).[186] However, if we want to see what the Celtic materials looked like before they were transformed from traditional tales into Christian Romances, we must look at the tales of the Welsh *Mabinogion*. These stories were not generally known until translated into English by Lady Charlotte Guest at the end of the nineteenth century. Written down in the eleventh century, but surviving only in later manuscripts, the tales of *The Mabinogion* date from much earlier oral compositions and appear only slightly the worse for being written down. In them, at one remove from the original Irish materials, these oral stories of magical giants, shape-shifters, clever women, taciturn men and snow white horses, all set in the Welsh language world of what is clearly ancient Britain, but particularly the forests and mountains of Wales and the western coasts, these tales appear stark, cruel: tales like 'Bran the Blessed', with its connections to Arthur, Merlin and to the Fisher King of the later Grail Legend, are clearly unprocessed and unadorned by Christian fabulators.

The Arthurian tales are part of a range of surviving Druidic elements which also include stories of the Green Man, Shelagh na Gigue, John Barleycorn, Robin Hood, May Day, Well Dressing, Morris Dancing and The Feast of Misrule.

In the same way that Christian churches were built on, and made use of, pre-Christian places of religious significance, elements of Druidism, barely remembered, half- understood and badly mangled -- the wandering knight, the chapel in a secluded grove, initiation and other tests, the Nature and rebirth rituals, the boy born to be king, the hardship of exile, the sick king and dying land, the riddling question that must be asked and answered, the seat of the Siege Perilous -- were transformed into the components of a mysterious Christian Romance. In the same way Celtic ritual elements were also transformed: the Dagda's Cauldron of Plenty became the Holy Grail; the Dagda's magical club (one end of which killed, the other cured) and Cu Chulainn's Gae Bulga, a barbed spear whose wound was always fatal, and Lugh's fiery spear,

---

186 Sir Thomas Malory, *King Arthur and his Knights*, ed. R. T. Davies, (Faber: London,1967); *Sir Gawain and the Green Knight* ed. J. R. R. Tolkien & E. V. Gordon (OUP: Oxford, 1968); R. S. Loomis, ed., *Arthurian Literature in the Middle Ages: A Collaborative History* (OUP: Oxford, 1959).

became the bleeding lance; Fergus's talking sword, itself a variant of the invincible sword of Lugh and Cuchulain's talking sword, which had become the magic sword Caledfwlch in the Welsh stories, became Excalibur. The Druid Myrddin became the magician Merlin. The Fianna or war-band which accompanied the hero Finn, and the warriors of the Red Branch, defenders and companions to king Conchobor, in the new tales became Arthur and the Knights of the Round Table; although in the early Welsh versions Arthur had lived modestly at Celli Wic in Cornwall, now the great Irish Druidic centres at Emhain Macha and Tara were translated into the Norman style castle and court at Camelot. In the early stories Arthur had been a roistering Celt, a semi-outlaw 'boyo', who spent his time hunting boar in the wilderness, but as the tales were recycled Arthur was transformed into a protector of his people; and in the newer Christianized version he became a king: and so on.

These were all elements of the Celtic rituals celebrating the power of nature, the story of the year and the rites of death and rebirth, but translated, absorbed, reworked and combined to give them a new explicitly Christian spin. In this transition the gods of the old world were transformed into medieval knights and their monstrous antagonists, while the Celtic goddesses became courtly ladies, queens and magical *feys*, and the Druids themselves appear, like Merlin, as wizards and shape-shifters. As John Spiers put it:

> What was irrational, unhuman and Pagan in these often primitive tales tended to be rationalised, humanised and Christianised as they were turned by the French romancers into a new kind of courtly and sophisticated art.[187]

Spiers has also written of the oral origins of the tales and the process of making and remaking them into romances:

> This traditional material consisted, of course, of traditional tales that were told and had been told over long periods of time and in different places. Though continually re-shaped in the process of transmission, such a tale has often persisted. Even when written down, and thus given a literary and less unstable existence, it was

---

187 J. Spiers, *Medieval English Poetry* (Faber: London, 1971), p.109; J. Spiers, 'A Survey of Medieval Verse', *Pelican Guide to English Literature: The Age of Chaucer* (Penguin: Harmondsworth, 1966), p.36.

liable to be used again for recital to audiences and thence caught back into the stream of oral transmission. Since medieval makers did not invent the tales they made into romances, we should have to seek for the origin of these tales elsewhere and in an earlier, perhaps ancient, age. But from an examination of the tales which have been transformed into romances, we can say something about their nature. For the most part, they certainly appear to be the kind of tales that have originated as myths -- stories of what happened or what was done in ritual ceremonies ... The tale appears generally to have been accorded the kind of status we accord to that reconstruction of bits and pieces out of the past which we call history, indeed to have been regarded as a kind of history – not as fiction but as objective truth, having its own rights and claim to be respected. Only a few makers were daring or original enough to re-shape a tale entirely...[188]

Jessie L. Weston saw this as the combination of ancient Druidic Nature worship and a Christianity that in the tenth and eleventh centuries, as it emerged from the Dark Ages, was still absorbing pre-Christian elements -- particularly Celtic ideas -- and which was still changing and consolidating itself. The blend is not accidental or random: it is, as Weston points out, 'purposeful', as if the authors, whether they knew fully what they were doing or not, were determined to present old knowledge in the shape of the new orthodoxy. Weston admitted that the evidence was far from complete, but nevertheless found the connections compelling, and commented that at the root of the Grail story:

lies the record, more or less distorted, of an ancient Ritual, having for its ultimate object the initiation into the secret of the sources of Life, physical and spiritual. This ritual, in its lower esoteric form, as affecting the processes of Nature, and physical life, survives to-day, and can be traced all over the world, in Folk ceremonies, which, however widely separated the countries in which they are found, show a surprising identity of detail and intention. In its esoteric 'Mystery' form it was freely utilised for the imparting of high spiritual teaching concerning the relation of Man to the Divine Source of his being, and the possibility of a sensible union between Man and God.[189]

---

188 J. Spiers, *Medieval English Poetry* (Faber: London, 1971), p.101.
189 J. L. Weston, *From Ritual to Romance* (Doubleday-Anchor: New York, 1957), pp.189-209.

However, Weston went on to warn that what remains of the original features is so fragmentary, so variously retold and distorted, that any attempt to use these things to attempt a more detailed reconstruction could only lead to further confusion.

*

In mainland Europe as the Celts were absorbed into Roman society, Druids faded away and Druidic traditions were transmuted. In France and Spain the Celtic identity -- and all trace of Druidism -- disappeared from the cultural scene. In Italy the Druidic line of the Cisalpine Gauls may have continued in writers like the historian Cornelius Nepo -- an important source for the Roman historian Livy, but whose works are all lost -- and the poet Catullus, a Romanized Celt writing in Latin.[190]

In Ireland and Wales some features of traditional Celtic oral culture survived until relatively recently. In Wales Druidic poetry lingered until 1580 when Wiliam Llŷn, the last of the major medieval poets with any claim to the tradition, died. After this, as the Tudor gentry became increasingly Anglicized, the poets found their patronage drying up. This, combined with the innate conservatism of the Bardic order, made its decline and disappearance as a profession inevitable. After the end of the sixteenth century their poetic skills and craft persisted only among amateurs.

In spite of the difficulties, throughout the Celtic world praise from a poet or storyteller was still important, and their anger was feared. It is said that even a Welsh minstrel poet was a force to be reckoned with, and if crossed, could compose a satire that would cause black blotches on the face, bring on an attack of diarrhoea or drive a man mad.[191] In Ireland in the fifteenth century the death of the Lord Lieutenant was attributed to a poet's spell, and 100 years later it was still thought that a poet could rhyme animals to death. As late as 1537 when O'Connor Sligo and O'Donnell made a treaty it was written into the agreement that if either man broke the agreement they both agreed to be satirized by the poets and would be excommunicated. It was a crime beyond understanding or pardon to kill a poet. When Cuain O'Lochain, chief poet of Ireland,

---

190 P. Beresford Ellis, *A Brief History of The Druids* (Robinson: London, 1994), p.200.
191 R. Graves, *The White Goddess* (Faber: London, 1999), p.18.

was put to death in 1024 by the people of Teffia, one source records that the murderers were soon afflicted with an 'evil scent and odour' that identified them as the murderers of a poet. Another source records that the killers were themselves soon put to 'cruel death' and their bodies left out 'until worms and vultures had devoured them'.[192] When the poet Fachtna Finn, chief poet of Ulster, heard of a plot to slay two kings at a feast, he saved both kings by seating poets at their side. The assassins dared not move against the kings for fear of harming the poets.

In conservative Ulster the Fenian Tales and the tales of the Ulster Cycle, dating from at least the seventh century but written down in the *Book of the Dun Cow* (*c.* 1100), along with the *Book of Leinster* (*c.* 1160), were still being re-told in the early eighteenth century, but the itinerant Irish Bardic harpists and poets who carried these tales did not survive much past the mid-eighteenth century.[193] Further south, in County Kerry, the last of the Bardic hedge poets seems to have been Eoghan Rua O'Suilleabháin. After ten years of wandering in his work he was press-ganged into the British navy and took part in the war against American Independence. He celebrated Admiral Rodney's defeat of the French Fleet at the Battle of the Saintes in 1782 with a ballad called 'Rodney's Glory', which he presented to the Admiral and in return was released from service. He returned to Kerry where he died in 1784 after a brawl with a man he had satirized. Only nineteen of his poems in Gaelic survive. The very last of the Gaelic bardic poets was the blind fiddler and *file* called Raftery who walked from village to village and produced the lines:

> I am Raftery the poet,
> Full of hope and love,
> With eyes without light
> And calm without torment.
>
> Going west on my journey
> By the light of my heart,
> Weak and tired
> To my road's end

---

192 S. MacManus, *The Story of the Irish Race* (New York, 1967), p.176.
193 C. M. Fox, *Annals of the Irish Harpers* (1911 rep: General Books: Memphis, 2010); A. Jones, *Dictionary of World Folklore* (Larousse: Edinburgh, 1995), p.176.

Look at me now,
My face to the wall,
Playing music
To empty pockets.[194]

In Scotland too, Bardic poets disappeared after the middle of the eighteenth century, brutally finished by the highland clearances. However, the Bardic oral impulse survived and within living memory in the Scottish Western Isles, communities handed on sagas, adventures, tales of kings and queens, battles and magic, when, each Sunday community children were gathered together and learned to recite their family tree back for twenty generations or more.[195]

Like a surviving 'meme', invisibly and almost unnoticed, Druidic lore was transmuted into Arthurian legend and the Grail Cult passed into the medieval literature of England, Germany and France. The idea of Druidism also survived. The poets Marvell, Blake and Wordsworth all declared themselves to be Druids. In the late eighteenth century, James Macpherson's *Fragments* of 'Ossian's' poems (1760) can be seen as a response to the brutal suppression of Scottish Gaelic culture and the eradication of the last of the Bardic clan poets by Butcher Cumberland after the Battle of Culloden (1746). Though widely condemned as fake medieval stuff, Macpherson's poems were in fact a continuation of the Druidic impulse and proved to be incredibly influential boosting a latent interest in Druidism: Blake, Coleridge, Byron, Burns all wrote 'Ossianic' poems. Walter Scott, Thomas Love Peacock and James Hogg were also followers of the trend. In Wordsworth's *Prelude* the Druids haunt Salisbury plain as 'long-bearded teachers'. In Italy, Germany Bohemia, Denmark, Holland, France, Hungary, Poland, Russia, Spain and Sweden, Macpherson's poems all found an echo in the national literary consciousness and contributed to the Gothic Revival in all its many forms: Goethe, the painter Ingres, Schubert and Mendelsohn were all influenced by the Ossian poems. In Finland the poems paralleled the creation of the equally problematic *Kalevala* (1835) and in Wales were echoed in the fake antiquarian poems of Edward Williams (1747–1826),

---

194 Trans Frank O'Connor in M. E. Collins, *Conquest & Colonisation* (Gill and Macmillan: Dublin, 1969), p.163.
195 N. L. Thomas, *Irish Symbols of 3500 BC* (Boulder Press: Colorado, 1988), p.15.

better known under his Bardic name, Iolo Moganwg.[196]

Arthur and his knights are still to be found in one form or another in modern English literary culture – in the writings of John Keats, Alfred Lord Tennyson, C. S. Lewis, Rudyard Kipling, T. H. White, T. S. Eliot, J. R. R. Tolkien, John Cowper Powys, Simon Armitage, Sir Harrison Birtwistle, Alan Garner, Neil Gaiman and in Marion Zimmer Bradley's novel *The Mists of Avalon* (1982). It is quite possible that the figure of the Druid as mediator influenced the Science Fiction writer Robert Heinlein (1907–88) and that Druidic training resurfaced, disguised as the Hogwarts Academy in J. K. Rowling's *Harry Potter* novels. Arthur is an academic cottage industry with over 11,000 books published so far on the topic. The figure of Arthur also appealed to the visual artists of the Gothic Revival, including Pre-Raphaelites William Morris, D. G. Rossetti and Edward Burne-Jones. Arthur has also passed into film culture in *Camelot* (1960), *The Sword in the Stone* (1963), *Monty Python and the Holy Grail* (1975), *Excalibur* (1981), *King Arthur* (2004), *The Last Legion* (2007) and the BBC TV series *Merlin* (2008). [197]

Celtic society was never a static entity and it was certainly changing even before the Romans arrived. The fact that the Druids had access to an ancient alphabet might have meant that in time literacy could have spread beyond them to the wider population. We will never know because the arrival of the Romans interrupted the transition, substituted a different set of conditions and set in train a different path to a written culture. Even so, the image of the Druid poet clearly offered something attractive and in the Celtic world, particularly in Ireland and Wales, oral culture -- perhaps as a counter culture -- never quite disappeared. Indeed for our purposes the survival of the idea of the Bard or Druidic poet may well be connected by some strange subterranean cultural passage, to the modern idea of the academy and the university. Certainly Matthew Arnold and Jorge Luis Borges have both made this connection.[198]

In modern Wales the late twentieth century saw a revival of literary life and with it the Welsh language National Eisteddfod began to grow. This

---

196 N. Groom, *The Forger's Shadow: How Forgery Changed the Course of Literature* (Picador: London, 2002).
197 G. A. Williams, *Excalibur: The Search for Arthur* (BBC: London, 1994); C. Hardyment, *Writing Britain: Wastelands to Wonderlands* (British Library: London, 2012), pp.13-19.
198 Matthew Arnold, *On the Study of Celtic Literature* (1866) Nuvisions LLC, 2011; Jorge Luis Borges, *Selected Non-Fictions* (Penguin: Harmondsworth, 2000), pp.458-463.

requires poets to compete in oral composition in the traditional classical Welsh poetic forms with only twenty minutes preparation, and is shown live on TV to an avid and well-informed audience. A revival of interest in Celtic culture, an end to suspicion between English and Welsh language writers, a cross over between language cultures was inevitable: it was certainly anticipated by the poetic techniques of Dylan Thomas, and later by Oliver Reynolds with his playful intermingling of the two languages in poems like 'Asgwrn Cefn y Beic'.[199] A Druidic impulse also clearly lies behind the 'Triads' and the interest in the Haiku form developed by Nigel Jenkins.[200] The revival of interest in national traditions and poetic forms in Wales has been encouraged by the move towards greater political devolution since 1997.[201] What else could explain the successful publication in English of Mererid Hopwood's *Singing in Chains: Listening to Welsh Verse*, a manual on traditional Welsh language poetic technique?[202] Also in 2005 Yr Academi Gymreig (The Welsh Academy) inaugurated the post of National Poet of Wales – in effect recreating something of the Bardic tradition: the present incumbent, Gillian Clarke (b.1937), certainly assumed the role in that spirit.

The Druidic Order was revived in modern times -- the Druid Society, based on Anglesey, and the Society of the Druids of Cardigan, were both founded in the 1770s; the Ancient Order of Druids was founded in 1781 in London; in 1792 Edward Williams recreated the Gorsedd of Bards, which survives to this day. Although 'the movement' has been through several splits since then and clearly lacks anything like the power of the original organization, it has been reinvented in the spirit of modern times as a focal point for 'Pagan' rites, shamanism and 'eco warriors'; in particular it marks the solstices and campaigns for access to Stonehenge. In figures like the contemporary oral story teller Eric Maddern (born Australia 1950), who has been called 'a green hero of Wales' for his work on the Cae Mabon Eco-Retreat Centre, and who is also an honorary Chief Bard of the Order of Bards, Ovates and Druids, and the figure of Rowan Williams, poet, Welsh speaker, White Druid and Archbishop of

---

199 O. Reynolds, *Skevington's Daughter* (Faber & Faber: London, 1985).
200 N. Jenkins, *O for a Gun*, (Planet Books: Aberystwyth, 2007); N. Jenkins, K. Jones, L. Rees (eds.), *Another Country: Haiku Poetry from Wales* (Gomer: Ceredigion, 2011).
201 M. Wynn Thomas, *Corresponding Cultures: the Two Literatures of Wales* (University of Wales Press: Cardiff, 1999); Flur Dafyd, 'Time to Leave the Hermitage', *The Guardian*, (11 October 2011), p.15.
202 M. Hopwood, *Singing in Chains: Listening to Welsh Verse* (Llandysul: Gomer, 2004).

Canterbury, these historically related themes of poetry, responsibility and intellectual leadership converge.[203] On 1 October 2010 'Druidry' was recognized as a religion in Britain: the Charities Commission, recognising Druidism's concern for nature and the environment, accorded the Druid Network charitable status for tax purposes.[204]

---

203 www.ericmaddern.co.uk.
204 Druidry to be classed as religion by Charity Commission', BBC News (2 October 2010), www.bbc.co.uk/news/uk-11457795.

Directed Study

What has the history of the Druids, Bards and Celtic literary culture to do with the theme of representation in writing and the notion of writing as a subject of study?

What can we sense about the connections between the roles of oral performers, prophets, interpreters, ambassadors, town criers, praise singers, storytellers, poets, priests, scribes, genealogists, oral historians, remembrancers, copyists and writers?

What are the main differences between a literate and an oral culture? In what ways can a written text really tell us anything about the oral world?

What do the figures of the Druid and the Bard signify for you as a writer and in what ways does the training of the Bards speak to you?

The history of Celtic Bardism outlined here seems to contradict much of what Jaques Derrida says about orality and writing. What do you think?

So are we now a totally literate culture, or do we still inhabit a transitional phase?

6
THE ROOTS OF CREATIVE WRITING AS A SUBJECT OF STUDY

This chapter considers Creative Writing as a subject of study and its roots and connections to the ancient scribes of the Middle East, the Classical Schools of Rhetoric, and the work of medieval scribes and monks. It brings the story up to the arrival of Creative Writing in modern universities. The basic questions asked here are: What is the relationship of a contemporary writer with the first writers -- the storytellers, poets, scribes and rhetoricians -- of old? What part of their traditions, habits, processes and powers is a modern writer, connected to? How have the social and political roles of the writer changed throughout history? What personal sense of discipline is involved in writing?

- Ancient Scribes and Scribal Schools
- Classical Schools of Rhetoric
- Medieval Scribes and Rhetoricians
- Creative Writing and the Universities

Writers have probably always worked both within and outside the institutions of their day. However, the intention here is to locate students and teachers of Creative Writing within the history of their subject and within a tradition of university teaching and learning. That is to develop an understanding of Creative Writing as a distinct subject by 'placing' it within the academy, showing Creative Writing not only as the original subject of academic study, heir to the Classics of the past, but concerned with producing (we hope) the literary 'classics' of tomorrow. The basic questions asked here are: Where does creative writing come from and how does it fit into university study? What is the relationship of a contemporary writer with the first writers -- the storytellers, scribes and rhetoricians -- of old? To what part of their traditions, habits, processes and powers are contemporary writers connected?

Although it is difficult to trace these things with any certainty, the traditional creative intellectuals of the pre-literate world, such as the ancient Druid poets and storytellers, had their own guild, an apprenticeship system, code of professional practice and degrees of qualification. However, in addition to pre-literate professional practice, the roots of Creative Writing as a subject of study lie in three very ancient institutions, each of which built on the traditions of the pre-literate world.

The first is that of the professional scribes of the ancient Middle East, in particular Egypt, Mesopotamia, Syria, Lebanon and Palestine, where the ancient scribes were in close relation with the prophets and political powers. Later these scribal traditions were echoed, reinvented and continued in the work of the medieval monks of Europe.[205]

The second is that of the Classical Greek and Roman Schools of Rhetoric, where although rhetoric was not creative writing exactly, but students were trained in the creative use of language by professional tutors -- rhetoricians who saw their subject as the manipulation of emotion through the use of well-chosen and effective language, mainly but not exclusively in political debate, and who often used literary texts as examples. Aristotle, though he wrote separately on Poetry and on Rhetoric, seems to have seen the study of rhetoric as the study of effective language which had applications in public and in private.

The third influence on writing as a profession comes out of the monastic traditions of Ireland and Gaul, themselves largely derived from Druidic learning and tradition, operating through the Celtic idea of a monastery as a seat of learning where the monks of the *scriptoria* copied, preserved and annotated the texts of ancient times. After the collapse of Rome, through the Dark Ages right up into the medieval period Irish monks kept learning alive in Europe with a supply of scholars and copied texts; many European monasteries owe their foundation to Irish monks and scholars: their work was later reinforced, translated and transformed by

---

205 J. Mace, *The Give and Take of Writing: Scribes, Literacy and Everyday Life* (Niace: Leicester, 2002).

the development of universities.

The histories of these traditions are fragmentary, discontinuous, contradictory and ambiguous and they fade into the history of other professions too -- painters, legal secretaries, clerks, clerics, stationers, engravers, printers, accountants, teachers to name but a few -- and into the foundation of universities. However, for all their discontinuities, and even taking into account the independence of writers as professional practitioners, it is in relation to these traditions that Creative Writing as a university subject of study has its roots. The key elements in the development of Creative Writing played a significant part in the foundation of universities.

Ancient Scribes and Scribal Schools

The word *scribe* and the activity it refers to reach back a long way into the past and intersect with the growth, history and development of writing and with the history of universities. The ancient Greeks referred to a scribe as a *grapheus* (scratcher), but the Cypriots, who were very conservative in their language use, preferred to call them *aloiphoi* (painter). Very possibly this is the more ancient term.

In modern English we get the word scribe from the Middle English, French and Latin words *scriba, scriber, scribere, scribillare, scrivein, escrivein, scribano*, all meaning to write. From the same root English also derives the words: *script, scribble, scribbler, scrivener, ascribe, transcribe, inscribe, describe, prescribe* and *proscribe*. The word scribe has several senses. A scribe could be:

- a person who writes or who can write
- an ancient or medieval copyist of manuscripts
- an ancient Jewish maker, keeper and interpreter of records, professional theologian, jurist or lawyer
- someone who scribes -- that is who makes marks on wood, clay or metal with a sharp stick
- a sharp stick or pointed tool used in carpentry for making marks, drawing lines or marking out wood.

WRITING THE WORLD

One definition of a scribe is:

> A learned individual who studied ancient wisdom and teachings,
> and who served as a copyist, editor, teacher or jurist. This profession
> was held in highest esteem since only those who possessed great
> character and outstanding intelligence were allowed to do such
> work for those in power.[206]

A scribe was clearly a member of one of the most ancient professions
which seems to have first emerged in Egypt and the fertile crescent of
Mesopotamia about 3000BC, using writing as an accountancy tool. Later
professional scribes also developed in ancient Greece, Persia, Lebanon,
Palestine and Rome. In all civilizations scribes have been the accountants,
transmitters of law and repositories of culture. However, they were
always few in number compared to the general population. It has been
estimated that in ancient Egypt only about one per cent of the population
was literate in hieratic -- that is about 10,000 people -- and that most of
these were Greek. Fewer still could read or write hieroglyphics.[207]

Basically the scribes of the ancient world were employed as support
for public officials -- in secretarial and administrative work such as
taking dictation, keeping business records, making judicial and historical
records for kings, nobility, the court, temples, city authorities, law courts
and businessmen. They wrote, transcribed, translated or copied out
manuscripts and records. Some produced simple functional records;
others were very skilled in penmanship and produced beautiful scripts.
Later these professions were to diverge and develop to produce civil
servants, journalists, accountants, archivists, historians, lawyers, judges,
teachers and creative writers. Egyptian scribes seem to have been held
in high regard. One scribe had three burial sites with his name on --
presumably for members of his family -- and one of these was capped
with a pyramidal stone carved with two images of the scribe himself. The
stone can be seen in the Egyptian museum in Turin. The same museum
also has a damaged statue of a seated scribe.[208] The fact that we have
images of these people is indicative of their status.

Excavations at Pylos in Greece have revealed a substantial group of

---

206 www.ruthlee-scribe.com/publications/scribe.
207 A. Robinson, *The Story of Writing* (Thames & Hudson: London, 2007), p.106.
208 Turin Museo Egyzio, gallery 13.

buildings now referred to as Nestor's Palace. There over a thousand clay tablets written in a script known as Linear B and dating from *c.* 1750-1450BC were found in an archive room. It is thought that the archive was the tax record of a period of several months.[209] Altogether the handwriting of forty different scribes has been identified, though a smaller group of eight seem to have done most of the work. The tablets left to us by these scribes allow us some insight into their life and work that of their community:

> Besides listing tax payments received, these scribes must have had to check the measure of each new delivery of tax oil, before it lost its identity in the huge olive oil-receiving jar in the ante-room; and they must also have had to count or weigh deliveries of all the other sorts of commodities and/or edible creatures which were used to pay taxes in Pylos.[210]

Excavations of the palaces on Crete, particularly at Knossos, have provided more tablets in this language and alphabet:

> At both Knossos and Pylos, there are also immensely detailed censuses of the flock and herds. One place in Crete for instance, is shown as having exactly 60 rams, 270 ewes, 49 he-goats, 130 she-goats, 17 boars, 41 sows, 2 bulls, and 4 cows. The similar Pylos censuses begin with entries listing very large numbers of animals with no owner shown, whereas there is a note of the owner of each of the smaller groups of animals that complete each list. The animals with no owner shown are presumed to belong to the king himself. If this is correct, the King of Pylos possessed literally tens of thousands of sheep and goats. Incidentally, large cattle are extremely rare in these censuses, to the point that the bulls and cows in the Knossos tablets are individually named. They had names like 'Dapple', 'Dusky' and 'Ginger', which makes them sound charming.[211]

---

209 J. Chadwick, *The Decipherment of Linear B* (CUP: Cambridge, 1990); E. Doblhofer, *Voices in Stone: The Decipherment of Ancient Scripts and Writings* (Paladin: London, 1973).
210 J. Alsop, *From the Silent Earth: The Greek Bronze Age* (Penguin: Harmondsworth, 1970), p.179.
211 J. Alsop, *From the Silent Earth: The Greek Bronze Age*, (Penguin: Harmondsworth, 1970), p.150.

WRITING THE WORLD

In ancient Akkadia cuneiform tablets were often signed by the scribe responsible. In Ugarit, the surviving written records were often provided by someone who signed himself 'Master-scribe'. However, the surviving Linear B tablets from Greece and Crete are all anonymous.

At the time of the Roman occupation of Judea and Palestine, for the Essene community in Qumran on the Dead Sea the copying of manuscripts was a vital part of community life. Over fifty individual hands have been identified in the surviving manuscripts dating from the period 250BC–AD 100. In their desert settlement the Essenes set aside a particular room with special tables for the production and copying of manuscripts. In times of strife the community stored their precious manuscripts in jars and hid them in nearby caves. After the caves and their contents were discovered in 1947, J. M. Allegro made a detailed study of the scrolls, and gave us a description of the place that the scribes and the copying of texts had in the daily life of this tiny community:

> From the *scriptorium* would come the steady scratching of pens, as the scribes copied their precious scrolls, and nearby their fellows prepared the inks and skins for their use. Perhaps the women of the community would be weaving the flaxen cloths for wrapping scrolls for storage, and either in the Settlement or in the caves a librarian was at his task of sorting and classifying the texts.[212]

The best records of the ancient scribal schools come from the Old Babylonian period in Mesopotamia and from Egypt. The role of the scribe was one of the most desirable and powerful professions. Consequently it was very difficult to become a scribe: the training was long and very hard and seems to have been kept largely within particular families. In ancient Egypt boys (and a very small number of girls) started their studies at the age of ten and it took ten to twelve years of intensive training to qualify for the profession. Most students only spent a few years in study and then left to work, equipped with the basics, but some stayed on at the school until they were masters. One of the Egyptian proverbs from those days advised young students: 'Give thy heart to learning and love her like a mother for there is nothing as precious as learning'.

In ancient Babylon the scribal schools were very small and were probably one-man operations. They consisted of a few rooms and

---

212 J. M. Allegro, *The Dead Sea Scrolls* (Penguin: Harmondsworth, 1956), p.109.

a limited number of pupils copying texts set by their master. All that remains now are the stumps of the walls, piles of discarded clay practice pellets called lentils and masses of broken clay tablets. Even so, most of the information we have about Mesopotamian scribes and their work comes not from the Royal or private libraries, but from the remains of the students' practice texts found in the ruins of the teachers' homes and the scribal schools.

In Egypt the students were lined up in rows, their texts on their kilts, chanting their set text until they knew signs, words and grammar by heart. They copied out older, classical texts, practising the mechanics of reading and writing, but as the texts they studied were also instructional, learning about their duties and the professional standards expected of a qualified scribe. It is probable that in New Kingdom Egypt all students were taught the hieratic script, and that only those who went on to work in the temples or the palace studied hieroglyphs.[213]

In learning basic cuneiform the ancient Mesopotamian student had at first to master some 300 basic signs and strokes. Students also had to learn cuneiform in both the Sumerian and Akkadian languages. Eventually Akkadian would fade away as a literary language and Sumerian, even though it was no longer spoken, would become the literary language. But then Sumerian and Akkadian would both fade away to be replaced by other languages written in cuneiform.

At all stages in the history of the scribe students started their practise by copying exercises set by their teacher. The names of gods, lists of technical terms, fragments of poems and proverbs were written on one side of a tablet by the teacher and copied on the other side by the student.[214] Students also had to copy temple hymns, prayers, wisdom literature, traditional stories, myths, mathematical texts, astronomical texts and literary texts. On Crete the scribes writing in the script known as Linear A often had produced lists of rations, palace inventories and census returns. One of the most common tasks set for students in Mesopotamia *c.* 1400BC was to copy the Scribes' Prayer:

> To the young pupil sitting before thee, be not indifferent in thy greatness. In the art of writing, all secrets reveal unto him.

---

213 P. Wilson, *Hieroglyphs: A Very Short Introduction* (Oxford University Press: Oxford, 2004), p.81.
214 A. Robinson, *The Story of Writing* (Thames & Hudson: London, 2007), p.3.

Numbering, counting, every solution reveal unto him. Secret writing, reveal unto him therefore.

Students had to memorize particular texts, words and signs. For example they might have to learn the names and signs of a metal-worker's tools, the names of all the streets in a particular district, or the locations of temples and shrines in Babylon. A popular text for study in Egypt was the 'Satire of the Trades' which laughed at all the manual jobs and ended with the advice: 'be a scribe'. Another such exercise in Mesopotamia was to memorize a particular text containing the measurements and dimensions of the major temples in Babylon. The same exercise seems to have been set long after the original temples had been rebuilt and the dimensions had changed. A similar exercise seems to have been carried from Babylon by Jewish scholars, since it was later set for student scribes in Jerusalem, where they were expected to memorize a document with the details of every aspect of the Temple -- including the number of gates and the sizes of rooms. Much of the student's time seems to have been taken up with chanting in unison and in taking dictation.

In Mesopotamia we know discipline was harsh and physical punishment was frequent.[215]

The door monitor said, 'Why did you go out without my say-so?' and he beat me. The water monitor said, 'Why did you help yourself to water without my say-so?' and he beat me. The Sumerian monitor said, 'You spoke in Akkadian!' and he beat me. The teacher said, 'Your handwriting is not at all good!' and he beat me.[216]

It does not seem to have been very different in Egypt, where a proverb of the period said: 'A boy's ears are on his back; he learns best when he is beaten'. In Mesopotamia, where students often spoke one language but were required to study, master and write in another, students were beaten with a Hippopotamus hide whip. The real dunces and troublemakers faced imprisonment. One Mesopotamian teacher was so frustrated he wrote to a pupil:

---

215 G. Jean, *Writing: The Story of Alphabets and Scripts* (Thames & Hudson: London, 1992).
216 *The Epic of Gilgamesh*, trans., A. George (Penguin: London, 1999), p. xviii.

I know that you frequently abandon your studies and whirl around in pleasure, that you wander from street to street and every house stinks of beer when you leave it ... You boy! You do not listen when I speak! You are thicker than a tall obelisk 100 cubits high and 10 cubits wide.[217]

In addition to learning how to write and the huge range of signs, students also had to learn how to gather their own raw materials and how to produce their own writing equipment. In ancient Egypt, for example, students had to gather marsh plants and bark to make papyrus, soot and binding agents from which ink could be made and also the raw stuffs to make glue, and feathers, reeds and fur to make brushes and quill-pens. The reed quill pens were generally about 20cm long with one end crushed to make a brush or cut and sharpened to make a nib. The making of papyrus was a state monopoly and the price was very high, so often the papyrus was scrubbed clean and then reused. In Egypt each scribe owned his own writing kit comprising of a slate palette with two shallow cups for holding red and black ink cakes; a connecting thong; a thin wooden brush case and a jug for water. The red ink, used for emphasis in titles and to divide a text under headings, was made from cinnabar (mercuric sulphide) or minium (lead oxide). Black ink was a mixture of soot and gum Arabic. If we are to believe the many illustrations of scribes at work, they were all right handed -- perhaps this was a necessary qualification.

In Mesopotamia a student scribe eventually had to master over 700 cuneiform signs acquired over several years of intense study -- all of which had to be reproduced exactly and without deviation or flourishes. Students began their studies by copying their teacher's sample texts -- usually a proverb, a literary fragment or a list of God's names – on the reverse of a soft clay tablet.[218] Students of cuneiform then graduated to practise their writing on a board covered with gesso (plaster and glue) a surface that allowed easy erasure. They also wrote on papyrus made from pounding strips of plant matter. The process of production was lengthy and labour intensive. Papyrus was made from the stems of tall reeds. The stem was stripped out and the pith cut into pieces about 20ins (50cm) long sliced lengthwise and placed on a hard flat surface. More

---

217 A. Robinson, *The Story of Writing* (Thames & Hudson: London, 2007), p.107.
218 S. R. Fischer, *A History of Writing* (Reaktion Books: London, 2001).

strips were laid horizontally over these, and then weighted down until the pulp fused into sheets. After this the sheets were trimmed to size and rubbed smooth with stones.

Learning to write was not simply a matter of recognizing and reproducing accurately all the necessary signs, students also had to learn to co-ordinate their movements:

> The scribe unwound the roll of papyrus with his left hand and wrote the inscriptions on it, re-rolling it with his right hand as he went along. Because of the length of the rolls (the longest found measures 40m) he usually worked in a cross legged seated position, with the papyrus wedged on his knees and resting on his loincloth.[219]

Unlike Mesopotamia, where their status was important but nevertheless rather lowly, in Egypt the scribes achieved great wealth, prestige and social position, and only the most highly regarded of them became priestly scribes. In Mesopotamia the scribes do not seem to have been attached directly to the temples or courts, but seem to have been employed by both since the priests and court officials were largely illiterate or, at least, did not concern themselves with the business of writing. In Egypt and Mesopotamia the scribes had the possibility of a position at court, in the law or in the administration, and in this they were part of a developing professional class. As the French historian Fernand Braudel commented:

> One could not become a technocrat, a scribe or a literate person, without rigorous training. It was the price to be paid for enormous privileges.[220]

And whatever the hardships of this training, the privileges were enormous. Once they had qualified the range of work open to scribes was considerable. Some worked at the royal court, some became personal secretaries, some worked for city and regional governors, some went to work in the temples, but many went to work in the textile industry, ship building, pottery workshops or transport. No businessman's entourage was complete without at least one scribe to record deals, orders and tax

---

219 G. Jean, *Writing: The Story of Alphabets and Scripts* (Thames & Hudson: London, 1992), p.41.
220 F. Braudel, *Memory and the Mediterranean* (Knopf: New York, 2002), p.65.

details. The majority of the scribes worked in the agricultural sector of the economy, keeping records for the irrigation of canals, keeping tally of rations and allowances for the labourers, maintaining storage records, tallying the harvest, recording tools and issuing receipts. Many scribes worked in the area of the law writing documents for conveyance of property. In times of war the role of the scribe was pivotal in arranging supplies and rations, conveying orders and messages, counting prisoners, arranging treaties, and, according to a stone frieze found in Nineveh, for counting war booty.[221] However, while the privileges may have been enormous we have to assume that there was also considerable risk to scribes at times of what we now call 'regime change'. The writer Walter Abish (b. 1931) has described with some horror seeing a recently discovered Mayan mural which showed victorious warriors slaughtering the defeated enemy leadership, while the enemy scribes were 'singled out for special attention -- they queued to have their fingernails pulled out and their fingers broken, 'since their writing was an instrument of power' used to 'extol the power of the enemy ruler'.[222]

In the great Assyrian Library at Hattusa the bulk of the documents recovered were the professional writings of the scribes undertaken for the priests -- lists of omens, determinations from the stars and other heavenly bodies, lists of sacrificial animals, natural events, predictions, textbooks detailing vocabulary lists in local languages -- plants trees, animals, gods, place names -- multiplication tables, astronomical texts and catalogues of musical compositions. Very few were literary compositions. At Nineveh, in Assurbanipal's library, multiple copies of over 1,500 texts were discovered including no less than thirty-five of the surviving seventy-three versions of the epic poem *Gilgamesh*. The texts again were mainly concerned with rituals, incantations and prayers, dictionaries, reading lists, word lists etc.[223]

Theft seems to have been a major problem in the ancient libraries and the scribes, acting as agents, seem to have been the main culprits. Carelessness in handling and storage seem to have been another major problem. One inscription was both a warning and a curse:

---

221 A. Gaur, *Literacy and the Politics of Writing* (Intellect: Portland, Oregon, 2000).
222 W. Abish, *Double Vision* (Knopf: New York, 2004), p.216.
223 L. Casson, *Libraries in the Ancient World* (Yale Books: Harvard, 2002), pp.8-11; *The Epic of Gilgamesh*, trans., A. George (Penguin: London 1999), p. xxvii.

He who breaks this tablet or puts it in water or rubs it until you cannot recognise it and cannot make it be understood, may Ashur, Ishtar, Shamesh, Adad and Ishtar, Bel, Nergal, Ishtar of Nineveh, Ishtar of Arbela, Ishtar of Bit Kidmurri, the gods of heaven and earth and the gods of Assyria, may all these curse him with a curse which cannot be relieved, terrible and merciless, as long as he lives, may they let his name, his seed, be carried off from the land, may they put his flesh in a dog's mouth.[224]

Throughout the Middle East the tradition of the scribal schools combined with the need to train religious teachers and leaders. The resulting centres of study, where religious texts were copied and clerics received their training, were eventually what the Crusaders saw, noted and brought back to Europe as the germ of the idea that was to create the University.

Classical Schools of Rhetoric

By the sixth century BC literacy in Greece was growing at a remarkable pace. Around the mid-fifth century BC Athens became a democracy and almost at once it became clear that the established education system, which placed great emphasis on physical culture and music, did not match the demands of the new political world. However, while the new Greek democracy may have expected and even required high cultural and educational standards, apart from the public theatres, the state made virtually no attempt to provide schools or places of learning. Education at all levels was provided by private establishments and by visiting scholars.[225] In 427 BC the Sicilian orator Gorgias of Leontini arrived in Athens to teach rhetoric. In 393 BC Gorgias's ex-pupil, Isocrates opened a school in Athens. He believed it was necessary to bridge the gulf between the art of rhetoric and the difficulties of reaching correct political decisions. For him, rhetoric was a form of culture, part of the practice of politics and the outward image of a 'good and faithful soul'. His aim was to study the art of discourse, *logos*, and to teach rhetoric for the political improvement of Greece, the understanding and debate of the laws, and so that Greek orators might become 'the teachers of the world'.[226] It was from Isocrates that the Greek liberal tradition in

---

224 L. Casson, *ibid* (Yale Books: Harvard, 2002), p.14.
225 T. A. Sinclair, *A History of Greek Political Thought* (Routledge: London, 1967), pp.45-7;
E. Barker, *Greek Political Theory* (Methuen: London, 1967), pp.41-46.
226 E. B. Castle, *Ancient Education and Today* (Penguin: Harmondsworth, 1961).

politics, literature and education grew. Aristotle, Plato, Zeno and Epicurus soon opened schools nearby and helped to ensure that Greek political culture was that of the writer, reader and scholar, and instead of confining themselves to lists of stores and property as most early scribes in Phoenicia and Mesopotamia had done, the Greeks began to make the alphabet also capable of recording stories, poetry and songs, and the dialogue of developing philosophical thought.

The result was an incredible outpouring of writing and the development of habits of mind that affect us even today. In Athens between the sixth and fourth century BC, Homer's *The Iliad* and *The Odyssey* were written down; Herodotus gave public readings from his foundation works of history; Aristotle wrote his influential *The Art of Rhetoric* (384BC), one of the earliest discussions of the art of public speaking, and his *Poetics* where, though he saw them as using and shaping thought and opinion through language, he also took care to distinguish between the practice of rhetoric and the writing of poetry, prose and drama: and Plato (427–347BC) debated whether Rhetoric, which rapidly became the standard education for statesmen, philosophers, generals, lawyers, judges and historians, was to be taught as a spoken or a written skill.

Neither Plato nor Aristotle were entirely enthusiastic about the ways in which language could be manipulated and both saw the study of rhetoric not simply as a way of training politicians in the art of public speaking, but as a way of curbing the power of politicians by understanding exactly how they used language. For all the success of the schools of Rhetoric in classical Athens, both Plato and Aristotle were aware that the teaching of Rhetoric was no solution to either educational or political problems, since Rhetoric could only offer guidance on how things might be said: it could offer no guidance on what should be said. Plato and Aristotle were both wary of the negative effect that rhetoric might have on democracy and they reacted strongly not just to propagate the study of rhetoric, but to educate listeners to understand the techniques being practised upon them by wily orators.

Plato had been marked very deeply by the condemnation and death of his tutor, Socrates, at the hands of the new democracy in 399BC, and consequently felt that all manipulators of words were to be mistrusted.[227] Plato held a very dim view of both politicians and creative writers and

227 Plato, *The Last Days of Socrates* (Penguin: Harmondsworth, 1969).

in *The Republic* made his unease clear. He linked writing with citizenship and valued plays and poetry only in so far as they helped people to distinguish 'discipline, courage, generosity, greatness of mind' and their opposites. For him most writers dealt in third-hand experience and imitative forms, and this, he said, had a lamentable effect on the public since they provided models not of good, strong, responsible men, but of bad, weak, frivolous men: theatre turned men into confused buffoons; poetry relaxed morals. Allowing poetry and theatre into a well-run city-state was, Plato said, like 'giving power and political control to the worst elements of society and ruining the better elements'. Plato was prepared to ban writers of poetry and drama until the writers could prove their worth to Athenian society.[228] His mistrust of writing and writers was thorough but perhaps a little too idealistic to be practical. Most writers now would prefer to see this as an indication of how seriously Plato regarded writing and word-mongering in general, rather than a blanket condemnation of their work.

In 324BC the Athenian Aeschines, having lost an important legal case, left Athens in disgust and founded a School of Rhetoric in Rhodes. The school, building on a well-established interest in writing and scholarship in Rhodes, seems to have been located in the ancient acropolis; unusually the school was part of the civic complex that housed the public sports facilities, the gymnasium, a library and a public amphitheatre which was probably used for practice by the student rhetoricians.[229] Only in Alexandria and in Pergamon were there similar arrangements, and there seems to have been considerable rivalry between these three centres of learning. According to Seneca, the warehouses of the port in Alexandria housed over 40,000 manuscripts ready for export. The Great Library, based in the Museion (house of the Muses), is said to have contained 700,000 manuscripts in shelves under colonnades and was equipped with several reading and study rooms, copying areas, storage space and communal dining facilities. The remains of the library in Rhodes indicate a much more modest collection, but even so the Alexandrians felt threatened, and in an attempt to ensure the superiority of Alexandrian scholarship and monopoly of knowledge, the city rulers banned the export of papyrus -- Alexandria had a virtual monopoly of production.

228 Plato, *The Republic* (Penguin: Harmondsworth, 1968), p.382.
229 *Ancient Rhodes: 2400 Years: A Short Guide* (Greek Ministry of Culture: Athens, 1993), p.30.

This should have seriously inconvenienced scholarship throughout the civilized world of the Greek, Egyptian and Mesopotamian cultures, but in fact the manoeuvre had the opposite effect: in the city of Pergamon scholars and scientists invented parchment (*pergamenum*), which proved to be cheaper and more durable than papyrus and over the next thousand years replaced it completely.[230]

In Rhodes the school of Rhetoric was recommended by Pindar, Pliny and Marcus Tullius Cicero. Cicero, (106–43BC), who had his early training in Rhodes and went on to become a famous teacher of rhetoric, referred to the people of Rhodes as 'highly educated'. The school does not seem to have produced many famous writers, but it did produce and attract noted public speakers and teachers; in addition to Astymedes and Archelaos, around 21BC the teacher Apolonius Malakos settled there, followed shortly by Apolonios Molon, both from Alabanda in Asia Minor. Molon taught Cicero and Julius Caesar. Aristippos, a follower of Aristotle, settled in Rhodes, as did the philologist Dionysus of Thrace (170–90BC), whose work *On Grammar* was to survive as a principle text book down to the Renaissance. However, not everyone was impressed by Rhodes or by the School of Rhetoric. While it was agreed the school of Rhetoric excelled at teaching clarity of expression, it was said to be less certain on matters of content and thought, and with its inevitable links to Asia Minor, it was said to favour 'Asian' pomposity, simile, exaggeration, passion and complex argument over the more austere and sober 'Hellenistic' style. The activities of the school did not please everyone though, and possibly resenting the hive of rhetorical activity it generated, Rhodes scholar Athenodoros wrote a book claiming that Rhetoric was not an art at all.

In the first and second centuries BC Rhodes attracted a number of intellectuals -- philosophers, philologists, grammarians, astronomers, mathematicians and geographers.[231] The School of Rhetoric and the gymnasium library in Rhodes received gifts of money and books from all over the ancient world and the school clearly played a significant role in social, political and cultural life. It is likely that there was considerable literary and scribal activity around the school, the gymnasium and the library. Apollonius of Rhodes (295–215BC), worked as director of the

230 M. Battles, *Library: An Unquiet History* (Vintage: London, 2004), pp.24-9.
231 *Ancient Rhodes 2,400 Years: A Short Guide* (Dodecanese Ministry of Culture: Athens, 1993), pp. 49-50.

great library in Alexandria, but either ran away in shame after the poor reception of the first publication of his *Argonautica* or left Alexandria after an argument about poetry. He took up residence in Rhodes and there rewrote the *Argonautica*. This second version -- the one that has survived down to modern times -- was much more successful and Applonius was later honoured by the city for his literary achievements. Apollonius seems to have had a connection to the School of Rhetoric -- indeed as a literary person it would be a surprise if he did not -- and he may have taught there.[232] Calixenous, a near contemporary of Apollonius, wrote his book *On Alexandria* in Rhodes and also seems to have been connected to the school. Aristophanes, may have maintained some connection to the School of Rhetoric. Aristophanes' exact connection to Rhodes has yet to be established. Several other locations also claim his birth, but in the Rhodes Archaeological Museum there is a small stone column dated to the first century BC with lines 454–459 from *The Frogs*, carved on it. The play was first performed in Athens in 405BC, but the text quoted is almost identical with that of the oldest surviving manuscript of the play -- the late tenth century AD Ravenna Codex -- which certainly indicates a very early connection between the writer and the place.

There is evidence that in the third century BC Ptolemy Philadelphos purchased books or manuscripts from Rhodes for the great library in Alexandria.[233] In the Rhodes Archaeological Museum a stone tablet -- possibly the remains of a large tile once set into the wall of the library -- has a carved list of the holdings of the library. Although not a full list, it shows holdings arranged alphabetically by author and their manuscript titles with the number of copies and the names of donors. The works include politics, rhetoric and philosophy ranging from the fourth century BC up to about 250BC. Another tablet shows the rules for the use of the library. A funery epigram carved in stone records the burial of the very successful dramatic poet Dioklos -- who somewhere in the period 250–150BC was crowned with an ivy wreath at the Athens Lenaia drama festival. Almost certainly a local talent like this would have been enlisted by the School of Rhetoric, the library or the gymnasium. Several

---

232 Apollonius of Rhodes, *The Voyage of the Argo* (Penguin: Harmondsworth, 1971). We could stretch a point and say the influence of the Rhodes School of Rhetoric can still be felt every time the film version of Apollonius's work, *Jason and the Argonauts* (1963), is repeated on TV.
233 C. Karousos, *Rhodes: History, Monuments, Art* (Esperos: Athens, 1973), pp.33-37.

funery stones recovered from the necropolis in Rhodes show carvings of bundles of papyrus scrolls, indicating that the deceased was a teacher, librarian or scribe of some note.

Several famous historical figures attended the Rhodes school and the Romans used it to train their politicians. Tiberius, who had also been a student at the school, was exiled to Rhodes with a huge retinue of catamites and other 'servants' and the remains of his palace have been discovered only a few hundred metres from the School of Rhetoric, so it is hard to imagine that he was not connected with it in some way during his exile. At various times Julius Caesar, Brutus, Cassius, Anthony, Cicero, Lucretius and Pompey all studied there and it is possible that the animosities so vividly recorded in Shakespeare's *Julius Caesar* and *Antony & Cleopatra* had their inception there. A part of Roman history that Shakespeare does not retell is that in 42BC, after the assassination of Caesar, Cassius, a former pupil of the School of Rhetoric, demanded finance from the city of Rhodes but was rebuffed: Rhodes, rich and proud from the spice, resin, ivory, silver and amber trades, refused to join the plotters. Cassius besieged and conquered the city: in the looting that followed the Romans stole all the local ships and 3,000 works of art, destroyed 800 public statues, confiscated all public and private finance, looted homes, butchered the citizenry, knocked down temples and public buildings and set fire to what remained of the city. One commentator noted that Cassius left the Rhodians 'nothing but the sun'. When the plotters were eventually defeated and committed suicide, festivities were organized in what was left of the city, but after this no more is heard about the Rhodes School of Rhetoric.[234] However, other schools of rhetoric survived and over 100 other Greek cities had a gymnasium with a library attached to it.[235]

Although it is difficult to know the degree to which creative writers of Ancient Athens and Rome studied rhetoric, or even to what extent they were directly influenced by the study of rhetoric, we can be fairly certain that democratic politics would have created a sharpened interest in the wording of the law and in the power of words to sway public opinion.

---

234 L. Durrell, *Reflections on a Marine Venus: a Companion to the Landscape of Rhodes* (Faber & Faber: London, 1960), pp.37-8; C. Karousos, *Rhodes: History, Monuments, Art* (Esperos: Athens, 1973), p.22.
235 L. Casson, *Libraries in the Ancient World* (Yale University Press: New Haven, 2002), pp.58-60.

As early as Homer's *Iliad* (probably written c. 550BC) the power of the word to sway and persuade is at the heart of the many debates that shape the Trojan War, though Homer was probably projecting contemporary concerns onto an ancient tale, since at the time of the Trojan War Greece was not yet a democracy and rhetoric had yet to emerge as a subject of study. Writers took a keen interest in rhetoric. Aristophanes, for example, satirized the power and influence of rhetoric in *The Clouds* (423BC) and in *The Wasps* (422BC).

When Plato wrote about Socrates he made use of the dramatic monologue, rather than straightforward theoretical prose: this not only enabled him to remain close to Socrates' own teaching methods, but allowed him to deploy his own rhetorical skills. While Aristotle in his *Rhetoric* did not directly address questions of style in dialogue, prose, poetry or in the writing of history -- though he did address some of these things in his much slimmer volume *Poetics* -- much of what he said was clearly applicable to writers. Also, in teaching rhetoric he was very aware of literary devices and used a great number of literary examples: he stressed the effectiveness of rhythm without metre in prose and emphasized the necessity of appropriate pace in narration. The prose of antiquity is thought to have been very much influenced by the study of rhetoric, and it has been said that Aristotle's discussion of ethical propriety influenced the creation of character, particularly in Classical comic drama and the novel.[236]

The great Classics scholar C. M. Bowra has made it clear that the Greeks regarded writers as public teachers, 'not in any pompous or arid sense but with a lively conviction that the highest lessons about men are best conveyed in a noble and satisfying form':

> For this reason Greek literature is always to some degree a public art (...) Writers were keenly aware of their responsibilities (...) in speaking for themselves they addressed their words closely and candidly to their compatriots (...) they belonged to an attentive, appreciative, and critical society (...) This enhanced their sense of public duty since they knew that with such an audience anything fake or feeble would soon be detected and derided. They could always draw support from the knowledge that they were at once the interpreters and the instructors of a national consciousness

236 H. C. Lawson-Tancred 'Introduction': Aristotle, *The Art of Rhetoric* (Penguin: London, 1991), pp.42-3.

(...) and this provided a basic culture which intellectual leaders could take for granted and through it have some assurance that, if they had something serious to say, it would be taken seriously by a circle far wider than that of their intimate friends.[237]

Between the seventh and fifth centuries BC, Greece differed enormously from the 'civilisations of the Orient' (Egypt and Babylon in particular). Writing had built on the changes possible within Greek society and the cultural traditions that emphasized the life of the individual: these had helped to make democracy and widespread literacy possible. Writing systems may have developed much earlier in the Orient, but nevertheless a stratified social structure with a scribal elite guarding a difficult writing system kept the bulk of the population essentially in traditional 'oral mode'. The alphabet and the spread of literacy helped to change Greece so that it might no longer be termed a 'traditional society':

> To begin with, the ease of alphabetic reading and writing was probably an important consideration in the development of political democracy in Greece; in the fifth century a majority of the free citizens could apparently read the laws, and take an active part in elections and legislation. Democracy as we know it, then, is from the beginning associated with widespread literacy.[238]

By the fourth century BC, bookselling was becoming a seriously profitable business and there were private scriptoria copying manuscripts to order in many major towns. However we know that in Rome buyers were often unhappy with the quality of the texts they bought, which were full of careless mistakes, and they sometimes brought along their own expert to evaluate the merchandise before completing a purchase. It seems that in Rome, rich men often sent their own scribes to established libraries to make copies.

The growth of Roman military power eventually transplanted Greek concerns and traditions to Rome, where the debates about the nature and teaching of writing and rhetoric continued. Marcus Fabius Quintilianus, also known as Quintilian (AD 35–95), was the first Professor of

---

237 C. M. Bowra, *Landmarks in Greek Literature*, (Penguin: Harmondsworth, 1968), pp.31-2.
238 J. Goody and I. Watt, 'The Consequences of Literacy', in J. Goody (ed.), *Literacy in Traditional Societies* (Cambridge University Press: Cambridge, 1968) , p.55.

Rhetoric in Rome. For more than twenty years he taught *progymnasmata* (argument, paraphrase, composition and oratory) to upper class boys in preparation for their entry to the School of Rhetoric. At his retirement he wrote *Institutio Oratoria*, detailing his teaching methods and showing how his students were trained to paraphrase fables into a simple spoken narratives, to develop the sententious sayings of poets into speeches, and to compose speeches and moral judgements and apply these in different situations.

Quintilian condemned 'the regular custom' of flogging students, advised that effective study could not be compelled but depended on the good will of the student, warned that the depressed student would never succeed and left instructions as to how to distinguish the clever imitator from the genuinely gifted orator. Quintilian recommended that writers should draft their work on wax tablets leaving plenty of space for corrections and said students should develop their memories and resort to ink and parchment only for final drafts.[239] With this emphasis on drafting and revising Quintilian showed himself to be a practical, practising and experienced teacher. He was clear that the success of his school sprang not only from his reluctance to differentiate between preparation for writing and preparation for public life, but also from his preference for teachers who were practitioners rather than 'pure' academics -- that is, for writers who taught rather than teachers who perhaps did a little writing. He warned of the damage caused by using inexperienced or inadequately experienced teachers, and of the subsequent decline that would follow in standards of writing, speaking and public debate.

It is in the Greek and Roman academies that Creative Writing as a university subject, as something that could be taught, learned, studied, practised, debated and theorized over, has its roots.[240] The connections between the alphabet, literacy, citizenship and democracy were to create a model of literacy and politics which underlies modern democratic traditions. For many classics scholars the study and practice of Rhetoric, learning how to listen actively and how to shape, use and analyse language, is seen as the equivalent to what might be termed a 'liberal education'.[241] But tuition in Rhetoric was not welcomed by everyone

---

239 Quintilianus, *Institutio Oratoria*, vols I-X, (Loeb: Harvard, 1996).
240 L. Casson, *Libraries in the Ancient World*, (Yale Books: Harvard, 2002), pp.27, 78, 103.
241 T. R. Glover, *The Ancient World* (Penguin: Harmondsworth, 1953), p.152.

in the Classical world, nor was its importance to the health of society uppermost in everyone's mind. The satirical poet Aulus Persius Flacus recalled that as a child he was so desperate to avoid having to listen to other students endlessly practising their oral composition as they paced back and forth, that he rubbed olive oil into his eyes and pleaded soreness to his mother to get the day off school.[242]

Quintilian may have been the first person to spell out in his text books some of the essential requirements for teaching and learning about composition in the modern sense. The boundaries and relationship between literature and rhetoric were increasingly fluid, indeed the interpenetration and overlapping of these two areas of study was inevitable. That rhetoric should play a part in literature was inevitable since while the study of rhetoric was, as it had been in Greece, part of preparation for public life as conducted by the ruling class, and a pre-requisite for success: rhetoricians looked to literature for the examples and illustrations of their principles, and in late antiquity the two areas of rhetoric and literature merged almost completely.[243] The study of rhetoric, it is clear, particularly in Rome around the end of the first and start of the second centuries AD, inspired literary activity among the educated classes.

However, the development of the Roman Empire and a Roman political dictatorship rendered the study of composition and rhetoric as a contribution to multi-voiced democratic debate increasingly irrelevant in Roman public life. Political and cultural life began to separate, as an education based in rhetoric proved irrelevant to a centralized state that chose its leaders from the army rather than the cultural elite. In response writers produced literature designed primarily to be read aloud in fashionable private gatherings, rather than for 'publication' or public performance, where the influence of 'rhetorical mannerism' encouraged the creation of writing like that of Seneca, in which ornament and effect were more important than elegance of expression or novelty of insight. The Roman Empire disrupted the homogeneity of earlier Greek and Roman public interest in writing and literary production and, as the

---

242 H. Martin, 'How Creative Writing invented English, or The Classical Provenance of Creative Writing', seminar paper, Sheffield Hallam University, Creative Writing Conference (Spring 2000).
243 E. Auerbach, *Literary Language and its Public in Late Latin Antiquity and in the Middle Ages* (Princeton University Press: Princeton, 1993), p.192.

collapse of the Empire approached, operated to divorce writing from its earlier, wider, popular social base through the creation of a distinct 'literary' elite within what had been the political class, operating through private readings and performances for its own amusement rather than the public good.[244]

Medieval Scribes and Rhetoricians

With the collapse of the Western Roman Empire around AD 406, Europe entered a period known as The Dark Ages where Latin was no longer the common language and literary culture virtually disappeared; as illiterate 'barbarian' rulers took over, public schooling disappeared and learning of all kinds passed into the hands of the Christian Church. Throughout the medieval period everyone who achieved a degree of literacy -- even those who were not themselves monks or church clerics -- did so through the Church. The Church, however, did not see the teaching of rhetoric as part of the literary repertoire deployed in the telling of grand tales, but simply as a means of enhancing the power of the sermon in reaching the lowest common denominator of the growing congregation.

It has been suggested that for several hundred years, from the collapse of Rome up to the tenth or eleventh centuries, while a few could still write in Latin but most of Europe was illiterate, the monks of Ireland, who were little affected by the collapse of Rome, worked steadily to preserve and copy the manuscripts in their possession. European intellectual endeavour, meagre though it might have been, was supported by the scribal effort of Irish monks who supplied manuscript copies to *scriptoria*, private libraries and royalty. While it is not clear yet what texts the Irish monks had -- probably standard classical texts, a few rare Roman and Greek texts and the surviving fragments of early Irish literature -- it is clear that the diligence of Irish scribes helped support learning and populate libraries across Europe. We also owe the spaces between words to the Irish monks: they introduced this innovation into their manuscripts around the year 600, but it was not adopted elsewhere until the twelfth century. Also, as Europe emerged from the Dark Ages, Irish monks and teachers founded several key monasteries, which in

---

244 *Ibid*, pp.243-49, 335.

turn created their own off-shoot houses, where learning could prosper.[245]

Most European monasteries in the medieval period had a *scriptorium* where, as at the monastery of St Martin of Tours, perhaps as many as 200 monks laboured.[246] For many monastic orders work in the *scriptorium* was a religious duty. The work of the scriptorium was supposed to be silent, but we know the monks produced a constant gentle hum, like the sound of bees, as they murmured the words they were writing. It is hard for us to appreciate the immense labour involved in copying, translating and modernizing these early manuscripts. Even though the monks could read, most were unused to writing: many would have been happier in the fields or the kitchens engaged in manual labour, and often progress was painfully slow:

> One copy of St Augustine's commentary, of 109 sheets -- say 218 pages -- of twenty lines to the page, has a note attached to it with the information that in 832 it was copied in seven days and corrected on the eighth by the same scribe. This represents the amazing speed of thirty pages a day. On the other hand another manuscript of 304 sheets (608 pages), begun on 2 June 819, was not completed until 12 September, which taking holidays into account, represents an average of six or seven pages a day.[247]

Young monks beginning work in the *scriptorium* had a great deal to learn before they could actually start copying or writing: the preparation of the animal skins for velum, the cutting of skins to size, the ruling of lines, the preparation of quills -- selection, drying, hardening, cutting, splitting -- the preparation of ink. In general a monastery manuscript, by the time it had been illuminated, illustrated, sewn, bound and gilded had probably passed through the hands of at least ten monks. Though they dedicated their work to God, it must be said that the monks were not all good at their work, or even happy in their work, and many made mistakes or were simply slap-dash. Every well run *scriptorium* had a senior monk whose task was to check and correct the manuscripts. At

---

245 T. Cahill, *How the Irish Saved Civilisation* (First Anchor: London, 1995), pp.160-63; H. Waddell, *The Wandering Scholars* (Penguin: Harmondsworth, 1954),pp.32, 53, 55; L. Adcock, *Arthur's Britain* (Penguin: Harmondsworth, 1973), pp.134-5; M. Battles, *Library: an Unquiet History* (Vintage: London, 2004); S. Young, *The Celtic Revolution* (Gibson Square: London, 2010).
246 L. Adcock, *Arthur's Britain* (Penguin: Harmondsworth, 1973), p.3.
247 P. Wolff, *The Awakening of Europe* (Penguin: Harmondsworth, 1968), p.59.

Salisbury Cathedral an official tasked with correcting manuscripts was financed out of the income from an area of farm land set aside specifically for the purpose.[248]

In the margins and in their comments on the literature they copied, the monks left many clues as to the pains they took with their work. 'The lamp is not very bright', complains one: 'This parchment is very rough', say another. Sometimes they criticized the quality of each other's writing: 'It is easy to spot Gabriel's work here', writes one. 'This work was not copied slowly' writes another. Often their comment on Greek and Roman texts was favourable, but one monk, tortured with the convolutions of ancient Greek grammar wrote: 'There's an end to that -- and seven curses with it!' The Irish monks in particular recorded fragments of popular song, their own poems and daydreams, reminding us not of their scribal function but their humanity:

> All are keen
> To know who'll sleep with blond Aideen.
> All Aideen herself will own
> Is that she will not sleep alone.

Perhaps the most vivid picture we have of the life of the Irish scribe is to be found in a beautiful poem written on a page slipped into a copy of a Latin commentary on Virgil:

> I and Pangur Ban my cat,
> 'Tis a like task we are at:
> Hunting mice is his delight,
> Hunting words I sit all night.
>
> 'Tis a merry thing to see
> At our tasks how glad are we,
> When at home we sit and find
> Entertainment to our mind.
>
> 'Gainst the wall he sets his eye,
> Full and fierce and sharp and sly;
> 'Gainst the wall of knowledge I
> All my little wisdom try.

---

248 D. Jackson, *The Story of Writing* (Studio Vista: London, 1981), p.85.

So in peace our task we ply,
Pangur Ban my cat and I;
In our arts we find our bliss,
I have mine and he has his.

One Irish monk expressed an awareness of his own brief existence compared to the life he had created in copying a text:

Sad it is, little parti-coloured white book, for a day will surely come when someone will say over your page: 'The hand that wrote this is no more'.[249]

Although we tend to think of the monks as anonymous scribes, the Benedictine monks of Le Bouveret in Swizerland have began publishing an index of known medieval scribes from their records: so far the names of 19,000 scribes -- some of the female -- have been identified.[250]

Cassiodorus was an Italian monk who, having devoted his life to learning, retired *c*. AD 540 (or 550) to his ancestral estate at Squillace in Southern Italy. There he set up his own model monastery with a library of his own purchases from North Africa and books copied under his own supervision. He also set up an inter-library loan system. He composed the *Institutiones*, in which he explained the importance of scholarship and the work of the scribes. He also produced *De Orthographia* in which he laid down the rules of copying and set out the standards to which the monks should aspire in the *scriptorium*.[251]

Until about the twelfth century most books were made by monks. The European market for books up to this time had mainly been for luxury items destined for the courts, and theological and philosophical works destined for the monastery libraries or for use in church. After this date however, commercial and professional scribes began to proliferate and the supply of books increased considerably. While a monk might have produced three or four books per year, a commercial scribe, paid by the job, might produce a book in a week.[252] From the twelfth century

---

249 P. Wolff, *The Awakening of Europe* (1968) 59-60; T. Cahill, *How the Irish Saved Civilisation* (1995), pp.160-63.
250 C. De Hamel, *Scribes and Illuminators* (British Museum Press: London, 2009), p.43. Also: www.leeds.ac.uk/ims/med_online/medresource.
251 L. Casson, *Libraries in the Ancient World* (Yale Books: Harvard, 2002), pp.143-44.
252 C. De Hamel, *ibid*, pp.7, 35.

onwards it was possible for noblemen to arrange for copies of texts to be made either in the monastery scriptorium or to arrange to borrow a text in order to have a copy made. Much of the income from making and copying texts derived from the production to order of official texts for students in the new universities and in the schools, in loaning texts for copies to be made in a system known as *pecia*. Licensed stationers often published lists of the texts they were offering. In the late Middle Ages universities also began to order books -- particularly translations of ancient texts preserved in Arabic -- for their own libraries. In general a rich young man going up to university ordered copies of the books he needed from a stationer licensed by the university. The stationer then arranged for the copies to be made. Poorer students would buy a blank gathering of pages and then spend their evenings copying out their texts, borrowed a chapter at a time from the licensed university stationer.

However, after the twelfth century, as vernacular works of literature began to appear in European languages, and the translations of Arabic, Jewish, Greek and Latin texts became a little more common, a wider audience for books in the emerging mercantile classes -- whose tastes generally were for books on hunting, agriculture, food, health, astrology, romance and household economy - began to develop. As a result scribes and illuminators began to work outside the monasteries; they formed teams and operated in workshops of their own. In the mid-thirteenth century, for example, there are records of such a team working in and around Catte Street in Oxford: eighteen illuminators, eleven parchment-makers, twenty-three scribes and nine stationers and samplers. These teams soon formed an important part of the nascent middle class, and increasingly they signed manuscripts and books with their own names: there are records of Egbert the left-handed, John the one-eyed scribe and of 'Alan the scribe and his wife the illuminator'.[253] In medieval Europe scribes served an apprenticeship of seven years before they could set up as a 'master'. After achieving the status of 'master', instead of joining a workshop or remaining with their old master, some scribes became itinerant scholars or notaries, travelling from court to court or city to city, selling their skills and then moving on. It is known that in the 1320s the Countess of Clare employed a scribe to copy a book at her castle. She paid him eight shillings plus board and lodging. The book was 317,000

---

253 D. Jackson, *The Story of Writing* (Studio Vista: London, 1981), pp.76, 86.

words long. If he worked six days per week including Holy days and managed an average of 3,300 words per day, he was paid less than a penny per day.[254]

While scribes greatly increased the flow of books and manuscripts throughout Europe, very little of their learning and teaching was written down. Mainly they seem to have taught by example. The few textbooks and treatises on scribal workshop practice are strong on 'lifestyle' advice, but short on professional detail. Cennini D'Andrea Cennino's *Il Libro dell'Arte*, for example, urges students to submit themselves to their master as early as possible, and not leave his service until they have to, to eat and drink modestly, to preserve the steadiness of their writing hand by refraining from heavy work such as lifting stones with a crowbar or indulging too much in the company of women. However, all detail of workshop practice is absent.[255]

The ancient scribes of the Middle East had been embedded in politically and economically highly centralized societies; support of centralized authority seems to have been one of the major, but usually unspoken, functions of the scribal strata in any society. Europe, as centralized states began to emerge, was not much different in this respect. From 1199, for example, when the king of England travelled he used to take with him a small band of Chancery scriveners (clerks and scribes) to prepare documents and record meetings. These records were kept on skins and parchments which were sewn together and then stored in rolls. This was part of a general attempt by the monarchy to create systematic records and develop more effective control. During the thirteenth century the workload of the Chancery scriveners increased and the number of documents mounted at an alarming rate. The scriveners ceased to travel with the king and instead were located permanently in their own offices at Westminster. Because of their central and permanent location within the courts the Chancery scriveners were able to exert an unprecedented effect on the shaping of the English language by standardizing spellings, grammar and usage around their own, mainly Central and East Midlands dialects.

Scribes in London had been expected to master several different styles of written text, but the increasing workloads and the pressures of commercialization meant that by the end of the twelfth century scribes

---

254 D. Jackson, *The Story of Writing*, pp.78.
255 *Ibid*, pp.80-81; Cennini D'Andrea Cennino, *The Craftsman's Handbook, Il Libro dell'Arte* (Dover Publications: New York, 1960).

began to abandon the rounded Carolingian style script in favour of the upright Gothic style. For the Scriveners of the Chancery this merely meant only an alteration in their writing style, but for the independent commercials scriveners and scribes this meant they could squeeze more words to a line and save on the cost of additional pages. So influential were the scriveners of the Chancery that by the time Caxton came to set up the first printing press in Westminster in 1476, 'Chancery Standard', rather than the literary works of Chaucer or Gower, was already the benchmark of correct and prestigious style in writing and the favoured style of printed text was almost always Gothic.[256] While Caxton's printing press was to have a drastic effect on the independent scribes, it little affected the Chancery scribes simply because their work was mainly in the production of handwritten records and unique legal documents for which no further copies were required.

Creative Writing and the Universities

It is important to remember that Creative Writing emerges as a university subject from the same nexus of traditions that created the European universities.

In the universities several strands of history intertwine. The foundation and early growth of European universities was based on cross-fertilization with ideas derived from the great centres of learning and the teaching methods observed where the Islamic and Christian worlds interacted -- in southern Italy and Spain -- and observations brought back by pilgrims, scholars, religious leaders and diplomats from the courts of the Caliphs in the Middle East and ideas brought back by the more thoughtful members of the entourages of the Crusading Knights in the period 1095–1291. This connection to ideas from the Islamic world as part of the spin-off from the Crusades is clear: the oldest universities, usually based on an expansion of Cathedral schools, date from this time. The University of Bologna, Europe's first university, was founded around 1088, just as the Crusades started; Paris University dates from 1100; Oxford and Cambridge universities came into formal existence in 1249 and 1284 respectively. But to this was added the work of resident experts

---

256 D. Crystal, *The Cambridge Encyclopedia of The English Language* (Cambridge University Press: Cambridge, 1997), p.43; D. Crystal, *Stories of English* (Penguin: Harmondsworth, 2005), p.231.

at the European royal courts, the expertise of the Cathedral schools who trained their own administrators, and the teaching expertise of those who ran professional apprenticeship schemes in Law and Medicine. And to the established tradition of scribing in Europe and the Middle East, and the resilient activities of scholars, whose main interests were channelled through monastic centres of learning, European universities added the training of churchmen, theologians, civil servants, lawyers and physicians -- the trained minds that the increasingly centralized modern state demanded to run and support the royal courts, the political classes, the law courts and the rapidly expanding civil service.[257]

From the closing days of the Roman Empire, through the Carolingian Renaissance up to the late medieval period the Church showed an interest in rhetoric only in so far as it enhanced and improved the ability to deliver sermons. However, during the late medieval period there was a revival of interest in the possibilities of rhetoric and writing and several influential manuals were produced. In addition to the study of Law, Medicine and Theology -- the basic university subjects of the time -- Rhetoric was re-established as part of the scholar's compulsory trivium of grammar, rhetoric and logic. Rhetoric, along classical lines, was a five part subject consisting of: Invention, Organization, Style, Memory and Delivery. However, by and large medieval poets were not university teachers. Indeed, as in ancient Greece where there seems to have been an uneasy relationship between rhetoricians and practising writers, there seems to have been some animosity between them in medieval England too, perhaps resulting from the way that poets had been taught.[258] Geoffrey Chaucer (*c.* 1343–1400), for example, wrote at a time when most 'literature' was written to be read aloud and could therefore still make use of many of the tricks to be learned in the study of rhetoric.[259]

Medieval schools of all kinds inherited an unbroken, but much altered tradition of rhetoric, and rhetoric became a basic element in any kind of writing or speech that pretended to be anything other than plain daily

---

257 G. Makdisi, 'Scholasticism and Humanism in Classical Islam and the Christian West', *Journal of the American Oriental Society* (April-June 1989); H. Goddard, *A History of Christian-Muslim Relations* (Edinburgh University Press: Edinburgh, 2000); M. Bragg, 'Medieval Universities', *In Our Time*, BBC Radio 4, 17 March 2011.
258 B. Vickers, *In Defence of Rhetoric* (Clarendon: Oxford, 1988).
259 A. I. Doyle, 'The Social Context of Medieval English Literature', in B. Ford, (ed.), *The Pelican Guide to English Literature: vol 1, The Age of Chaucer* (Pelican: Harmondsworth, 1966), pp.86-8.

speech. Chaucer is thought to have studied at the Inner Temple, which specialized in training lawyers, so he would have been unable to avoid the study of rhetoric, along with grammar and logic. Chaucer was aware that his teachers of rhetoric felt innovation in writing was something that happened strictly within a convention of established and applied 'rules of composition', rather than in the creation of something new. Although Chaucer was not aware of it, his teachers were using manuals that were 'based on a corruption of classical theory', which often took their examples from 'bad postclassical models', and were almost exclusively concerned with 'prescriptive rhetoric' and the amplified 'high' style.[260] Though he made extensive use of rhetoric in his compositions, Chaucer also mocked his teachers' version of rhetoric by satirizing one of the most popular of the manuals of the time -- the twelfth century Geoffrey de Vinsauf's *Poetria Nova* -- in *The Nun's Priest's Tale*. It is clear that Chaucer saw literary invention and innovation in rather a different light from the academic teachers of the time.

One of the reasons for this is clear. Schoolmasters and university teachers in Grammar and Rhetoric were not popular figures. Up to the fifteenth century a scholar graduating with a Master's degree was presented with a birch rod -- and he was expected to use this on his pupils. And one of the reasons they used the birch was that, in addition to maintaining classroom discipline in the manner of their Babylonian and Egyptian forerunners, rather than producing literary creators, schools and universities trained scholars who copied and learned by rote: university teachers of rhetoric saw themselves not as innovative practitioners of a form of creative writing, but as the custodians of ancient learning. Chaucer had been quick to spot that they could not impart to emerging writers much that was professionally or practically useful, since for them everything was theory which they had at second or third hand rather than from their own literary practice. Aristotle and Quintilian may have made little operational distinction between 'the study of grammar' and grammar 'animated by poetics or rhetoric', but others, particularly practising writers, did.[261] These were exactly the tutors that Quintilian had warned against -- non-writers teaching something of which they

---

260 C. Muscatine, *Chaucer and the French Tradition* (University of California Press: Berkeley, 1969), p.173.
261 G. Steiner, *Extraterritorial: Papers on Literature and the Language Revolution*, (Peregrine: Harmondsworth, 1972), p.99.

had little or no experience except through studying the often corrupted texts passed down to them. It was no accident that in the early Tudor period many university educated writers contented themselves with translating and 'Englishing' classical Latin plays, rather than creating new work.

During the Renaissance, as more classical texts became available in translation and as university graduates and 'upstart crows' like Shakespeare (1564–1616), tried their hand at writing, there was great revival of interest in teaching and learning the ancient techniques of composition. Shakespeare, as part of his 'small Latin and Less Greek', had probably encountered rhetoric at school in Stratford, and he had certainly read Thomas Wilson's influential treatise *Art of Rhetoric* (1553), though he does not seem to have held it in high regard or, beyond making use of Latin comedies, to have been fettered by the classical 'rules of composition'.[262] The general disregard of the 'rules of composition' drove Sir Philip Sidney (1554–86), a soldier, courtier and experimental poet, to produce *A Defence of Poetry* (1595), in which he took contemporary writers to task for knowing little and caring less about the classical unities which, in his opinion, determined good writing and literary composition.[263]

Shakespeare and Chaucer were the liveliest and most attuned minds of their times: both were relentless innovators, both were enormously well read. But neither was a scholar in the conventional sense: they were literary practitioners -- and in Shakespeare's case it seems largely self-taught. And yet, while both men knew the rules of rhetoric and composition, both were also aware of the limitations of the rules. Neither of them felt any great need for scrupulous observation of the rules. Indeed, they both broke and subverted literary convention through parody, experiment and innovation in order to find and create their own new and more responsive literary forms. Had they been taught by practising writers rather than theoreticians, things might have gone differently.

---

262 M. C. Bradbrook, *The Growth and Structure of Elizabethan Comedy* (Chatto & Windus: London, 1962), pp.27-41.
263 P. Sidney, *A Defence of Poetry* (OUP: Oxford, 1997).

In Western Europe, the development of copper plate and litho printing began with G. A. Hercolani's *Lo Scrittor' Utile et brieve Segretari*, published in Bologna in 1574, and soon spread widely.[264] This development rapidly changed the status of the 'Writing Master':

> The professional writing master, who set up in business to teach writing and arithmetic, enjoyed a much humbler position in society than perhaps he felt himself to deserve, as heir to the medieval master-scribes. He was unclear whether he was an artist, a law writing scrivener or merely a teacher. He no longer enjoyed the status of the priestly scribe in medieval society, nor was he a member of a team of artists and craftsmen who produced sumptuous luxury volumes which were sought after by the highest in the land. The artist illuminator in the fifteenth and sixteenth centuries had found a new role as an easel painter, independent of the book, but the calligrapher had lost his association with the making of beautiful and valuable things. The arrival of the printed book, and the social changes of the following century, forced him into a no man's land which to some extent he might be said to occupy still, falling uncomfortably between the stools of scrivener and schoolmaster.[265]

The business of scribing has been almost entirely male: literacy clearly put great power in priestly male hands and in the hands of the mainly male political elite they instructed and advised. That power, as Jack Goody puts it, 'represented power vested in the minority of the literate over the majority of the illiterate (disproportionately female), who had only indirect access to the canonised text'.[266] This situation seems to have persisted in almost all literate communities from the invention of writing for about 5,000 years, through the European Renaissance and on into the nineteenth century, before the idea of universal education and the spread of universal suffrage challenged the status quo. Only in India does there seem to have been a slightly different arrangement. There female participation in the religious rites and their access to literacy and the sacred texts can be traced back to the sixth century BC and the very beginnings of alphabetic writing in that part of the world. In Europe it might be possible to compile an anthology of female writers and

264 A. Fairbanks, *A Book of Scripts* (Penguin: Harmondsworth, 1968), p.20.
265 D. Jackson, *The Story of Writing* (Studio Vista: London, 1981), pp.120-21.
266 J. Goody, *The Power of the Literary Tradition* (Smithsonian: Washington, 2000), p.129.

priestesses going back through the female novelists of the nineteenth century to the female poets of the eighteenth century, the female saints and divines and then to the Greek poet Sapho, but it would be a slim and uneven collection compared to the male-dominated traditional canon of literature. For example, it is only now, in the twenty-first century, that Jewish women have begun scribing the *Torah* for themselves.[267]

It is not the case that women never had any access to literacy, sacred rites and texts. Women probably always had some access to these things. While they may have been more easily excluded from the public religious expressions at major festivals and from the ranks of the literate priesthood, they almost certainly found ways to access sacred texts and to acquire literacy. Within the Christian tradition we can see that in spite of a male priesthood there was a feeling that women could not be denied salvation. In terms of property, in those societies where women could inherit, the longer average life span of women meant that much property, including texts, came into their hands, and that their salvation became particularly important and possibly remunerative to the priests. In families where there was no male heir a woman might be allowed to take on the role of the son. It is a complex area and not much explored.

Walter Ong summed up some of the ambiguities of this scribal and rhetorical legacy when he said:

The physical properties of early writing materials encouraged the continuance of scribal culture. Instead of evenly surfaced machine-made paper and relatively durable ball-point pens, the early writer had more recalcitrant technological equipment. For writing surfaces, he had wet clay bricks, animal skins (parchment, vellum) scraped free of fat and hair, often smoothed with pumice and whitened with chalk, frequently reprocessed by scraping of an earlier text (palimpsests). Or he had the bark of trees, papyrus (better than most surfaces but still rough by high-technology standards), dried leaves or other vegetation, wax layered onto wooden tablets often hinged to forma diptych worn on a belt (these wax tablets were used for notes, the wax being smoothed over again for reuse), wooden rods and other wooden and stone surfaces of various sorts. There were no corner stationery stores selling pads of paper. There was no paper. As inscribing tools the

---

267 www.womenstorah.com/halachah; and www.womenintheancientworld.com/literacy

scribes had various kinds of styli, or goose quills, which had to be slit and sharpened over and over again with what we still call a 'pen knife', brushes (particularly in East Asia), or various other instruments for incising surfaces and/or spreading inks or paints. Fluid inks were mixed in various ways and readied for use into hollow bovine horns (inkhorns) or other acid resistant containers, or, commonly in East Asia, brushes were wetted and dabbed on dry ink blocks, as in watercolour painting.

Special mechanical skills were required for working with such writing materials, and not all 'writers' had such skills suitably developed for protracted composition. Paper made writing physically easier. But paper, manufactured in China probably by the second century BC and diffused by Arabs to the Middle East by the eighth century of the Christian era, was first manufactured in Europe only in the twelfth century.

Longstanding oral mental habits of thinking through one's thoughts aloud encourage dictation, but so did the state of writing technology. In the physical act of writing, the medieval Englishman Orderic Vitalis says, 'the whole body labors'. Through the Middle Ages in Europe authors often employed scribes. Composition in writing, working out one's thoughts pen-in-hand, particularly in briefer compositions, was, of course, practised to some extent from antiquity, but it became widespread for literary and other prolonged compositions at different times in different cultures. It was still rare in eleventh-century England, and, when it occurred, even this late, could be done in a psychological setting so oral that we find it hard to imagine. The eleventh-century Eadmer of St Albans says that when he composed in writing, he felt he was dictating to himself. St Thomas Aquinas, who wrote his own manuscripts, organizes his *Summa Theologiae* in quasi-oral format (...) Similarly an early poet would write down a poem by imagining himself declaiming it to an audience. Few, if any, novelists today write a novel by imagining themselves declaiming it aloud. Though they might be exquisitely aware of the sound effects of the words. High literacy fosters truly written composition, in which the author composes a text which is precisely a text, puts his or her words together on paper. This gives thought different contours from those of orally sustained thought.[268]

Rhetoric, while it made use of writing and often drew on literary texts, was at root the art of public speaking, of oral address. In one sense the

---

268 W. J. Ong, *Orality and Literacy* (Routledge: London, 1982), p.94.

rhetorical tradition represented the old oral world while the scribes were representative of 'the modern'. However, this distinction is not clear-cut. As rhetoric became an 'art', and as the principles of the alphabet and literacy spread, so the techniques of rhetoric were refined, catalogued and written down by scribes so that even what was clearly rhetorical and oral (for example knowledge, oral recitation and interpretation of *Rig Veda*, the Bible or the Koran) was very soon based in memorizing written texts, in reference to authorized texts and in literacy:

> No one could or can simply recite extempore a treatise such as Aristotle's *Art of Rhetoric*, as someone in an oral culture would have to do if this sort of understanding were to be implemented. Lengthy oral productions follow more agglomerative, less analytic patterns. The 'art' of rhetoric, though concerned with oral speech was, like other 'arts', the product of writing.[269]

Inevitably perhaps, from the medieval period onwards Writing and Scholarship trod different paths. The impact of printing and the increasing availability of books shifted the emphasis of study, directing efforts towards what was written rather than what was said, towards what could be consumed in private rather than what was debated in public. Instead of testing oral, improvisational and compositional skills, universities set written papers testing their students' knowledge of a body of established factual information and interpretative skills transmitted through lectures. By the eighteenth century both Oxford and Cambridge had given up on oral exams and had stopped testing oral and compositional skills altogether. Rhetoric as a subject of literary study seems to have fallen out of the syllabus very quickly after this: it does not have an entry in *The Oxford Companion to English Literature* or in *The Cambridge Guide to English Literature*.[270]

*

---

269 *Ibid*, pp.107-8.
270 P. Harvey (ed.), *The Oxford Companion to English Literature* (Oxford University Press: Oxford, 1960); I. Ousby (ed.), *The Cambridge Guide to English Literature* (Cambridge University Press: Cambridge, 1993).

WRITING THE WORLD

Knowledge of the literature of the past is essential to any writer. However, while writers are aware of texts other than their own, and are particularly aware of the writing out of which their own has grown, they are not concerned with the 'place' in the canon or the critical interpretation of finished texts which have already achieved publication. Creative Writing is concerned with making what the Italian poet Julius Caesar Scaliger (1484–1558) called 'imaginative interventions' in the present. Creative Writing is concerned with what will be written, what is being written, how a creative idea will be shaped and expressed, how it will get out into the world. Creative Writing -- in addition to pondering the nature of humanity and interrogating the peculiar activity we call writing as an essential part of its daily business -- is the midwife of new texts: it is concerned with planning and drafting of creative work, the process of bringing new work into existence, with the act of making, with solving particular creative problems, the difficult business of bringing feelings, states of mind, ideas and ways of seeing into the world and with finding effective forms.

Creative Writing clearly has its own historical, philosophical and theoretical elements to discover, recover and burnish: but in addition, it attempts to affect awareness of feelings, the way people organize their thought and view their life. It attempts to bring into being new products of the mind, new ways of seeing and understanding, to say things never thought or said before -- or if not, then to say things again but better fitted for contemporary readers. Creative Writing is substantially *before* the fact. The work of English, on the other hand, is largely forensic (from the Latin *forensis*, of the Forum, meaning the courts of law or public judgement) not only because it deals in debate about and judgement of the texts that form the accepted literary canon, but also because it comes *after* the fact of literary creation. English deals with work that is established, that has already been written and which has achieved some historical significance. Basically an English team is mainly concerned with the literature of the past, while a Creative Writing team is concerned with the literature of the future.

One of the major questions the traditional study of literature often misses out, but which Creative Writing can address, is the issue of the social role and social function of the writer as a creative and interpretive intellectual. And from this recognition other questions grow. What is writing? What do writers do? What does writing do? How do they represent the world in words? Why do writers write? Who is their audience? What might their audience expect of them? And once asked these questions open up debates of considerable complexity.

In US universities, Creative Writing, or Imaginative Writing as it is sometimes called, has been a feature of academic life for over 130 years. Interpreted as the widest possible variety of creative work and creative discourse for print, performance and broadcast, involving listeners, writers and readers, it began with informal courses at several universities towards the end of the nineteenth century. In the 1920s, a successful undergraduate course at Harvard led by Dean Le Baron Russell Briggs was taken up by Utah University, and in the 1930s State University Iowa established its School of Letters with both undergraduate and MA programmes in writing, taught by writers rather than academics. The subject formally announced itself with a conference at Breadloaf, Vermont: this became an annual event. The subject then became an important component in the rapid post-war expansion of US universities and was particularly important to English programmes and to general or combined studies degrees. However, increasingly Creative Writing sat rather uncomfortably in English departments where it was part of an English degree and often delivered by academics rather than by writers. English academic staff quickly became frustrated that they could not produce 'good' results -- particularly when compared with the classical canon of English Literature they taught in their other classes.

At the same time, and in contradiction to this, it was often assumed that Creative Writing was an 'undemanding' subject: while students could usually get into a Creative Writing programme in large numbers because of open admissions policies, they often lacked the background reading that made further development likely. Many students were unrealistic about their ambition to write, lacked basic writing skills or a real interest in the subject; most did not read very much; many were simply looking for an easy way into university or for an extra class to fill out their timetable; many students had no interest in writing after university and really wanted a passive lecture based programme, rather than active involvement in writing workshops or the development of their creative imaginations. While Creative Writing recruited well, it rapidly acquired a reputation as 'the major flunk-out' subject, particularly for first year students. However, from the late 1960s Creative Writing provision began to address these problems with its own distinctive ethos, marking guidelines and learning outcomes; increasingly it developed independently of English Departments and began recruiting its own staff.[271]

In the UK Creative Writing first made an appearance in 1970 at the University of East Anglia. The subject existed only at postgraduate level, but even so, the shock of its appearance has still not quite gone away. In spite of a hesitant start, over the next two decades Creative Writing established a modest presence in undergraduate studies (usually as part of an English degree) at several British universities: after Derby University pioneered a standalone undergraduate degree in 2000 six other UK universities also developed degrees in the subject, and by 2008 it was offered as a degree component at twenty British universities. The NAWE website lists 421 Higher Education Creative Writing courses.[272] There have been professors of Creative Writing at several universities including Sheffield, Bath, Glamorgan, London, East Anglia, Southampton, Nottingham Trent, Manchester, Swansea and Derby. Creative Writing is The Open University's most popular module. At most of the institutions where it is taught there are sixty to ninety undergraduate students and a well-established interest in Masters Programmes: PhDs in the subject have started to appear. At British universities there are now over 5,000 students studying Creative Writing at undergraduate level -- that is more than the number studying English Language.[273] The subject is well established in the USA, Canada, Australia and New Zealand, and it has begun to establish itself in the universities of India, Poland, Italy, Romania and elsewhere. These are confirmations that the subject is popular, is recreating a distinct place for itself and is developing its own presence and agenda of study.

The subject, as the British universities soon realised, was a gift. A Creative Writing programme could bulk out not only English courses, but a whole range of other subjects within the general area of an Arts or Humanities faculty. It could also, without difficulty, be fitted into most Combined Studies and Joint Honours programmes. This allowed

---

271 W. Stegner, *On the Teaching of Creative Writing* (University Press of New England: Hanover NH, 1997).
272 NAWE -- National Association of Writers in Education: www.nawe.co.uk.
273 *Student Record 2003-08* (Higher Education Statistics Agency: London, 2009).

universities to process the more creative (less academically inclined) students, helped maintain student numbers, allowed cross financing with worthy but less popular subjects, and above all brought in student fees -- lots of them. At the same time, employing professionally published writers who taught, rather than university lecturers who dabbled a little in writing, boosted the universities' bids for government research funding, which was allocated on the basis of publication. Universities found they needed little to support the subject since its basic requirement was simply a workshop room in which to teach and discuss: it involved no complicated machinery, heavy scientific equipment, massive investment, technical support or complicated health and safety arrangements. Since Creative Writing taught transferrable skills the jobs market soon began to appreciate that graduates from this subject were often more disciplined and more immediately useful than graduates from traditional Humanities and Arts subjects. This also allowed universities to tick the 'Graduate Employability' box for the subject. Also, as writers were often more productive in terms of publications than traditional academics, the subject often brought in research funds which were not necessarily re-invested in it, but could support academic research projects. Thus, while Creative Writing is often regarded by universities as a milk cow, it is also something of a poor cow.[274]

While it made some kind of administrative sense initially to place Creative Writing 'in' the English departments of the UK and USA, and perhaps even to teach Creative Writing as part of an English degree, the elements, skills, practices and agenda of Creative Writing were clearly attractive to other areas of study. Elements of Creative Writing practice can now be found in several other academic areas -- Theatre Studies, Performing and Media Arts, Media Studies, Sociology, Religious Studies, Fine Arts, Art & Design, Art Therapy, Journalism, Film and TV. There is no longer any particular reason to associate Creative Writing with English, and while the two subjects can (and do) exist side by side, the emphasis on theory in literature teaching means that Creative Writing is increasingly taught as an independent stand-alone subject.

There are several current ideas about what Creative Writing at university might be. One popular view is that Creative Writing is simply

---

274 The phrase 'milk cow -- poor cow' as a description of Creative Writing in UK universities was coined by Andrew Melrose.

Life Writing, something that allows people to write out their experience and which encourages *catharsis* (the purging of emotion). The most extreme form of this view sees Creative Writing as a kind of Art Therapy, an academic variety of care in the community. While most tutors acknowledge a therapeutic element to the subject, this is not the main thrust of Creative Writing within universities. Indeed, tutors usually try to persuade students to move beyond the safety of autobiography, however therapeutic, to put their revelations into fictional or poetic form, to develop narratives that are more than 'the way it actually happened', to think themselves into someone else's life and feelings, to take an imaginative leap out of their own skin and develop a cloak for their experience.

It is often assumed that Creative Writing is something anyone can do, that 'we all have one novel in us'. Usually this is accompanied by the explanation that Creative Writing is merely 'free' or 'personal' expression, that we only have to emote on paper, write 'what we feel', and that a student can never 'get it wrong'. This view is not something that tutors easily accommodate: those who come to the subject with this idea usually come to grief very quickly. It is often something of a shock to discover that Creative Writing is a subject which sets standards -- and not only in terms of literacy, academic performance, satire or witty observation of social *mores*. Because, in practical educational terms, the subject insists on moving students towards professional standards of presentation, writing, spelling, organization, planning, reading, engagement and expression, Creative Writing can do things, including combating plagiarism, that now give traditional academic subjects real difficulties.[275]

Creative Writing within the university plays a broad role, not as Arts Therapy, a service unit for Dyslexia, Remedial Academic Support, nor even as a part of Adult Literacy, but simply in its own right. Perhaps the most important and the easiest to understand of the various erroneous views of Creative Writing is the one that sees it simply as 'part of English'. This, for people who remember 'doing' poetry at school, makes a kind of sense. But while there is clearly a great deal of common ground and productive cross-over between the two subjects, the work,

---

275 M. McCrory, 'Strategies for Checking Plagiarism in a Creative Writing Programme', seminar paper: Conference on Plagiarism, English Subject Centre, University of Liverpool (2 Nov 2001).

agenda and practices of English teachers are very different from those of Creative Writing teachers. Both subjects are concerned with general cultural values, the interpretation of experience, and with words and language: but after this they part company. The difference in aims and methodology of the two subjects is almost total and it is important to distinguish between the *work* of English and the *work* of Creative Writing.

The idea that English somehow 'embraces' or in any way 'owns' Creative Writing is clearly un-historical: Creative Writing is not the newest comer to the academy, but rather the oldest, the original, university subject. In the beginning all writers were creative writers simply because there was nothing else and there were no divisions into different kinds of writing: to write was to create where no writing had been before. Without the scribal schools of the Egypt, Mesopotamia and Palestine, the Classical Schools of Rhetoric in Athens, Rhodes and Rome, without the ancient storytellers, historians, philosophers, dramatists like Homer, Herodotus, Plato, Euripides, Virgil, Ovid, Euripides, Pliny and the rest -- the writers we now call 'the Classics' -- there would be no English, Politics, Philosophy, History, Theatre, Sociology, American Studies, no Sciences, there would be no university. If anything, historically speaking, English, along with most other academic subjects, is a very successful offshoot of Creative Writing.[276]

English emerged as a literature in the fourteenth century and as a university subject was accepted in Cambridge with some reluctance in the 1860s.[277] For many years the subject struggled to gain acceptance from the more established disciplines, who considered it to be the equivalent of 'geography or forestry', a subject for those who were not intellectually equipped to study the more serious subjects.[278] The study of English was planned at Cambridge University in 1917, and started at around the time of the 1918 Armistice. The Cambridge English syllabus stopped at around 1830 and English staff, mainly part-time 'freelance' lecturers, at first allied themselves with the Classics and Philology by setting

276 H. Martin, 'How Creative Writing invented English, or The Classical Provenance of Creative Writing', seminar paper, Sheffield Hallam University, Creative Writing Conference (Spring 2000).
277 S. Potter *The Muse in Chains* (Cape: London, 1937); E. M. W. Tillyard, *The Muse Unchained: An Intimate Account of the Revolution in English Studies at Cambridge* (Bowes & Bowes: London, 1958); F. Mulhern, *The Moment of 'Scrutiny'* (London: New Left Books, 1979).
278 A. Alvarez, *The Writer's Voice* (Bloomsbury: London, 2005), p.81.

about Anglo Saxon and Medieval texts in the hope that this would give the subject some academic credibility; they dabbled with philosophy, history and religion in developing an interpretative methodology and then, in the developing intellectual foment that followed the First World War, took up from Matthew Arnold the battle for Culture. They claimed to be 'central' to national cultural life and the moral health of English society and set about ranking texts in order of 'moral seriousness'. In the years, 1926–27 English was ratified as a degree course and a centralized Faculty structure established to administer and teach it. Throughout the 1930s and 1940s as more UK English departments opened up, the subject fought a desperate battle to establish the idea that it was something more than 'a charming parasite' or a training ground for book reviewers.[279] By the mid-1970s the avenues of exploration outlined by F. R. Leavis, Q. D. Leavis, L. C. Knights and those gathered around the journal *Scrutiny*, were largely exhausted or simply by-passed by new ideas from the European mainland, and the 1990s saw English enter what is now referred to as the 'the Culture Wars' in which the canon was contested, the literary application of Political Correctness was investigated, and increasingly English devoted itself to literary theory, which seemed somehow more serious, more tangible, more academic than any previous version of the subject.

By the mid-1990s Creative Writing had proved its worth and answered its critics within the academy. It had, through academic publications, justified its presence and practices.[280] However, just at this point the UK rapidly extended the corporatisation of the universities. Compelled to respond to a managerial culture that moved education away from the world of ideas, issues, standards and personal development towards the simpler, measurable, vocational aspects of study, UK universities were put under increasing financial pressure by successive Governments. They focused on the issue of their own survival and on education as a business that had somehow to be financed: they had little option but to justify their continuation by reference to league tables and 'throughput' targets. The traditional three 'r's (reading, writing and arithmetic) were

---

279 F. R. Leavis, *Education & the University: A Sketch for an English School* (Chatto & Windus: London, 1948).
280 D. Lodge, *The Practice of Writing* (London: Vintage, 2011), pp.170-78: C. Tighe, *Creative Writing @ University: Frequently Asked Questions* (Manchester: IMPress, 2009) www.carltighe.co.uk.)

transformed to become recruitment, retention, results. And this was increasingly delivered by tick-box management and a bonus culture working to 'corporate targets'. Universities began to redefine study in the Arts and Humanities, not as graded, progressive, linked courses, a disinterested mental and intellectual activity shaping and extending the mind, but simply as a 'finance based commodity', perhaps even as a qualification, a collection of discrete easily digestible, bite-sized, semester-long 'off the peg' modules aiding rapid progression, good graduation statistics and employability. Students found themselves transformed from scholars hoping to master their subject into paying 'customers' and browsing 'consumers' with 'rights' that undercut the learning process. The notion that a university might deliver something more challenging than what the 'customer' wanted became awkward.[281]

Also from the end of the 1990s the complex but widespread cultural deficit produced by the Schools National Curriculum and the 'race to the bottom' engendered by the production of league tables, performance indicators and exam boards competing to show 'better' results, began to show themselves in a generation of young people who were often in possession of good 'A' level certificates, but who were much less capable of university level study than previous generations. In 2012 the government announced that it was instituting a new Baccalaureate exam and admitted openly that twenty- eight years of grade inflation at 'A' level had become a serious problem for universities who were increasingly concerned at the remedial education they had to undertake to process undergraduates to degree level.

Inevitably the emphasis on these changes undermined research and serious academic study making a whole raft of subjects in the Arts and Humanities increasingly difficult to justify, except in terms of the seriousness of theory. From the late 1970s English, along with Philosophy, Media Studies and History, had little option but to move steadily away from considerations of what it was 'to be', the nature of being human, and the study of the activities humans engaged in. English in particular became less concerned with the historical processes of literary creation and individual talent. Forced to justify itself by reference to theory just at the very time it was beginning to experience an urgent need to 'get beyond theory', English in a very short time built for itself 'an iron

---

281 F. Furedi, *Wasted: Why Education Isn't Educating* (Continuum: London, 2010).

curtain' between scholarship and 'the art of writing'.[282]

It was in this inauspicious climate that Creative Writing, with its professional discipline, body of knowledge, literary and practical transferrable skills, and its specific working practices and educational strategies, developed as an undergraduate subject.

While the UK universities seemed determined to repeat the mistakes of the US experience, the traditional academic establishment still harboured a lingering resentment against the development of Creative Writing, characterizing it as somehow illegitimate, 'un-academic' and undermining academic standards -- which in the circumstances was ironic.[283] It is possible to see now that rather than unravelling traditional university subjects and standards, Creative Writing, by restoring and reasserting itself within the academy, is fulfilling some part of the inner reflection on, and training for, citizenship that the ancients so valued and which is reflected in so many classical texts. For classics scholars the study and practice of Rhetoric and Poetics (from which in part the idea of teaching Creative Writing descends) was what was once termed 'a liberal education'.[284] By helping to create the 'classics of tomorrow' within the modern academy Creative Writing quietly, in its own way, and by a completely different route, has begun to find, revive and extend the idea of 'the classics', to challenge, revitalize, review, renew and develop the idea of national (and international) literature and the canon, and to re-assert a standard-setting civic role for literature such as the ancients believed in and which distinguished literary critics, writers, thinkers, scholars and teachers as diverse as Matthew Arnold, Cardinal Newman, Antonio Gramsci, Leon Trotsky and F.R.Leavis once sought for the study of Literature.

---

282 L. Kampf, 'The Scandal of Literary Scholarship', in T. Roszak (ed.), *The Dissenting Academy* (Penguin: Harmondsworth, 1969) pp.45-60; L. Kampf & P. Lauter (eds.), *The Politics of Literature* (Vintage: New York, 1968) p.24; A. Alvarez, *The Writer's Voice* (Bloomsbury: London, 2005), p.118.
283 P. Dawson, *Creative Writing and the New Humanities* (Routledge: Abingdon, 2005), pp.2-4.
284 T. R. Glover, *The Ancient World* (Penguin: Harmondsworth, 1953), p.152.

Directed Study

What have scribal schools and the training of ancient scribes got to do with Creative Writing?

In what ways might an understanding of the work of the ancient scribes be of interest or use to a modern writer? In what senses do you suppose modern writers might still be scribes?

'The hippopotamus hide whip and regular flogging may have fallen into disuse, but a modern writer still needs a sense of discipline.' Why? In what ways is the modern creative writing disciplined?

In what ways do you think the role of the writer has changed since ancient times?

How and why were the ancient scribes powerful? In what ways is it likely that scribes might have a role in helping to shape a national or ethnic consciousness or the standardization of the language?

In what ways, if at all, do modern Creative Writers represent a tradition that goes back to the scribal schools and schools of rhetoric? In what ways has that tradition changed?

Why are Jewish women inscribing the *Torah* for themselves? And why now?

7
A WORLD WITHOUT WRITING?

This chapter deals with a group of modern novels and stories
where the opposite of writing -- the very absence of writing -- is
an essential element of the tale, and where this absence reveals
something about what writing is, what writing gives us, the
relationship of writing to orality and about what the absence of
writing might mean for society. Some of these works deal with the
world before writing was invented; some deal with a world where
writing has been lost, reinvented or suppressed; some deal with a
world where writing and oral culture sit uneasily side by side.

- Prehistoric Society
- Traditional Society
- Literary Products of Oral Culture
- Post-Disaster Society

On the radio I heard a programme about a man who declared a 'no music
week': he would not sing or whistle or hum; he would not turn on the
radio or TV in case music was playing; he would not use his iPod or CD
player. He would not go to pubs, clubs or cafes in case music was being
played. He would not pick up a musical instrument -- not even a comb.
At times it was difficult, but he managed (just about) to go a whole week
without consciously using music.

This led me to wonder what would it be like to live in a world where
little or nothing was written down? How could we as a modern culture
manage to go a week without reading or writing? It would be impossible.
Writing -- a system of signs of one kind or another -- is absolutely
everywhere. Predictably as a teacher, I might think students do not read
enough, but even if they use BlackBerries or i-Pods, text each other on

their mobile phones, surf the internet or access Facebook on their laptops, they are still creatures of a written world; and no matter how marginal intellectuals might feel, the people who inhabit the modern world have no option but to engage with writing in their daily lives.

My reason for asking Creative Writing students to consider the contribution that the record of 'symbolic thinking' has made to the complex of plans, thoughts and acts we now subsume under the general word 'writing', is to try to persuade them to see language and writing as if for the first time, without taking them for granted, to see them for the amazing things they are and to wonder about the history of these things in the development of the human mind.

Clearly it is important that a writer should know something of the origins of the materials they work with -- language and writing. It is also important they see language as what humans make, as part of what makes us human, a product of society and also as the product of the human mind that makes society possible. Bearing in mind that language is the raw material with which a writer works -- what paint is to a painter, stone or wood to a sculptor, light to a photographer or sound is to a musician -- this is not an unreasonable place for a writer to start thinking about writing.

We have the forensic ability to piece together much of the life of an ancient scribe and the history of the alphabet. We can read backwards from the earliest literary texts – *The Odyssey* and *The Iliad, Táin Bó Cúalnge, Mabinogion, Beowulf,* the Bible, the Koran and the *Vedas* -- to find portraits of the poets and bards who once 'carried' these works in their heads, and we can work out much of the process of transition from an oral to a literate society through the scant details and many difficulties of individual transcriptions. However, it is an entirely different matter to imagine how that world worked, to imagine what it was like to inhabit a world where there was no -- or even very little --writing, and where the acts of writing and reading were arcane, deeply mysterious and jealously guarded.

The point of identifying and describing the novels and stories mentioned in this chapter is to show that this is not an arcane academic exercise. Several very distinguished writers have found these ideas revealing and have explored them in their creative work. These issues, while not much discussed, are still with us. If anything we are just beginning to realize how mysterious the acts of reading and writing really are. At the same time it is important we realize with each new technological innovation the ideas underlying reading and writing have not only become more complex, but also more easily taken for granted.

The authors of the books and stories discussed here all have ideas and views about how writing shapes the way we think, remember, record and order our world. In their writing they also make points about the way humans behave, comment on certain aspects of our humanity and emphasize the fragility of human achievements. In particular they emphasise the fragility of human 'civilization' and its reliance on written texts.

Prehistoric Society

In modern fiction one of the earliest attempts to imagine a world without writing was H. G. Wells's 1921 story 'The Grisly Folk'. There, even though the modern humans are said to 'chatter', apart from derogatory noises and laughter and the single instruction 'come', the only example of human language we are given in the story is a single word:

> At a sign from the two leaders the little straggle of menfolk halted and a woman who had been chattering in subdued tones to a little girl became silent. The two brothers surveyed the wide prospect earnestly.
> 'Ugh!' said one abruptly and pointed.
> 'Ugh!' cried his brother.[285]

Given the prevailing state of knowledge at the time Wells was writing it is perhaps not surprising that the only word he gives them should be 'Ugh'. In contrast to the modern humans, the Neanderthals are seen as an ugly threat, and later in the story they live up to their image, but as far as Wells is concerned, they are language-less -- they produce no sounds or speech at all.

In many ways William Golding's *The Inheritors* (1955) follows on from H. G. Wells' story. This is a beautifully written, but nevertheless quite disturbing psychological novel by one of the modern masters who later went on to win the Nobel Prize for Literature. It is about the final days

---

285 H. G. Wells, 'The Grisly Folk' (*Storyteller Magazine*, April 1921), *Selected Short Stories* (Penguin: Harmondsworth, 1977), p.291.

of the Neanderthal people as they realize they are no longer alone, that a new species -- Cro-Magnon humans -- has arrived in their territory, and their slow realization that as a species they are doomed. Golding reverses Wells' view of the Neanderthals and shows them as simple folk whose quiet existence is shattered by the arrival of warlike invaders -- us.

The novel is interesting for us because it is an attempt to imagine how the Neanderthals thought and felt. It attempts to see them as a kind of human, that is human-like, but not quite like us. The novel dwells on their shared mental map of their environment, their inability to make sense of unfolding events or adapt to the new situation. It hints that perhaps with their larger brains they used some kind of telepathy and shared an imagination, but that they could not develop any new picture of the world, could not develop new pictures in their shared imaginations.[286]

The book, reflecting thinking current at the time, assumes that the Cro-Magnon humans killed off a more primitive species. The Neanderthals are represented as 'innocent, sympathetic and incompetent'[287]. In this the book has dated a little: current opinion now tends to acknowledge that the species lived in a far harsher climate than modern humans and was in existence for four times longer than modern humans have managed. As such the Neanderthal species was very successful. Also it is now believed that there was a considerable overlap and interaction between these two species, and that the relationship, where they inhabited the same hunting areas and even the same caves for as long as 10,000 years, was much more complex and not necessarily violent or hostile.

These stories, while they are about the end of the Neanderthal world, are also about the start of our world and the start of what it is to be a modern human. In their different ways both Wells and Golding leave us with a series of lingering questions -- if the Neanderthals were still alive today would we notice them on the street, would we recognise them as different, in what significant ways are they different from us, would we acknowledge them as human, how would we relate to them or regard them, would we clash violently or would we find ways to co-operate and coexist?

---

286 W. Golding, *The Inheritors* (Faber: London, 1961), pp.49-50.
287 D. Miles, *The Tribes of Britain* (Phoenix: London, 2005), p.46.

WRITING THE WORLD

Lester Del Rey's short story 'The Day is Done' first appeared in *Astounding Science Fiction* magazine in 1939.[288] It too followed on from Wells's story, but it developed a much more sympathetic and probably more realistic portrait of the Neanderthals in their final days, showing them as in every way outclassed by the incoming Cro-Magnon humans -- they are not very good hunters, they cannot communicate effectively, they are the butt of the modern human children's jokes, and the are reduced to begging for food -- but they are still far from being the simple-minded brutes of Wells's tale and they live at peace with their new neighbours.

Jean Auel's *The Clan of the Cave Bear* (1980) was the first of a series of popular novels including *The Valley of the Horses, The Mammoth Hunters, The Plains of Passage* and *The Shelters of Stone* (2002). The entire ambitious sequence of novels is called *Earth's Children* and deals with life in what is now Crimea during the 10,000 year long interglacial period 35,000–25,000BC. In particular it deals with the life of Neanderthal humans and their first contacts with the newly arrived and rapidly encroaching Cro-Magnon humans.[289] It picks up from Lester Del Rey's ideas of the Neanderthals and paints a rather more nuanced and sympathetic picture than Wells's or Golding's version of the encounter.

The Clan of the Cave Bear deals with a family group of Neanderthals as they take in and adopt a lost Cro-Magnon child called Ayla. It was enthusiastically reviewed. It was also greeted most respectfully by archaeologists, anthropologists and palaeontologists as it is clearly based on extensive reading and on the most up-to-date archaeological research. It shows in a very sympathetic way how Neanderthals hunted, made clothes, collected medicines and communicated. The novel is particularly good at imagining the differences in how the Neanderthals thought and how they communicated -- in particular it supposes that their use of gesture was an important part of language. It also shows how these things were different from the ways of the Cro-Magnon humans, so different, in fact, that the Neanderthals take pity on their foundling and see her as somehow damaged and so un-Neanderthal in her looks they consider her to be ugly. It is also a very thorough imagining of a world long before writing had been invented, a world where humans communicate as much by sign as they do by speech.

---

288 L. Del Rey, 'The Day is Done' in Lester Del Rey, *The Best of Lester Del Rey* (Ballantine: New York, 2000).
289 J. Auel, *The Clan of the Cave Bear* (London: Coronet, 1980).

Traditional Society

Bruce Chatwin's *The Songlines* (1987) is a fascinating and unorthodox book which records Chatwin's journey across Australia. It is about the origins of humanity, the nature of humanity, about language and humans, and about the relationship between walking, talking, singing, memory and being human. The subject of the book is Australian aboriginal songlines. These are invisible pathways and tracks known to the aboriginal Australians, which connect up all over Australia. These songlines are the equivalent of documents defining ideas of history, identity, stewardship and territory. They tell the story of creation and record how the land came to be the way it is. The preservation of the song cycles is an aboriginal religious duty and part of the definition of their tribal identity:

> Every song cycle went leap-frogging through language barriers, regardless of tribe or frontier. A Dreaming-track might start in the north-west, near Broome; thread its way through twenty languages or more; and go on to hit the sea near Adelaide ... [290]

By singing these songs the people remember creation and sing their world into creation. To alter a verse or to alter the sequence is to un-create and that is punishable with death. The book talks of the songs, stories and oral culture of Australian aboriginal people and links these with ideas about what it is to be human and how humans developed. It records a very different relationship with the world from the one that Europeans are used to -- stewardship rather than ownership.

Frank Delaney's *Ireland: The Novel* (2004) is a hugely ambitious epic novel which deals with the life and times of an itinerant storyteller in Ireland. It starts in 1951, but the narrative, through the tales of the storyteller, travels back in time to tell of the Ice Age that created Ireland, of the subsequent Irish history and Irish myth, the raiders and invaders, the poets and leaders, the freedom fighters, politicians and ordinary people that went to make up the modern state of Eire. Through the storyteller's tales and through the slowly revealed story of his own life, the novel explores the social, political, communal and national function of storytelling, showing how it contributes to, and helps to form, community and identity. It is also very good at explaining how the basic

---

290 B. Chatwin, *Songlines* (Vintage: London, 1988), p.58.

practical elements of the oral storyteller's art work together for overall effect.[291]

Literary Products of Oral Culture

This category includes books which are themselves the products of the transition from an oral to a literary culture or where this transition figures in the story. I have chosen examples from Nigeria, where, in spite of growing literacy and burgeoning university education and where modern writing is almost always in English rather than any of the indigenous languages or Arabic, there is still a flourishing oral culture.

Oral culture is still particularly strong in West Africa. There are, alongside professional writers like Senghor, Achebe and Soyinka who work in French or English, also a great number of professional *griots*. This word has come to include many different types of narrator within oral culture: oral performers, interpreters, praise singers, oral historians, storytellers, singers, dancers and drummers, spokespersons, ambassadors, masters of ceremony, tutors, genealogists, musicians, composers, town criers and exhorters of troops about to go into battle. Each of these has a particular specialism or skill. Some work in a local area, others travel far and wide to earn a living. Each adjusts their performance to accommodate their audience and increase their income.

West Africa also has a very strong tradition of women's songs of abuse. This is a tradition where, when female members of a community feel that someone has slighted their power or standing, women paint their bodies and gather at the culprit's house to draw attention to the offender by publicly singing improvised songs of abuse. This is a very powerful weapon since the songs are forceful, direct and may include bawdy material and even curses. In 1929 a British Colonial administrator in Olomo was so unnerved by such a gathering that he ordered troops to open fire. In Ghana children often sang abuse songs against President Nkrumah, but he employed his own praise singers to counteract their effect until all songs of abuse were officially banned in 1962.[292]

There are two modern Nigerian writers who are said to have their roots in traditional Yoruba oral story telling. Their work can tell us much about the world and work of the traditional story and the transition from a spoken to a written culture.

---

291 F. Delaney, *Ireland: The Novel* (London: Time Warner, 2004).
292 S. Newell, *West African Literatures* (Oxford University Press: Oxford, 2006).

Perhaps the most influential Nigerian writer is D.O.Fagunwa (1903–63). He is one of the very few writers to use Yoruba, one of the many indigenous languages, and the only one to find a readership in Nigeria. Fagunwa was an enthusiastic raconteur, a pious moralist, a misogynist, blessed with a fertile imagination and a good ear, and his talent was clearly rooted in Nigerian oral storytelling traditions. His *Ogboju ode Ninu Igbo Irunmale* (1938) has been translated into English by Nobel prize-winner, Wole Soyinka (b. 1932).[293] Here is how the third adventure in *Forest of a Thousand Demons* starts:

> My comrades all, I have beheld the ocean and have known the sea; water holds no further terror for me. My eyes have witnessed much in this world. Yesterday, I told you what scourging I underwent during my second sojourn in the Forest of Four Hundred Gods and I told you how I resolved never again to hunt or set my hand on any arduous task. I must confess this to you, that promise I made, it was a futile thing. I performed yet another deed of a tough nature.
>
> It happened this way -- it was in fact the season of the harmattan and I rose late in the morning; too much thinking kept me awake most of the night. I had lately returned from my second hunting adventure and when the woman of the town saw in me a new man of wealth, they began to beset my house in thousands and I took them to wife with equal zeal. Many of them did I marry because they were not really interested in my nature. They declared, 'It's your wealth we understand, we have no interest in your character. Even if you wallop us with your gun and bash our heads about with your hunting bag, wed you we must.
>
> But before long, as they began to see my hunter's ways and my riotous temperament which came from a long intimacy with beasts and ghommids of the forest, they began to sneak off one by one, until, on this morning of which I speak, only nine wives were left me. I was chatting with one of them when this hard business on which I was to embark reared its head. This is how it happened ...[294]

Significantly the novel opens with an encounter between an oral narrator called Akara-Ogun and a scribe who is asked to set the hunter's story down for posterity, but by the end of the novel the hunter has disappeared from the narrative, leaving behind only a slip of paper on

293 Wole Soyinka's translations first appeared in the journal *Black Orpheus* in 1966. Later they were published as *Forest of a Thousand Demons* (Nelson: London, 1968).
294 U. Beier (ed.), *Political Spider* (Heinemann: London, 1970), p.2.

which is written 'when we try to grasp him we grasp nothingness'. It is as if the act of writing down the tales has wiped out the necessity of its oral narrator. In its own way this highlights not only the narrative device used to tell the story, the idea that writing somehow permanently 'fixes' the oral tale, but also questions the need for oral narrators outside the novel once the novel is written.[295]

It must be remembered that this is not an oral story, but a translation into English of a story that had its roots in oral tradition, but which had been written down in Yoruba. Soyinka, it is clear, has done a little of his own reworking of the tale and the style in his translation.

Fagunwa was to have great influence on the following generation, particularly on Amos Tutuola. Tutuola was born in Abeokuta in 1920, the son of a cocoa farmer. As the son of a Christian, at the age of twelve he attended the Anglican Central School in Abeokuta, but there he received only a primary school education. As his father died five years later, Tutuola became a farmer and then moved to Lagos to become a blacksmith and coppersmith. In the years 1942–45 he worked at his trade in the RAF and after the war became a messenger in Lagos for the Department of Labour, then he became a storekeeper for the Nigerian Broadcasting Corporation in Ibadan. He married, had six children and retired in 1978.

Tutuola read Fagunwa in Yoruba as a young man and in 1952 published *The Palm-Wine Drinkard*, a kind of extension, embellishment and reworking of Tutuola's style and content into English. In this novel he gathered together and explored the experience of living in two cultures, forcing literary English to bend and accommodate to Yoruba idioms and folk culture in a clearly literary text. While Fagunwa had been local in observation and ambition, Tutuola was to become international in his impact and was to inspire young writers in Nigeria and throughout Africa. The book enjoyed considerable acclaim in Britain and the USA and was highly praised by Dylan Thomas, who said it was a 'brief, thronged, grisly and bewitching' novel and added that 'nothing is too prodigious or too trivial to put down in this tall, devilish story'.

Tutuola's is not the standard English literary idiom, but that of day-to-day Nigeria -- a powerful, rhythmic idiom, part-classical English, part-Nigerian Pidgin, part-contemporary Nigerian invention, part-direct

---

295 S. Newell, *West African Literatures* (OUP: Oxford, 2006), p.70.

translation from Yoruba -- and it possesses an incredibly lively energy. Tutuola's struggle is to squeeze the endless vitality of Yoruba oral culture into the yoke of a literary text. His story forms are not stiff or literary and make extensive use of Yoruba folklore and traditions. He blends modern life in English with a Yoruba spiritual inheritance in a complex revelation of change -- what Nobel Prize Winner Wole Soyinka called a series of 'shotgun image-weddings'. As well as the more traditional ghosts and spirits of the forest Tutuola gives us spirit churches, Crown Agents, a TV-handed ghost, bombs and airplanes.

In *The Palm-Wine Drinkard* he tells the story of a boy who is the oldest of eight children, and a palm wine drinker from the age of ten. One day his palm wine tapster, after tapping the 560,000 palm trees of the estate for over fifteen years, falls from the tallest tree and dies. The narrator, soon out of drink, is given to understand that there is a place where dead people go before they pass on to the after-world, and desperate to get his palm wine tapster back, he goes off in search of the place. This is the start of the Drinkard's search:

One fine morning, I took all my native juju and also my father's juju with me and I left my father's hometown to find out whereabouts was my tapster who had died. But in those days, there were many wild animals and every place was covered by thick bushes and forests; again, towns and villages were not near each other as nowadays, and as I was travelling from bushes to bushes and from forests to forests and sleeping inside it for many days and months, I was sleeping on the branches of trees, because spirits etc. were just like partners, and to save my life from them; and again I could spend two or three months before reaching a town or village. Whenever I reached a town or village, I would spend almost four months there, to find out my palm-wine tapster from the inhabitants of that town or village and if he did not reach there, then I would leave there and continue my journey to another town or village. After the seventh month that I had left my home town, I reached a town and went to an old man, this man was not a really man, he was a god and he was eating with his wife when I reached there. When I entered the house I saluted both of them, they answered me well, although nobody should enter his house like that as he was a god, but I myself was a god and a juju-man. Then I told the old man (god) that I am looking for my palm-wine tapster who had died in my town some time ago, he did not answer to my question but asked me first what was my name? I replied that my name was

'Father of the gods' who could do everything in this world, then he said: 'was that true' and I said yes; after that he told me to go to his native blacksmith in an unknown place, or who was living in another town, and bring the right thing that he had told the blacksmith to make for him. He said that if I could bring the right thing that he told the blacksmith to make for him, then he would believe that I was the 'Father of gods who could do everything in this world' and he would tell me where my tapster was.[296]

One of the many adventures concerns a woman 'beautiful as an angel' who could not be persuaded by her father to marry. One day at the market she spots a beautiful 'complete gentleman', dressed in 'the finest and most costly clothes' worth at least £2,000. The man refuses to tell her where he lives and repeatedly advises her to go home, but after the market she follows him into the forest. To her surprise, as he reaches the owners of the various parts of his body, he returns the parts and pays a hire fee. Bit by bit he is reduced to just a head, arms and neck. The lady almost faints and wishes she had listened to her father. The man then returns the arms, neck and the skin that covered his head. Now he is just a skull, and although she tries to run away the skull can jump a mile with ease and so captures her. Trapped in the skull's hole in the ground, surrounded by his skull friends and relatives, she is sat on a large frog with a cowrie shell alarm around her neck.

However, the Drinkard, who is not only a tall storyteller, but a brave and valiant shape shifter, had his eye on the woman, followed the skull man back to his hole, and now rescues the woman by changing into a lizard, then by becoming invisible and finally by flying away as a sparrow, after he has changed the lady into a kitten. For his reward he is given fifty kegs of palm wine and of course he marries the lady. The marriage lasts for six months before he has to resume his search.

The Palm-Wine Drinkard was Tutuola's first book. As he went on to produce further tales in the same vein, many readers felt that Tutuola was simply plundering Yoruba myths and traditional oral storytelling for his materials. The oral storytelling tradition is still strong in sub-Saharan Africa, but is under pressure from TV, Radio and the modern, literate, educated world. Tutuola's significance is that he straddled the oral and the written worlds and his writing of what is clearly an oral

---

296 A. Tutuola, *Palm-Wine Drinkard* (Faber: London, 1952), p.9-10.

storytelling tradition is probably the nearest we can get to the unwritten world as it transits into literate society. While we can say that this book is in many ways a foundation text, it is unlike *Beowulf*, the Bible, the Koran, *Rig Veda* and the other foundation texts in that the author inhabits the modern world and is aware of writing, of modern influences, different models and alternative structures, in ways that the other foundation authors could not have been.

Chinua Achebe's novel *Things Fall Apart* (1958) was one of the first novels from Nigeria written by a member of the emerging university-educated, middle-class intellectual elite, and it appeared at a crucial historical moment, just two years before Independence. His novel, which was to be the first of a trilogy on related themes, was an instant success and since it first appeared has not been out of print. It has been translated into thirty languages and has sold over two million copies.

The novel, which as Achebe has said covers the lifetime of his grandfather, deals with the life and fate of Okonkwo in the days when colonial Europeans had just begun to appear in tribal Nigeria. The collision of the two cultures is partly presented through the dilemmas of Okonkwo's daily life, the colonial rulers' anthropological approach to African life and their attempts to impose their idea of law. The novel is of interest to us here because Achebe presents part of the clash between the Nigerians and the new Colonial rulers as a clash between a literate and an oral culture, between a culture where history, wisdom and knowledge of all kinds are preserved in ancient sayings and folklore, and in the memory of the elders, contrasted with a culture that holds the written word -- understood or not -- to be law. That is, two very different ways of thinking and of preserving law, history, culture and identity.[297]

Post-Disaster Society

Stanisław Lem's *Memoirs Found in a Bathtub* (1971) is an off-beat science fiction novel set in the year 3149, when a terrible paper-destroying blight has obliterated the culture and the entire written history of the planet. However, deep in the heart of a granite mountain, preserved for centuries in isolation, a paper document is discovered. It is the bizarre record of a man trapped in a hermetically sealed underground complex, who has

---

297 C. Achebe, *Things Fall Apart* (London: Heinemann, 1988).

been entrusted with a secret mission which makes no sense to him.[298]

The diary reveals an absurd, bureaucratic world of orders and counter-orders, spies and counter-spies, codes and counter-codes, tactics and counter-tactics -- all directed at an enemy that probably no longer exists. The books reveals the inner workings of bureaucratic paranoia, but also deals with the conflicting needs and despair of a man who is guarding secrets he does not understand in a world that makes no sense to him. When it first appeared communism was still a very strong repressive regime in Poland and the political satire on the massive, suffocating bureaucracy that communism created was very clear. It is possible that the novel was referring obliquely to the events of 1968 in Poland.

The book reveals the curiosity of a future world that has no paper about a world that was once dominated by paper. It reveals how the world without paper finds it very difficult to understand or interpret the meanings recorded in the documents it discovers, and almost impossible to recover how a world with paper actually functioned. This is an interesting reversal of the idea we normally deal with -- where we are curious but cautious about the evidences of the pre-literate world. However, in an age when email and mobile phones are increasingly used instead of paper and when surveillance through the internet and CCTV is growing rapidly as part of a war against an ill-defined 'Terror', the novel is relevant again to the experience of a whole new audience.

Walter Miller Jnr's *A Canticle for Liebowitz* (1960) was hailed as a masterpiece of science fiction and ranked alongside 1984 and *Brave New World*. After the Japanese attack on Pearl Harbor, Miller had enlisted in the Army Air Corps and trained as a radio operator. He took part in fifty-five aerial combat missions in the Second World War, over the Balkans and Italy, including the bombing of the Benedictine monastery at Monte Casino. More than a decade later this experience led him to write this book. In his lifetime (1923-96) he published only this book and two collections of short stories.

The novel deals with a society looking back to a previous era. It is set in the barbarous future after a nuclear holocaust called 'the Deluge' has destroyed civilization, knowledge, learning and all sense of history. In a monastery out in the Texan dessert the monks of Saint Liebowitz

---

298 S. Lem, *Memoirs Found in a Bathtub* (London: Andre Deutsch, 1992). Originally published in Polish as: S. Lem, *Pamiętnik znaleziony w wannie*. (Kraków: Wydawnictwo Literackie, 1971).

have inherited a series of sacred relics that date from before the time of destruction. They spend their lives reverencing, laboriously copying, illuminating and interpreting holy fragments, which they do not understand, in the belief that these texts hold and preserve an ancient knowledge. They hope that one day they will be able to interpret these documents and that they will somehow contribute to a renaissance and to the reconstruction of civilization.

The monks' efforts to interpret and understand what they work so hard to preserve, teeter between comic and tragic, since we know, but the monks do not, that most of their sacred relics are merely electric wiring diagrams, fragments of shopping lists or plumbing schematics. Brother Francis, for example, while out in the desert, finds a hole in the sand which turns out to be an old shelter. He musters his modest command of pre-Deluge English and reads haltingly the words 'Fallout Survival Shelter':

> The first word was enough for Francis. He had never seen a 'Fallout', and he hoped he'd never see one. A consistent description of the monster had not survived, but Francis had heard the legends. He crossed himself and backed away from the hole. Tradition told that Beatus Leibowitz himself had encountered a Fallout, and had been possessed by it for many months before the exorcism which accompanied his Baptism drove the fiend away. [299]

He is clearly referring to radiation sickness.

Russell Hoban's *Ridley Walker* (1980) is set in Kent in the remote future, a long time after a nuclear war has destroyed civilization. It is a vivid and harrowing tale that makes effective use of an entirely in a new kind of English -- a degraded, broken down, idiomatic spoken language. This is not the kind of English spoken before the 'one big one', a nuclear war, but it is a kind of English that has grown up afterwards. This a bitter, melancholy post-literate fable where the local population struggles to understand its history and worries that they might repeat the mistakes that led to the 'one big one', though of course none of them can say what this was or how it might be avoided.

The book appeared at the height of the Cold War and worries about nuclear confrontation to rave reviews: 'Extraordinary', 'a cult book', 'remarkable', 'unique', 'dizzying'. It is useful to us because it is an attempt to show how

---

299 W. M. Miller Jnr, *A Canticle for Leibowitz* (Corgi: London, 1960), p.14.

language changes --particularly where it is not defined and refined by writing. It is also useful because it attempts to show that both scientific and historical knowledge cannot be 'fixed' or transmitted accurately without writing: their culture, history and law are interpreted and preserved for them (rather like the travelling storyteller in Frank Delaney's *Ireland: The Novel*) through the oral tradition of a travelling Punch and Judy puppet show. Without knowledge fixed by writing, civilization simply cannot grow and society is doomed to struggle with itself.

Walter Tevis's *Mockingbird* (1980) is a science fiction novel which lays out a future world where humans are numbed and mentally immobilized by drugs and pornography. They have long ceased to do any work as this is performed by a vast series of robots. The novel follows the fortunes of two young people who have by some strange twist of fate managed to avoid the general state of human apathy: Bentley is a young man from rural Ohio who has taught himself to read and who has travelled to New York in the hope that he can persuade the University to let him teach the subject: Mary Lou is a very intelligent young woman who was scheduled for extinction at birth, but who has refused to take drugs, has run away from her dorm and taken up residence in the zoo.[300]

The third character is a robot called Spoforth, who is currently Dean of the University and Governor of New York, the last and most intelligent robot ever built. He wants to be human, or at least to recover the full memories -- the memories of the human on which his own intelligence and programming was based -- that lurk at the edge of his consciousness. However, Spoforth is also responsible for including chemicals in the drugs the humans take, and for supplying recreational drugs that render them incapable of breeding. Spoforth is responsible for an edict that teaching reading is a crime: as humans can no longer read they do not heed the warnings about sterility written on the food and drug packaging. No one can remember the last time a child was born and it seems that humans are destined to die out very soon. All across New York the few remaining depressed humans are drugging themselves into a final blissful 'high' and then setting themselves on fire.

These three characters play out a bizarre and complex relationship. Bentley, unaware of the prohibition on teaching reading, has taught himself to read and wants to teach reading: Mary Lou falls in love with

---

300 W. Tevis, *Mockingbird* (London: Gollancz/Orion, 1980).

Bentley, who has been set to work by Spoforth taping the written sections of silent movies for the archives, teaches Mary Lou to read. A whole new world opens up for Mary Lou as she begins to set down the 'memory of her life'. Spoforth imprisons Bentley for teaching Mary Lou to read and for breaking the 'Privacy Laws' by cohabiting with her. But then in an effort to become more human, Spoforth takes the now pregnant Mary Lou to live with him so that he can become a father to the child.

For these characters reading represents access to the past, to the events that led to this situation. But it also leads them to access their own personal feelings and to the enlargement of their intelligence and their personality. Reading is not only self-education in a world where humans are deemed to need no such thing, but an act of refusal and revolt and recovery. The book is about the passion, joy and enthusiasm that a man and a woman discover in each other, but also about the way that books and the acts of reading and writing help them to unlock the world and enhance their own inner lives.

Ray Bradbury's *Fahrenheit 451* (1954) is a classic work of science fiction by one of the pioneers of the genre. It is an eerie, prophetic novel about a future where happiness is allocated on TV, where individual eccentricities are outlawed, where reading, study and scholarship are illegal, and where all books, which have been identified by the government as the cause of all unhappiness and discontent, are burned by a special task force of Firemen. The book derives its title from the temperature at which paper is said to burn. This is the story of Montag, one of the task force Firemen. Trained by the state to be its obedient servant and to destroy books of any kind wherever he finds them, Montag, nevertheless, one day reads a book and automatically becomes an outlaw. The fact that Montag can read at all in a society dedicated to promoting illiteracy is perhaps a weakness in the plotting, but it is also an indication of Montag's predisposition to independent thought. This book shows a world that is fast becoming illiterate and where the privacy of the imagination is feared. It shows how books and reading perform a subversive, democratic and humanising role in preserving imagination, sympathy, insight, individuality, identity, privacy and independent thought.

Fahrenheit 451 also indicates how books might survive in even the most hostile regime. In the final scene of the book, set in a grove out in the wilderness, Montag, who has finally run away from the city and his job as a Fireman, is introduced to the people of the resistance not by their names but by the authors and titles they have committed to memory as they pace back and forth -- *Ecclesiastes*, *Revelation*, Plato's *Republic*, *Gulliver's Travels*, Marcus Aurelius, Byron, Machiavelli, Tom Paine.[301]

The Nobel Prize winner Günter Grass said:

> And even if one day people stop or are forced to stop writing and publishing, if books are no longer available, there will still be storytellers giving us mouth-to-ear artificial respiration, spinning old stories in new ways: loud and soft, heckling and halting, now close to laughter, now on the brink of tears.[302]

While it is reassuring for Grass to say this in his Nobel lecture, the novelists mentioned here have made it clear that a complex society, civilization, science and technology cannot be created or sustained by oral storytellers and an oral culture. However, while emphasizing the importance of writing, these novels also emphasize the fragility of our civilization and remind us that writing, literacy and books are not things we can take for granted: writing could so easily have failed to develop, and, as the Taliban has proved, can so easily be taken away.

*

It is possible to map all these tales to the major theoretical texts about oral culture and history -- Jan Vansina, *Oral Tradition* (1965), W. J. Ong, *Orality and Literacy* (1982), Jack Goody, *The Power of the Written Tradition* (2000), A. B. Lord, *The Singer of Tales* (2000).[303] However, the only academic text I have found so far which touches on the issue of human pre-history in literature, and in passing, on the theme of worlds without writing, is

---

301 R. Bradbury, *Fahrenheit 451* (Corgi: London, 1974), pp.144-47.
302 Günter Grass, 'To be Continued', *Nobel* Lecture, Swedish Academy, Börssalen, Stockholm, 7 December 1999: www.nobelprize.org/nobel_prizes/literature/laureates/1999/grass-lecture.
303 W. J. Ong, *Orality and Literacy* (London: Methuen, 1982); J. Goody, *The Power of the Written Tradition* (Washington DC: Smithsonian Books, 2000); J. Vansina, *Oral Tradition* (Harmondsworth: Penguin, 1965); A.B. Lord, *The Singer of Tales* (Harvard: Harvard University Press, 2000).

De Paolo's, *Human History in Fiction* (2002)[304] so this idea is still relatively unexplored.

The novels and stories discussed here are all imaginative attempts to consider the idea of a society without writing, particularly the transition from a literary to an oral culture and the cataclysmic transition from a highly civilized world back into an oral culture. Each in its own way alerts us to some aspect of the culture of writing and the links between the civilization we enjoy, the act of writing and the preservation in writing of knowledge, experience and intuitions painfully acquired over thousands of years. As Marshal McLuhan put it:

> Until writing was invented, man lived in acoustic space: boundless, directionless, horizonless, in the dark of the mind, in the world of emotion, by primordial intuition, by terror. Speech is a social chart of this bog. The goose quill put an end to talk. It abolished mystery; it gave architecture and towns; it brought roads and armies, bureaucracy. It was the basic metaphor with which the cycle of civilization began, the step from the dark into the light of the mind. The hand that filled the parchment page built a city. [305]

304 C.de Paolo, *Human History in Fiction* (McFarland & Co: N. Carolina, 2002).
305 M. McLuhan, *The Medium is the Massage: An Inventory of Effects* (Penguin: Harmondsworth, 1967), p.48.

Directed Study

Read *The Palm-Wine Drinkard*. Do you think it might be a 'transitional text'? Why?

Would you say *The Palm-Wine Drinkard* is basically an oral tale that just happens to have been written down? If so, on what evidence?

What evidence can you see in *The Palm-Wine Drinkard* of a Nigerian oral storytelling tradition?

What do you think a novelist like Amos Tutuola or a poet like Linton Kwesi Johnson could have in common with Homer and the poets of the ancient world?

If you had to be one of the 'talking books' in Ray Bradbury's *Fahrenheit 451,* which book would you choose to be? Why? What difficulties do you imagine you would face in trying to become that book?

On the evidence of Frank Delaney's *Ireland: A Novel* what do you think were the main ingredients for oral storytelling? What, according to Delaney, might the national, political and cultural role of the storyteller be? What social and political changes have affected the role of the traditional storyteller in Ireland?

Look again at the early parts of the Bible. Can you see any elements that might connect with the song-lines of Australia as described in Bruce Chatwin's Songlines?

Without writing in what ways did traditional Nigerian society and culture function, according to Chinua Achebe's *Things Fall Apart*, with regard to knowledge, wisdom, law, history and identity?

The Neanderthals in William Golding's *The Inheritors* and in Jean Auel's *Clan of the Cave Bear* are imagined with very different communicative abilities. Which you think is the more likely version? Why?

8
LANGUAGE AS RAW MATERIAL: WRITERS AND WORDS

Language is the material writers work with. Language is a writer's business. This chapter indicates that perhaps what marks off writers from most other language users on the planet is the degree to which they pay attention to words, understand, create, manipulate and develop language. Indeed many writers are of the opinion that a writer's responsibility for and towards words is a task which is intrinsically ethical. Their success depends on developing an awareness of language, a skill in using language, an ability to make new language and the power to make language do what they want it to. But problems of representation abound -- for example, what is a word, exactly? And in what ways can a word represent even a small part of what we want to say?

- Different Approaches to Defining a Word
- A Unit of eaning
- A Group of Sound Features
- Dictionary Entries
- Some Short Word Histories
- The Emotional Content of Words

The English language is like squirrel hoarding nuts. It has a huge store of words -- many of them 'borrowed' from other languages. At a conservative estimate English has over 500,000 words. It has been said that in the twentieth century alone some 200,000 new words were added -- most of them technical or scientific.

Shakespeare's plays indicate he had a vocabulary of over 30,000 words -- a much wider vocabulary than most of his contemporaries -- though that does not mean he used all of this vocabulary in everyday speech. Now, most people use a vocabulary of about 5,000 words and have a further 10,000 words in their passive vocabulary. Members of the professions that make extensive use of words -- university educated teachers and lawyers -- are thought to use only about 36,000 words. It has been said that the average student by the end of their studies has (for a short time at least) a passive vocabulary of around 40,000 words, while university lecturers have a passive vocabulary of over 73,000 words. On the other hand, BT says that 96 per cent of phone conversations get by on 737 words.[306]

The main problem in studying words is that of defining words. Most of us assume we know what a word is, but when it comes down to it, we have no hard and fast, generally agreed definition. Even linguists lack a single unified, universally applicable definition of what a word is. And if you Google for '*word: definition*' you get no less than 1,140,000,000 hits -- so you can see the size of the problem. Beyond a rough understanding that words, when they are not being spoken, are probably those things between the white spaces on a printed page, there is no agreement.

To approach the idea of the word through texts alone is to hamper ourselves right from the start. Most words are spoken, not written. And even the simple statement that words are surrounded by white space is not necessarily true -- we have no white spaces when we speak. In many cultures individual written words have not been marked out by spaces in the text. Ancient Sanskrit, Phoenician, Greek and Latin did not have spaces between the words. Indeed spaces were invented by Irish monks around AD 600, but took a long time to catch on elsewhere in the world. Some written languages like ancient Oscan and modern Amharic use dots•as•word•dividers•rather•than•white•spaces. Modern Japanese, Korean and Chinese scripts manage perfectly well with an entirely different system.

We may have no adequate agreed definition of a word, but to say we have no concept of the word would be mistaken. Even in non-literate societies language is recognized as an entity of some sort, even an entity

---

306 G. Deutscher, *Through the Language Glass: How Words Colour Your World* (Heinemann: London, 2010), p.110.

of considerable power, but as Walter J. Ong has pointed out in entirely unwritten languages, as the early texts indicate by running words together, there is often no sense of, or term for, the 'word'. That is, the sense of a word as a discrete, unchanging item does not figure.[307]

The problem of the definition of 'a word' is one for literate societies and literate people, people who compile, consult and refer to dictionaries and who are aware of the way language and writing work. It does not necessarily concern the rest. However, with or without a definition, most of us are fairly confident that we know a word when we see or hear one. But let's not dismiss the possibility of defining a word completely. There are several possible approaches to the definition of words and each gives us a partially successful idea.

We sometimes assume that writing is a case of merely putting things into words: if we think about it we have to admit that this is too simple and it is really a case of finding 'the right word'. But even this is not enough to define the process that a writer goes through when thinking about representing a thought, feeling or idea in writing. The poet Ted Hughes spoke about words not as a linguist or dictionary maker, but as a writer:

> It is when we set out to find words for some seemingly quite simple experience that we begin to realize what a huge gap there is between our understanding of what happens around us and inside us, and the words we have at our command to say something about it.
>
> Words are tools learned late and laboriously and easily forgotten, with which we try to give some part of our experience a more or less permanent shape outside ourselves. They are unnatural, in a way, and far from being ideal for the job. For one thing, a word has its own definite meanings. A word has its own little solar system of meanings. Yet we are wanting it to carry some part of our meaning, of the meaning of our experience, and the meaning of our experience is finally unfathomable, it reaches into our toes and back to before we were born and into the atom, with vague shadows and changing features and elements that no expression of any kind can take hold of. And this is true of even the simplest experiences.[308]

But nevertheless we try to represent our ideas in words. We have no choice.

---

307 W. J. Ong, *Orality and Literacy* (Routledge: London, 1982, p.60.
308 T. Hughes, *Poetry in the Making* (Faber: London, 1969), p.119.

Different Approaches to Defining a Word

But the fact remains that there is, as yet, no standard, all-embracing, cast iron definition of what a word is. Where does that leave us? How can we use words, and trust words, if we don't know what they are? The Lexicographer Tom McArthur has said that, while we might not have a single definition of a word, most words have several of eight features in common, and that words can best be defined by reference to these features.[309]

1. The orthographic word. That is, words which can be understood in terms of a particular alphabetic or writing system at a particular time in history. He warns that words may take a non-standard or non-canonical form -- for example the word *merry* has at various times in the past been written as *myry*, *myrie*, *murie* and *mery*. And it may be that there is more than one form of the word e.g. US *color* and Br *colour*. It must also be said that spelling is fluid even in the present day. For example we could write *ice-cream* or *ice cream; landowners* or *land owners; pocket knife* or *pocketknife; toy shop* or *toyshop*. They refer to the same thing.

2. The phonological word. That is a word understood in terms of its sound, which occurs as part of an utterance rather than alone and which may be subject to rhythm or stress. English has both stressed and unstressed syllables, but experienced native listeners or speakers know the difference between: *It's no good at all* and *Snow good a tall*. They also know the difference between *a notion* and *an ocean*. On paper these words have a white space around them and different spelling to help the reader, but in speech their syllable boundaries are not so clear and it is the context that establishes which option the speaker intends.

3. The morphological word. That is the form that lies behind the word. The word *big* can be spelled out as *b.i.g.* or it can be spoken big, but the concept exists independent of either the spelling or the pronunciation since it can be indicated by sign language and can be applied to many different substances and situations. The word *colour* may be spelled

---

309 T. McArthur, *Living Words: Language, Lexicography and the Knowledge Revolution* (Exeter University Press: Exeter, 1998), p.42-9.

differently on either side of the Atlantic, and within European languages its cognate will be pronounced in many different ways, but the notion behind it is common to all speakers of these languages and can give rise to other words that make use of it – *colourful, discoloured, multi-coloured* etc.

4. The lexical word (also known as the full word, content word, lexeme, lexical item). This is a very open set and includes: nouns, verbs and adjectives relating to things, actions and states, often occurring in more than one version e.g.: *do, does, doing, did, done.* Lexical words may be simple in structure: *cat, mouse,* or they may be complex: *cold-bloodedness, incomprehensible, teapot, blackbird, Commonwealth, stamp collector, put up with, natural selection, Parkinson's disease.*

Another way of defining this category is to say that these are words you would find in the dictionary. However, sometimes the forms of the words listed in the dictionary are connected in ways that a dictionary is not really suited t explain. For example: *take, takes, taken, took, taking, taker* appear in the dictionary as five separate forms, when in fact they are variations on the same form, each with a different grammatical function.

Another part of the definition of a lexical word is that it is the basic form of any word, before inflection, plural, tense, gender etc affect it. For example, *dog* would be a base form, but *dogs* would be an inflection. *Oats* would be a base form that has no inflection. Yet *Police*, since it is the plural form and has no singular, is both the base form and the inflection.

In English *be* has up to eight different forms, but most words have five forms. However in some inflected languages, like Russian, Polish, Latin or French a word may have several dozen forms.

5. The grammatical word. (Also known as base form, form word, function word, structure word, the morpheme) One definition of this is: a word that has a function as part of the system of the language but carries no content, rather like a lubricant, a linking lexical word: this category includes conjunctions, determiners, interjections, particles and pronouns: e.g. *if, of, a, and, the, have, who, up, down, in, out.*

Grammatical words are often contrasted with content words. Thus in the phrase 'a bottle of wine' *a* and *of* are grammatical words with no content, but *bottle* and *wine* are content words rather than grammatical.

There is some debate as to whether *in, with, we, this, that* and *for* should be included as grammatical words since they do seem to have some content as well as function. Generally these words are said to be grammatical rather than content words since their function is more important than their content.

6. The onomastic word. These are words that name or establish a special status or unique reference, for example, the difference between *Jean-Paul* and *The Pope*; Smith and Smithsonian. These words are not a part of the normal vocabulary, they have to be learned even by native speakers, and while they are not always listed in dictionaries, they are usually found in encyclopaedias.

7. The lexicographical word. The word as it is found in dictionaries, usually presented in an alphabetic set-up. Cross referencing *did* and *do*, *them* and *they* etc. There are two kinds of entries: words the dictionary maker thought people might want to look up and then the citations and references under which the definition of the word proceeds.

8. The statistical word. The word as it occurs in a word count. The word counter deals in token words -- items on the page surrounded by white space including numerals, abbreviations codes, names etc.

9. The ninth category
There is a ninth 'catch-all' category, which McArthur calls *Other Words*. This category includes:

a) word-like units, that is, things that act like words. For example compound units that include the word word: base word, buzz word, compound word, long word, root word.

b) words that use *ism: Americanism, malapropism.*

c) words combining *onym*, eg: *synonym, antonym.*

d) terms that relate to the form of a word: *abbreviation, acronym, compound word, port-manteau word.*

e) terms that relate to social usage: *anagram, buzz word, confusable, loanword, nonce word, palindrome, stunt word, vogue word.*

There are several areas of language that McArthur does not attempt to categorize – for example logograms like I ♥ U and emoticons like the smiley face - ☺.

There are many other ways of defining words, but this is McArthur's system.

A Unit of Meaning

The first is to say that a word is a unit of meaning. This, however, runs into immediate problems since the only way to define a unit of meaning is by recourse to example, and what may be a unit of meaning in one language may not be acceptable in another: and what may be a unit of meaning in spoken language may be different from that in written language.

In Hungarian, for example, it is possible to produce compound words of enormous length by tagging bits onto the end. Palmer quotes an example from the Siberian Koryak language where they can produce one word for the phrase 'They always lie to us'. In the Alaskan Yup'ik language there is one word for a phrase like 'He wants to get a big boat' -- *angyaghllangyugtuq*.

There is also one word in Yup'ik for the phrase: 'The two of them were apparently really hungry' -- *kaipiallrulliniuk*. It is possible to break the word down into its component parts. *Kaig* 'be hungry'; *piar* 'really'; *llru* past tense marker; *llini* 'apparently'; *u* indicative 'that'/'those/ they'; k 'two'. The same website that provided these examples from Yup'ik also provided a one-word sentence for: 'I guess she probably didn't really want to go for those short little trips, did she?' So it would seem that in some languages it is difficult to draw a distinction between a word and a sentence: what may be a word in one language, with a clearly defined single sense, in another language may be a sentence with several elements.

In English the nearest we can get to this is probably the word *antidisestablishmentarianism*. Some would argue that there is only one unit of meaning here, while others would say that we are dealing with a compound word made up of several distinct units of meaning. However, a compound word is still a word and it does all the things any normal self-respecting word can do.

In French they use four words to say 'I do not know': *Je ne sais pas* (literally: I not know not). In English we can say: *Dunno* instead of *I do not know*. But the 'word' *dunno* does not appear in the dictionary, so is it in fact a word?

How accurate is it to say that a word is a unit of meaning, when in one language it is a short item, but in another is a long phrase of several units yoked together?

A Group of Sound Features

The second possible definition of a word is to say that it is a group of sound features from a given language.

In some languages it is possible to recognize a word by the stress pattern. In Polish for example, the stress is regular -- always on the last but one syllable -- but in English, Russian and Greek, the stress jumps about all over the place. Greek at least marks where the stress should fall with an accent, the other languages do not.

Also the way in which words may be joined together does not always allow us to easily distinguish between one word and another. It is possible to confuse words like: *a tack* and *attack*.

Another problem is that, depending on the speed and pronunciation of the individual speaker, it is not always possible to identify individual words in speech. When we speak there are no white spaces. Also: We. Do. Not. Pause. Between. Each. Word. We. Utter. And (capital A) we don't (apostrophe t) indicate punctuation in speech either, (comma) do we (question mark)? At least in English we don't. However, some languages show their grammar in both spoken and written forms. In Japanese they indicate the main subject of the sentence with the word *wah, and* indicate questions by putting the question marker *ka* at the end.

The idea that a word is a collection of sound features is useful, but only up to a point -- it also rather incomplete.

Dictionary Entries

A third approach is to simply assume that words are what appear in a dictionary. However, this is not always very helpful. Tom McArthur, a professional lexicographer and the editor of *English Today*, has pointed out that what may be instantly recognized as a word in one language may not be a word in another.[310] For example if we look at the words *reál, realitas, réalité,* and *realidad* we can see immediately that they are connected to our own words *real, really, realty* and *reality*. We might even say that they are in effect the same words, or at least clearly connected to them. However, they are not English words and we will not find them in an English dictionary.

Apart from the obvious problem that in order to find a word in a dictionary you have to know roughly how to spell it, which means you have to know on some level what the word *is*, there is the additional problem that even in a dictionary -- especially in a dictionary -- a word can have several meanings.

The word *ear* (as in, on the side of your head) and *ear* (as in corn) have absolutely different origins and histories and refer to entirely different things, yet they are written and pronounced identically. So, are they the same word, or different words?

A *foot* (one the end of a leg) and a *foot* (as in twelve inches) is another case in point. But that is not the end of it. We have *foot of the bed, foot of the staircase, foot of a cliff,* where in each case foot actually means 'the base of something'. Also there's: *what's afoot?, dirty work afoot* and *foot the bill.*

And what can we make of a word like *read*? In the past tense this is pronounced the same as the word *red*. But everywhere else it is pronounced the same as reed. Are *read* (reed) and *read* (red) the same words?

The same might be asked of *take, taken, takes, took, taking* where each word is an aspect of the word *take*.

Even small basic words, it seems, cannot be taken for granted. For example -- there are eight dictionary entries for the verb *to be (be, is, are, am, being, was, were, will)*. They are all part of the verb *to be* but are they all the same word?

If you were a foreign learner and you knew the word *go*, but wanted to find the past tense, you would have considerable difficulty discovering the relationship between *go* and *went*. If English had a regular past tense for this word you might assume that the past tense of *go* was **goed*. And since went does not look like a past tense, a learner might feel confused that it was not possible to say simply 'I will went to the shop'* instead of 'I will go to the shop', or feel that **wented* was more obviously appropriate

---

310 T. McArthur, *Living Words: Language, Lexicography and the Knowledge Revolution,* pp.42-9.

as a past tense form of went. But in English it isn't. So are *go* and *went* the same word or different forms of the same word? Clearly they are related to each other in the minds of native speakers, but they have separate entries in the dictionary and absolutely different forms.

Most words in English have only up four possible forms. But in other languages it is not unusual for a word to have a dozen different grammatical forms and endings and there are some languages with many more possible forms for each word. In Finnish, for example, some words can have as many as seventeen different forms. The dictionary records single items, but it does not necessarily gather together areas of meaning. In fact we can't turn to the dictionary with any great hope of help in defining words though their history or through an area of meaning. A dictionary records only the meaning current at the time it went to press. If we want to see how the meanings of words change through time we have to go to a specialist etymological dictionary like the Oxford English Dictionary (OED).

Short Word Histories

<u>KING</u> In its present form king is an Anglo Saxon word, but its history goes back much further than that. Its ancestor was the Germanic word *kuninggaz*, which survived into modern German as *könig*, into Dutch as *koning*, Swedish as *konung*, and Danish as *konge*, and from which English derives the words kin, kindred, kind and king (Shakespeare's Hamlet you may remember puns on *kin* and *kind*). Some etymologists think it unlikely the original word referred to a royal person, but instead it seems to derive from the Indo-European noun *kunjam* meaning race or people and is part of a series of modern words that trace their ancestry back to an even earlier Proto-Indo European word *gene, *gon, *gn denoting some kind of offspring or production.[311] The Latin derivative of this gave us *gender, general, generate, genital* and *nature*; the Greek offshoot produced *gene, genetic, gonorrhoea*.

---

311 In linguistics an asterisk * indicates that something is either conjectural --
that there is no written evidence for it -- or that it is not something a native speaker
would normally produce.

<u>SNOW</u> The Indo-European word for snow is thought to be something like *snigwh* or *snoighwos*. The Germanic descendant of this word was *snaiwaz*, which evolved into German *schnee*, Dutch *sneeuw*, Swedish *snö*, Danish *sne* and English snow. The Slavonic version of the word produced Polish *snieg*, Russian *sneg*, Latvian *sniegs* and Czech *snoh*. In Latin it became *nix*, from which descended French *niege*, Italian *neve*, Spanish *nieve*, Welsh *nyf* (now obsolete). But the word has survived in India in the Sanskrit word *snehas* meaning slippery or greasy.

<u>PEN</u> The English word *pen* derives from Middle English *penne* (feather or quill), which in turn came from Old French *penna* (wing or feather) which in turn had come from Latin *pesna* and perhaps Old Lain *petsna* meaning flying. This can be traced back to Greek περνω and πετώ (perno and peto, to fly) and Sanskrit *patram* (a feather). They all derive from the Indo-European root word *pet.

<u>PENCIL</u> Etymologically the word pencil means 'a little penis'. It probably derives from a lost Indo-European root word *pe, which gave rise to Greek πέος (peos) and Sanskrit *pasas* meaning penis. The current sense of the word as a wooden tube filled with a graphite rod used for writing and drawing did not emerge until the seventeenth century. It came from the Vulgar Latin *penicellum*, a diminutive of *peniculus* (brush or broom, itself a diminutive of *penis*, meaning a *tail*) via Old French *pincel* and modern French *pinceau*, meaning a paintbrush. It is probably also related to the Latin words beginning with *pen*, meaning interior, inside, within, which gave rise to the series of English words *penetrate, penetration, penetrator, impenetrable* etc.

<u>WRITING</u> The English word *writing* derives from the Anglo Saxon writan. This word is a cognate with several words in the Germanic languages: Old Frisian *writa*, meaning to scratch, score or mark by rubbing; Old Scandinavian *writan* meaning to cut; Old High German *rizan* meaning to tear or to draw; Old Norse *rita* meaning to score or to write; Icelandic *rikh* meaning to write. The word in Anglo Saxon seems to have derived from an ancient Germanic root word *writanan, which referred to scratching runes and symbols on stone or wood with sharp tools. This sense of scratching a sign has long been forgotten as the original meaning developed to include the action of marking parchment or paper with signs.

WRITING THE WORLD

READ With the invention and spread of writing a word was needed to signify the act of interpreting signs. To the early Germanic tribes it would seem the act of reading was a mystery that only the wisest could master. The ancient Germanic word *raedanan, meaning to meaning to advise, consider, discern, take council or guess. The idea of taking council can be seen in an Anglo Saxon king's name: Æþelræd -- literally 'of good council'. However, usually attached to this king's name is the epithet Unræd, which is often rendered by text books as unready, but actually meant 'without-counsel'. The word appears in a wide range of Germanic languages: Teutonic and Old English raedan; Old Frisian rida; Old Scandinavian radan; Old High German ratan; Old Norse ráða; Gothic reda; it is related to the modern German word rathen and the English word riddle; the nineteenth-century Scottish dialect revival produced the word rede, which, though the revival failed, allowed the word to survive as a conscious archaism into Tolkien's Lord of the Rings.

However, although most examples of the word come from the Germanic language group, in addition to the Germanic languages, the word also appears in several other Indo-European languages: Old Irish im-radim; Old Slavonic raditi, meaning to take thought or attend to something; Sanskrit radh, meaning to succeed or to accomplish something. Almost certainly the ancient Germanic word derived a much older Indo-European root word.

FART We find this word slightly rude these days, but it is in fact a very ancient word. The Indo-European root words *perd and *pezd, were imitation words, probably meaning to break wind softly. The word seems to be present in all the Indo-European languages:

Sanskrit:	pardate
Greek:	perdo & perdizo
Latin:	podere
French:	péter (as in pétard)
Lithuanian:	perdzu
Russian:	perdet'
Polish:	pierdziec
Albanian:	pjerdh (fart loudly)
German:	farzen & furzen
Swedish:	fjärta
Danish:	fjerte

The Greek word also evolved into *perdix*, the name of a bird, which eventually became the Latin word *perdrix*, the French *perdreau* and the modern English *partridge*. Apparently the noise the bird made when it was disturbed and whirred into the air was reminiscent of a fart.[312]

The word fart is first recorded in English in a beautiful song probably written by a monk at Reading Abbey in the years 1200–50:

Summer is icumen in --
Lhude sing! cuckoo.
Awe bleteth after lomb
Lhouth after calve cu, (cow lows after calf)
Bulloc sterteth, bucke verteth,
Murie sing! cuckoo.[313]

St Augustine used the Latin word in *The City of God* (AD 430); Geoffrey Chaucer used the English word in *The Miller's Tale* (c. 1390–95); Ben Jonson used it in *The Alchemist* (1610) and it was common enough in the eighteenth century for both Swift and Johnson to use it.

BEER The word beer seems to derive ultimately from the Indo-European root **bheu* (meaning to grow). In ancient Sanskrit the word became *bhu*. The Old Teutonic forms of the word might have been **beuro* and/or **beuwo*, derived from the word for barley. This form of the word in its Slavonic variant may well have been the root for the Polish, Czech and Russian word for beer -- *piwo*. The Gothic form for the word barley might have been **biggwis*, close to the Old Norse, Danish and Swedish words *bygg, byg* and *bjug*, all referring to four-rowed barley which could grow in northern Europe. But also, and from time to time, the word meant the better quality six-rowed barley sometimes known as *bear*. And this word seems to have been close kin to the Old English word *beow* meaning grain. Once divorced from its direct reference to grain, beer was probably a general word for drink. The same Indo-European root was probably the source of the Latin words *biber* and *bibere* (drink), from which English also takes the words *beverage, bibulous, imbibe, bibber* and possibly *bib*. Strangely, and to confuse things a little, the main Old English word for beer was ale. The word beer (Old English *beor*) did not gain wide usage until the fifteenth century.

---

312 M. Morton, *Dirty Words: The Story of Sex Talk*, (Atlantic Books: London, 2005), p.126.
313 R. T. Davies (ed.) *Medieval English Lyrics*, (Faber: London, 1963), p.52.

<u>PAL</u> The word seems to have come from Indo-European and survived into Sanskrit as the word *bhratr* or *bhratar*, meaning brother. It survived into several other languages too: Greek *phrater*, Latin *frater*, Breton *breur*, German *bruder*, Dutch *broeder*, Danish and Swedish *broder*, Slavonic *brat*, Tokharian *pracar* and *procer*, US buddy and English brother. It also survived in several Romany languages. Turkish Romany dialects had *pral* and *plal*; Transylvanian Romany dialects had *peral* meaning comrade, mate, partner, chum: an accomplice in crime or dishonesty. The word pal is first recorded in English in 1681 (OED) as criminal cant or slang and it derived from English Romany, *pral, phal* or *phral*, meaning brother, friend, mate.

<u>BREW</u> There seems to be a connection from the word beer to the word brew. The ancestral meaning of brew was to do with heating, and it comes from an Indo-European root word **breuro, *bhreu* or **bhru* -- meaning to make a drink by boiling. There is a possible Sanskrit cognate in the word *bhrjj*, meaning roast. The word has a cognate in Latin *defrutum* (new boiled wine) and the OED also cites a Thracian version of the word meaning beer. Fermentation may have been a secondary connotation for the word, and the form **beuro* (grain - beer) may well be derived from this word.

The English word brew, though it probably derives from Indo-European, was carried into English via the Old Teutonic form bru meaning to make a decoction or to infuse (from which modern English *broth* and *bread* -- as something cooked or fermented -- also seem to derive). The earliest recorded written example of brew in English comes in the year 893. Brew has a wide variety of written forms and is still common not only in English but throughout the Germanic languages. The Indo-European root word is probably also the source of the Latin word *fervere* (meaning to boil), from which English derives *fever, fervent* and *ferment*, and also the second part of the word *comfrey*. Some etymologists have also linked the word *brew* with the word *burn*.

GAY The origins of the word are disputed. Judy Grahn, in her book *Another Mother Tongue*, says the word *gay* derives from the Greek goddess Gaia -- the mother earth figure.[314] This is unlikely. Another version has it that English took the word from French *gaieté*, which could be traced back to Old French gai meaning happy, light hearted, merry, in high spirits, which perhaps derived from Frankish and Old High German *gahi*, meaning swift or headlong, which had also yielded Middle High German *gach* and *gaehe* and modern German *jäh*, meaning impetuous, sudden, impulsive. However, other scholars trace it back through French to Old High German *wahi*, with a possible meaning of slack or loose fitting.

Chaucer used the word of men and women, to mean happy or jolly. In The Miller's Tale, (c. 1387) he described the character of Absalon as *jolif* and *gay*. However, when Gervys suggests that Absolon is troubled in his sleep by thought of 'som ga gerl' (l.3779) there is more than a hint of sexuality about the word. It seems that Shakespeare thought of the word as meaning a female prostitute because in *Othello* (c. 1601–04) Iago refers to his ideal woman as someone who 'Never lacked gold, and yet went never gay' (*Othello*, II i 150).

However, by the sixteenth century, the word was also being used to refer to men who were self-indulgent or sexually promiscuous. By the eighteenth century the word had come to mean given to pleasure, pleasure-seeking, promiscuous, dissipated -- as in *he's a gay dog* and *gay house* i.e. a brothel. In the late eighteenth century the term applied to women working as prostitutes. A *gay bit* or *gay lady* was a prostitute; but a *gaying instrument* was a penis and *gaying* it meant to have sex.

The word was still used in these senses until the late 1960s. However, the meaning had begun to shift by the end of the nineteenth century. In 1889 a gay club in London was prosecuted and one of the male prostitutes working at the club, when questioned, referred to one of his male associates as 'gay', meaning that he too was a male prostitute. This is the earliest recorded use of the word in reference to homosexuality.[315] The late twentieth century sense of *gay* as homosexual, which first appeared in the 1950s, seems to have arisen from an earlier US slang term -- *geycat* or *gay cat*, meaning the young male companion of an older male tramp. The implication of a homosexual relationship was carried forward in the

---

314 J. Grahn, *Another Mother Tongue* (Beacon Press: Boston, Mass, 1984).
315 G. Hughes, *Swearing* (Penguin: Harmondsworth, 1998), pp.232-33.

1930s when the term was applied to any young homosexual.

By the 1960s *gaycat* had been abbreviated to *gay*, but the heterosexual use of the word lingered on and through the early 1960s a *gay deceiver* was a padded bra. *Gayola* was an illegal payment made to the police to enable the running of illicit gay clubs in the US. In 1969 police raided the gay club The Stonewall Inn in Greenwich Village, New York. It was the latest in a series of raids, but this time instead of accepting police harassment, the customers rioted. It was turning point for gay activism.

The word gay now means homosexual and to use it any other way is to court misunderstanding. In 1971 the term *gay pride* appeared, used to describe the second birthday of the Gay Liberation Movement. Homosexuals connected this movement and adopted the word *gay* as a self-description in the 1970s, mainly because they disliked the medical connotations of the term 'homosexual' but also as a way of stripping their identification of any pejorative sense.

However, on US university campuses, at about the same time the word also came to mean stupid, ugly eccentric -- a paradoxical response to the use of the word gay as a politically correct term for homosexual. A *gay basher* was a 'real man' who went out of his way to find and beat up homosexual men. In the 1980s many gay men and women developed *gaydar* -- radar for detecting other gays. Now the word is a standard part of the language -- we have *gay rights, gay liberation, gay activism, gay youth, gay bars* etc.

In recent years radical homosexuals and lesbians have preferred to return to the more confrontational term *queer*. Although some lesbians refer to themselves as *gay* or *gay chicks* the term is usually restricted to male homosexuals. With the decline in the acceptability of terms like *homo, faggot* and *queer, gay* is currently the Standard English term for male homosexuals.

The Emotional Content of Words

Clearly as writers our choice of words is made by reference to the emotions we want to suggest or to examine. However, just because a word has a particular emotional content for the writer that does not mean it will be the same for the reader. It may be that the writer has to show the reader, bit by bit, through their writing, the meanings they want them to understand and think about. For example, William Empson charted very effectively the way that Shakespeare played on the word 'honest' in Othello.[316] It is very likely that all words have some emotional content, that no word is free from this. However, the possibility that words can adequately represent our feelings is clearly very complex. A simple demonstration like this makes it clear that our ability to chart the emotional and semantic possibilities lurking in a word is very limited.

Semantic Differentials[317]

Beer

	1	2	3	4	5	6	7	
1 Angular		_	_	_	_	_	_	_		Rounded
2 Weak		_	_	_	_	_	_	_		Strong
3 Rough		_	_	_	_	_	_	_		Smooth
4 Active		_	_	_	_	_	_	_		Passive
5 Small		_	_	_	_	_	_	_		Large
6 Cold		_	_	_	_	_	_	_		Hot
7 Good		_	_	_	_	_	_	_		Bad
8 Tense		_	_	_	_	_	_	_		Relaxed
9 Wet		_	_	_	_	_	_	_		Dry
10 Fresh		_	_	_	_	_	_	_		Stale

*

No single approach to the definition of a word is entirely satisfactory. The novelist Anthony Burgess despaired of ever being able to define a word and said that as the term *word* could have no precise meaning a whole range of things counted as words:

The term word cannot have any significant denotation: a word is what my typing fingers think it is -- a cluster of symbols separated by space, or even a single symbol separated by space from other clusters or single symbols. The symbols represent phonemes. The words of connected speech do not even have the frame of silence around them: they are glued together in a single act of communication. But it is convenient to assume that words have real existence.[318]

316 W. Empson, *The Structure of Complex Words* (Chatto & Windus: London, 1951).
317 C. E. Osgood, *The Measurement of Meaning* (University of Illinois Press: Evanston, 1967).
318 A. Burgess, *Language Made Plain* (Fontana: London, 1978), p.101.

So I hope that by now we are all aware that when we say *word* or refer to *words* we are dealing with a very imperfect convention, a vague but convenient idea.

Even so, as writers we can learn a lot about history, national priorities, politics, characters, motives, society, social mores and taboos from studying words, by charting the rise and fall of popular words, by noting new words and newly imported words, by simply being aware of the language as it is used and as it changes. Words, like language as a whole, reflect social reality and can be looked at from several points of view:

- the areas of life with which they are associated and the social and linguistic needs they fulfil
- the origins and roots of word
- the ideas that go into making words and making words popular: i.e. is the new term produced by putting together a combination of old words in a novel way, or has it been imported (and changed in the process) from another language?
- the way an individual uses words.

Think about the various options open to us when adopting a new word or using an old word. Instead of adopting a new word from another language we could try to construct an English equivalent. German regularly invents new words, but English steals words all the time. French does to, but this is frowned upon by the French Academy which tries to prevent words like *le weekend* and *le football*. For example in English we have *kindergarten* and we have *crèche*. And they are both used to mean roughly the same thing. The one we took from German and the other from French. But if we did not have these words, what word would we use? *Nursery*? Is that the place where we grow nurses? No, it is the place where we grow plants? Do we also grow children there?

At the same time though, effective communication need not always take place in words. You will not find some words and phrases in the dictionary: *and I was like ... and he was like ... Oh? Unh? Oh-oh, ah-ha, mmmm,* mmm? *duh.* These and a host of other words like them do not appear in a dictionary, but they have meaning and they communicate very effectively.

Directed Study

In what way is this topic linked to the theme of Representation?

Often we know very little about the history, meaning and content of the particular words that make up our language. But information is available. The following words all have a long and interesting history -- look up their history: attorney, banjo, barbecue, blackmail, brogue, budgerigar, bungalow, butter, cartoon, coleslaw, concerto, dilemma, denigrate, dirge, doo-lally (doolalley etc), dragon, geisha, gorilla, junta, kettle, knapsack, macaroni, manure, mediator, moccasin, mosquito, nitty-gritty, nigger, niggardly, paprika, pound, rape, samovar, scot (as in scot-free), scotch, sinecure, scorch, taboo.

Remember you are looking at these words as writer and exploring the idea of *writing and representation,* so for each word find out: Where did the word come from? What was the root or the earliest meaning of the word? Is the word 'native' to English, and if not, when did it arrive in English - and why? In what circumstances was the word loaned into English? How has the meaning changed and what meanings has the word acquired? List the dates and changes in the historical meaning of the word. List the related words and phrases derived from this word. Are the spelling and pronunciation of this word important or just confusing? Are current meanings recorded in the dictionary and what does this word mean now? Is use of this word on the street different from its dictionary use? Is the word taboo? Was it always taboo? Try looking up a word that you know to be taboo. Can you find it in the dictionary? If not, why not? What taboos, if any, does this word and its dictionary entry reveal? Why would a writer use a taboo word? Were there any words you could not find in the dictionaries? Ask yourself why you could not find these particular words? Are there other words that interest you? Use this opportunity to look them up too. When you have done this for several words, ask yourself:

- As writers, do we really need to know anything about the history of words and language? Isn't it sufficient that we speak the language? If not, why not?
- Why do you think it might be important for a writer to know about the origins and history of words?

'Imagine what the English language would be like if you removed French words. You wouldn't be able to order your chauffer to bring around your limousine anymore. You'd have to say underwear instead of lingerie. You couldn't go to a restaurant. No more cuisine, no more gourmet, sauce, menu, chef, perfume. You'd have to find a new word for brassiere.'[319] Imagine what would English be like if you removed all the German, Italian, Japanese, Asian, Greek and Celtic words. Try writing a short account of going out to dinner with friends without using words borrowed from any of these languages.

Try charting the emotional content of other words. You might like to try this with the word beer or even with different kinds of beer. You could also try the same chart with different kinds of tea or various soft drinks. Now choose a word of your own and try making up a chart along the same lines. Some suggestions for other words you might like to chart are: mother, father, boy, girl, youth, noise, study, landlord, rent, library, home.

---

319 Frank McCourt, *Teacher Man* (Harper: London, 2005), p.156.

9
HOW WELL DOES LANGUAGE DO THE JOB?

This chapter considers how we use and categorize words. It opens up a debate about how we arrive at meanings and what we think meaning is. In doing so it challenges our assumptions about the commonest element language is supposed to convey -- meaning.

It also poses the question of how a writer's relationship to words and the ideas in and behind words might differ from those of the average speaker of the language.

This chapter questions the exact meanings that language conveys and our assumptions about the language we use every day. In particular it asks: How well does language do its job? What does language do well and what does it do badly? How far can we trust language to tell us about the world? Writers are concerned with all these issues, but they affect us all in one way or another.

- Words and Meaning
- Transparency
- Conceptual Spheres
- Colour as Metaphor
- The Colour Grue
- Arbitrariness in Language

WRITING THE WORLD

English is particularly rich in synonyms -- that is, other words that mean nearly the same. As a result English is often said to have 'a lot of words.' One way of imposing order on the massive vocabulary of the English language is to organize it into fields of related meaning. For example, when Peter Mark Roget first published his *Thesaurus* (1852), he grouped his entries under six main areas: *Abstract Relations, Space, Matter, Intellect, Volition* and *Affections*. Each of these had dozens of sub-headings, which in turn led to over 1,000 'Semantic Categories'. Groups of words were then listed under these category headings.

While crossword users were delighted with the book, and professional writers saved their brains in searching for alternative words, in general linguists found little use for the *Thesaurus* since it did not elucidate meaning. It only gave other words in roughly the same area. You could look up *body* and find listed there all the parts of the body, but it did not necessarily tell you what a body is. You could look up *fruit* and find all kinds of fruit listed, but you would not necessarily be able to arrive at a definition of what fruit is. If you started with a word like *tractor* you would soon find that it was part of an enormous 'lexical field' called Agriculture, but you would not find out what a tractor was.

If you look up the word *walk*, you find a whole range of related descriptive words: trudge, stagger, limp, hobble, hop, crawl, hike, march, stride, pace, stroll, wander, amble, creep, tiptoe. We can, however, divide up this group of words according to the manner in which the walking is done:

Walk with difficulty:	trudge, stagger, limp, hobble, hop, crawl
Walk quickly, with purpose:	hike, march, stride, pace
Walk slowly, without purpose:	stroll, wander, amble
Walk quietly:	creep, tiptoe, sneak[320]

From a structural point of view all these terms may be more or less interchangeable, but presented in this differentiated way it is possible to see varying levels of appropriateness, stylistic choices, and a range of registers for each and every word. While this is of little use to a foreign learner (unless they are advanced), it is a gold mine for a writer searching for a stylistic variant, a synonym or even a near synonym.

---

320 A. Underhill, *Use Your Dictionary: A Practice Book for Users* (OUP: Oxford, 1980), p.49.

Words and Meaning

The study of the words as signs, and the connections between signs and the things they signify is called semiotics. The connection between words and the things they refer to has always been a problem. Plato, writing in the dialogue *Cratylus*, believed there was an intrinsic connection between the form and meaning, the sound and sense, in words. Aristotle, on the other hand, writing in *On Interpretation*, argued that the relation between sound and meaning, a word and its content, between the sign and the thing signified, was arbitrary even though it had been established by tradition. Ludwig Wittgenstein (1889-1951) agreed with Aristotle. He insisted that there was an enormous degree of arbitrariness in words and their meaning, and that it was only in social use that words had meaning: the meaning of a word, he insisted, resides in its use in the language.[321] Tom McArthur put this another way when he said that words were 'procedural fictions' -- arbitrary signs that allow us to get through the day by thinking that when we speak or write, we know what we mean, or that someone somewhere knows what we mean.[322]

In fact, words usually mean what we want them to mean. Sometimes they don't even mean what we want them to mean. Indeed, the more closely you examine words, the less their meaning can be guaranteed. We can even ask: What do we mean when we say Meaning?

The study of words, the categories of their meaning and association, is called Semantics. Semantics considers language to be a Conceptual System and recognizes many types of meaning including: Conceptual, Connotative, Stylistic, Affective, Reflected, Collocative, Associative, Thematic, Intended, Interpreted and Contextual.

Modern Semantics has three main areas of focus: (a) it concentrates on the study of words as signs, each with a symbolic function; (b) it explores the view that language is a system, a structure, whose various elements are inter-dependent and help to delimit each other; (c) it considers language as primarily a social phenomenon. It is this last I want to concentrate on, but the other aspects will also figure in what I want to say.[323]

---

321 L. Wittgenstein, *Philosophical Remarks* (Blackwell: Oxford, 1975).
322 T. McArthur, *Living Words: Language, Lexicography and the Knowledge Revolution* (Exter University Press: Exeter, 1998), p.35.
323 F. R. Palmer, *Semantics* (Penguin: Harmondsworth, 1984).

Transparency

Every language is made up of words that are *opaque* -- that is, the meaning is not immediately apparent, the words do not explain themselves, we have to learn or acquire our vocabulary and its meanings through social interaction. It is not so much that because languages have changed so vastly down the centuries that the *original* meaning of words, if there ever was one, has been lost, altered, changed. It is rather that language has always been in a process of change, and the meaning of words is always shifting. A dictionary can do no more than offer us a kind of snapshot of the language at any given moment.

For example look at the word *book*. In English the word *book* can be traced back in time. The ancient Indo-European root-word was **bhagos* meaning *beech tree*. The Old Germanic peoples inherited this word from the Indo-Europeans as *boks* the name of a tree: they used to cut thin slivers of beech wood, hollow them slightly, fill in the hollow with wax and then inscribe symbols in the wax. Later, Germanic *boks* became Anglo-Saxon *boc*, meaning a gathering of leaves or documents. And so the word passed down to us as the German word *buch* and the English word *book*.

When I explain it this way the connection to beech trees is fairly clear. It might even offer us an explanation as to why pages of a book are sometimes referred to as *leaves*, why we *leaf* through a book and why the first page is sometimes referred to as the *fly leaf*. But the connection of a bound gathering of papers to the idea of trees, to beech trees in particular, or to gatherings of beech slivers is not at all clear to us when we see the word book. Still less is this so with the invention of eBooks and Kindles.

Only a few words are to some degree transparent:[324]

1) Onomatopoeic words tend to be similar across languages because these words imitate sounds and therefore imitate similar meanings. For example, cuckoo: *coucou* (Fr), *kuckuck* (Gm), *kókkyx* (Gk), *kakuk* (Hung), *kukułka* (Pol). There is no connection between these words, except that they are all attempts to imitate the sound the bird makes.

---

324 S. Ullma, 'Semantics' in: N. Minnis (ed.), *Linguistics at Large* (Paladin: London, 1973), p.79.

2) Derivative and compound words tend to be transparent to anyone who has a grasp of the basic components of the language. For example: *shoe-lace* and *dreamer*. Yet the original components, shoe, lace, and dream, must be known and understood before these words can be understood and may, for a foreign learner, still be opaque.

3) Figurative expressions -- e.g. *live wire, string puller, crossed wire, wired up, a wiry person* -- all owe their transparency to their function as metaphor, and to the immediacy of that metaphor.

However, the randomness of words can be illustrated very clearly by looking at brand names. If there were something right and fitting about words, as Plato suggested, then they would apply to particularly to commercial goods and their brand names - and these would surely be apparent, right and fitting, even across language and national borders. In fact names - and particularly brand names - don't travel at all well.

According to a survey in the journal *Hotline* (spring 1998), *Grated Fanny* is a can of tuna fish in South America; *Cock* is a deodorant in France; *Bum* is a biscuit in Turkey; *Moron* is a kind Italian wine; *Krapp* is a Scandinavian toilet paper; *Spunk* is a German salt liquorice. *Persil* is a washing powder in England but in France it is rather like the word for parsley. If words are supposed to have some innate, fitting relationship to the thing they describe, then crossing to another language reveals that this is just not so. Vauxhall learned this to their cost when they tried to market their new Vauxhall Nova internationally only to find that no-one would buy it in Spain. In Spanish Nova name means 'won't go'. David Lodge in his novel *Nice Work* refers to a windscreen de-icer from Finland called *Superpiss*, and he comments that 'what might be onomatopoeia in one language community may be obscenity in another'.[325]

C. S. Lewis once warned:

Language exists to communicate whatever it can communicate. Some things it communicates so badly that we never attempt to communicate them by words if any other medium is available. Those who think they are testing a boy's 'elementary' command of English by asking him to describe in words how one ties one's tie or what a pair of scissors is like, are far astray. For precisely

---

325 D. Lodge, *Nice Work* (Penguin: Harmondsworth, 1989), p.96.

what language can hardly do at all, and never does well, is to inform us about complex physical shapes and movements. Hence descriptions of such things in the ancient writers are nearly always unintelligible. Hence we never in real life voluntarily use language for this purpose; we draw a diagram or go through pantomime gestures. The exercises which such examiners set are no more a test of 'elementary' linguistic competence than the most difficult bit of trick-riding from the circus ring is a test of elementary horsemanship.[326]

His point was that language does not relate precisely to the world. Language allows, invites, encourages us to think it is describing the world very accurately, when in fact, as most of us sense from time to time, there are huge areas of human experience that language does not represent at all well, and which we, as writers, struggle to represent in language. We can't always say what these areas are, because what language does not represent is almost unthinkable, or at least very hard to get at in words -- and if we can't put a thought into words, that thought remains unformed, incoherent, unexpressed. For writers, the connection to this problem is intimate, since language is our working material. Part of the writer's struggle is to find ways of expressing things that have not been expressed, to drag to light what might be thought, to uncover and give expression to new ways of thinking and feeling.

Language represents the world to us -- but only partially: there are gaps and there are inconsistencies. The Whorf Hypothesis suggest that languages -- and particularly those parts of language known as grammar and vocabulary -- determine what information must be conveyed in that society, and what aspects of society must be expressed in that speech community.[327] In English, for example, we have things for which we have no name. For example, mothers and fathers often have brothers and sisters -- we call them uncles and aunts. But in English we have no words to show which uncles and aunts are on the mother's side and which are the father's side. They are all uncles and aunts. In Latin, however, they had father's brother *patruus*, mother's brother *avunculus*, father's sister *matertera* and mother's sister *amita*. And you can imagine that this could be extended to cousins on the male side and cousins on the female side.

---

326 C. S. Lewis, *Studies in Words* (CUP: Cambridge, 1994), 313.
327 J. B. Carrol (ed.), *Language, Thought and Reality: Selected Writings of Benjamin Lee Whorf* (MIT: Cambridge, Mass., 1976).

Likewise, we could specify the degree of removal on both the male and female sides, when in fact we only specify first and second cousins. For example, the Yanomamö language from Brazil specifies different types of cousin: *amiwa* (daughter of a paternal uncle of maternal aunt), *eiwa* (son of maternal uncle or aunt), *suwabiya* (daughter of a maternal uncle or aunt), *soriwa* (son of a maternal uncle or paternal aunt). In English, it seems, when it comes to family relationships, our language is rather impoverished. What does the absence of these words tell us about our society?

An example of the Whorf Hypothesis in action is George Orwell's novel *1984* (1949), where the government operates through a language called 'Newspeak'. In that language, all words to do with unhappiness, dissatisfaction and the possibility of political change have been eradicated, thus making these things almost (but not quite) unthinkable and rendering opposition almost impossible to articulate. Of course where language cannot deal with all the differences in the nature of things, we can always explain more fully by generating more language. But that is not my point. My point is that there are things in the world that are not represented in our language.[328]

At the same time that we do not have names or words for things we clearly have, we also have the opposite -- a vast range of things collected under one word that is sometimes more, sometimes less, appropriate. We have the word chair. But that word can include: *rocker, easy, stone, wood, upright, reclining, garden, lounger, armchair, stool, high stool, bar stool, milking stool, toadstool, hammock, swing, dining, office, high, swivel, shooting stick, sofa, settee, chaise-longue, poufé, saddle, side-saddle, throne, a bardic throne*. Not only that, but the said item can have one leg, two legs, three legs, four legs, six legs, or no legs at all. We also have a *chairman* or *chairwoman* often referred to simply as *The Chair*, and from this we have to verb to *chair* or *chairing*. We also have the academic term, *Professorial chair* -- which is not only invisible, it is entirely notional. We can distinguish between these things and we can add an adjective or even make a hand gesture to help indicate what we are referring to, but would an alien from another planet see the connection between these things?

Also English is a little vague with its pronouns. If I say 'We are going shopping' I might be including you or I might not. In Australian Creole,

---

328 H. Rheingold, *They Have a Name for It* (Sarabande: Louisville Kentucky, 2000).

on the other hand, it is said that there are many varieties of the word *we*. Depending on which of the Australian languages, there can be four different words to indicate 'we': 'you and me', 'me and somebody else but not you', 'you and me and pile of others', 'me and a heap of others, but not you'. The precise choice of which 'we' word is clearly very important.[329] In English the only real variant we have is, where the Queen does not refer to herself as *I* or *me*, but as the Royal *one* or *we*. Presumably the queen does not own an iPod, but if she does she refers to it as a 'we pod' or 'one's pod'.

Conceptual Spheres

A hugely important part of language is the way it organizes schemes or concepts of the world. Conceptual Spheres are closely organized areas of ideas in which items are drawn up, analysed and presented in a particular way. Conceptual Spheres, for example, allow us to see the choices we make as speakers of a language and the choices our language and culture make for us -- if you like, the choices we are allowed to choose from.

Some of the most interesting work in this area appeared in analysing colour. For example we might speak of red, but which red do we mean? Red has two main sub-divisions. Do we mean scarlet or crimson? If we mean scarlet, which of its two main categories do we mean -- vermillion or pillar-box?[330] And if we mean crimson, which of its two main categories -- blood-red or wine coloured?

Conceptual Spheres not only organize a series of linguistic choices, they pass on important cultural material. Berlin and Kay, for example, studied the colour systems of ninety-eight different languages, and their findings were surprising.[331] We might assume that as the human eye sees the same colour spectrum wherever humans are, colour would be a human constant, ranging across every culture, and that everyone who was not colour blind would see and refer to the same range of colours.

However, Kay and Berlin found that while the human eye saw the same range of colours, different cultures did not divide up the spectrum in the same way and did not talk about colour in the same way. What

---

329 M. Bragg, *The Adventure of English* (Sceptre: London, 2004), p.278.
330 J. Britton, *Language and Learning* (Penguin: Harmondsworth, 1974), p.197.
331 B. Berlin & P. Kay, *Basic Colour Terms* (University of California Press, Berkeley, 1969).

they found was that black and white were virtually the only universal colour terms in all languages. They found that there were a total of eleven basic colour categories: *white, black, red, green, yellow, blue, brown, purple, pink, orange, grey*, and that from these basic eleven colour terms, most languages selected a range of colour terms. However, they also found that some languages recognized more than the basic eleven colours.

They found that it was possible to predict that if a language contained one set of colours then it would probably also contain another particular set. For example, if a language contained black and white it could also contain red, but without red it would not contain any other colours. If it had red then it could also have green and yellow: but without green and yellow it would probably not contain any other colours. If it contained green and yellow then it could also have blue, but without blue it would probably contain no other colours. If it contained blue then it could also contain brown. Without brown it could contain no other colours. If it contained brown then it would probably also contain purple, pink, orange and grey. It was later discovered that there were a few exceptions, but this is true for most languages.

Berlin and Kay managed to show this on the page: if a language contained a colour to the right of the > sign it would also contain all the colours to the left, but not vice versa.

white / black > red > green/yellow > blue > brown > purple / pink / orange / grey

English uses all eleven basic colour terms, but some languages get by on a colour system consisting of only two or three colour terms. Several languages from the New Guinea Highlands have only black and white, which also serve for dark and light. The Philippine language of Hanunóo, for example, makes do with four basic colour terms and illustrates Berlin and Kay's ideas very clearly:

mabiru	=	black, or dark tints of other colours
malagti	=	white, or light tints of other colours
marara	=	red
malatuy	=	green

Some languages organize their range of colours differently. In Japanese *awo* means green, blue or just pale. Navajo has only one word for grey and brown, and one word for blue and green, but it distinguishes two kinds of black: the black of darkness or the absence of light, and the colour black of objects such as coal.

I have heard of only one language that does not have colours -- Piraha, discovered in 2008, the language of a small tribe in the remotest Brazilian rainforest. They apparently do not have colours, but have phrases to indicate colour: for example, it is the colour of a leaf, it is the colour of blood, it is the colour of the sky etc.[332]

Colour as Metaphor

Language is largely a system of metaphors -- words for carrying ideas from one area of thought into another. Language itself is a metaphor, since unless language is talking about language it is generally not the thing it describes, but a metaphor by which things can be described.

Strangely language is incredibly resistant to 'the real world', especially in the area of colour. Often colour terms are applied in a very vague way, and in general colour is a metaphor. In fact we are sometimes even slightly confused as to what we mean by the term *colour* itself.

In snooker, for example, it is established that you pot a *coloured* ball only after you have potted a *red* -- snooker assumes that for the purposes of the game *red balls* are not *coloured*. However, when we refer to getting a little colour in our cheeks we *only* mean pink or red, we do not mean, for example, blue, grey or green.

It is worth reminding ourselves that just because we say a thing is red or blue or green, that is far from the end of the complexities of our colour system: it really tells us very little about the kind of red or blue or green we mean. Russian, for example, has different words for dark and light blue and so has twelve colours in its system. Hungarian has two words for red -- one for dark and one for light.

In fact to say a thing is red or blue or green or black or white, may not, in itself, be true at all, since there are other cultural and political aspects to issues of colour to be considered. In the southern states of the USA after the ending of slavery, it was normal to refer to 'gentlemen of colour'. Yet, the term *coloured* implies that the rest of humanity is not 'coloured', which means what? That white was not a colour? Or that

---

332 J. Carey, 'Don't Sleep, There are Snakes', *The Sunday Times* (23 November 2008): www.timesonline.co.uk/tol/arts_and_entertainment/books/non-fiction.

some people were 'coloured' and everybody else was see-through? The word *coloured* was a metaphor that signalled something about race and status, rather than something about colour itself.

In South Africa under apartheid, where gradations of skin colour indicated rank and worth, the term *coloured* did not include black people or white people but referred to people of mixed race, since for the apartheid regime this was an entirely different category.

Applied to people, colour is always a metaphor. If you look closely at people described as *black* they may, in fact, be various shades and tones of brown and red and blue, but in fact, if there is one colour they are not it is *black*. Andres Siegfried has said that even within the word *black*, referring to skin colour, it is possible to identify different kinds of *black*:

> Black, brown, deep brown, yellow, reddish brown, deep yellow, chocolate, gingerbread, fair, light brown, red, pink, tan, olive, copper, blue, cream, pale black, dead black, bronze, banana.[333]

Nigerian novelist Chimanande Ngozi Adichie described her skin colour as 'the colour of gingerbread'.[334] And any painter will tell you it is the same with *white* people. When applied to skin colour white people are not *white* but various shades of pink-grey-green. Nor are people from the Orient the colour of daffodils or indigenous Americans the colour of a fire engine. When black, white, yellow, red are applied to people they are not accurate colour descriptions, but a metaphor, a sign, indicating something else.

And different cultures have different associations for different colours. In English, for example, we tend to associate the colour white with purity and innocence. Charles Dickens plays on these associations in *Great Expectations* (1860-61). When Pip goes to visit her, Miss Haversham, jilted on her wedding day, but still clad in her white wedding dress, has become a recluse: she lives alongside the crumbling remains of her wedding feast and the white wedding cake, as if time had stopped at the moment of her abandonment:

> She was dressed in rich materials -- satins, and lace, and silks -- all of white. Her shoes were white. And she had on a long white veil

333 R. Wright, *Black Boy* (Longman: London, 1970), p.vii.
334 Chimanande Ngozi Adichie, 'What I see in the Mirror', *The Guardian Weekend* (23 January 2010), p.43.

dependent from her hair, and she had bridal flowers in her hair, but her hair was white (...) I saw that everything within my view which ought to be white, had been white long ago, and had lost its lustre, and was faded and yellow.[335]

White is not normally associated with death, disease and decay in European traditions, but rather with innocence and purity. Yellow, on the other hand is connected with disease and melancholy.

In Nigeria both black and white have totally different associations. A Nigerian might find it puzzling that Europeans often use black as a term for sin, for evil, disease, decay and death, and even more puzzling that we often use white to refer to innocence or purity. In Nigerian theatre, red and green (the colours we use in traffic lights) are used to indicate good and evil. And Chinua Achebe tells us in *Things Fall Apart* (1958) that, even before Europeans arrived, the polite name for leprosy in Nigeria was 'the white skin'.[336]

In the Muslim world and in several Asian cultures white is the sign of sadness, mourning, widowhood or bad luck. Red is the colour of good luck -- as in the Russian roulette sequence in the film *The Deer Hunter*.

The Colour Grue

The history of terms for colour is notoriously difficult in several languages. The Indo-European languages -- and the colours blue and green -- are a perfect example of the difficulties.[337] The root word for blue seems to have been a Proto Indo-European word *bhel* (shine, flash, burn, light coloured, blue, blond, yellow). A great many words derive from this root – *bleach, bleak, blind, blink, blush, blaze, flame, fulminate, flagrant, phlegm*. In time this word gave rise to the Indo-European word *bhlewos* (light coloured, blue, blonde, bright or yellow). This developed into Latin *flavus* (yellow), French *blanc* (white), Polish *biały* (white), Russian *белый* (white), Welsh *blawr* (grey), the Middle High German word *bla* (yellow), the English words *flavid* (a yellow dye), *flavescent, flavine, pale* and *livid*. However, in the Scandinavian adaptation of the word, like Old Norse *blamaðr* and Icelandic *blamaður*, the word meant black, swarthy or Negro. Old English had the words blaw and

335 C. Dickens, *Great Expectations* (Cygnet: New York, 1968), p.76.
336 C. Achebe, *Things Fall Apart* (Heinemann: London, 1958).
337 G. Deutscher, *Through the Language Glass: How Words Colour Your World* (Heinemann: London, 2010); www.Wikipedia, 'The Colour Grue'.

blaew, also from this root, but they did not survive into modern English.

The Latin word *flavus* seems to have been borrowed into the Germanic languages as **blaewaz*, which might also have meant green, orange and blue, and in time became Old Frisan *blau*, Old High German and Old Scandinavian *blao* (shining) and eventually modern German *blau*. However, in spite of its Anglo Saxon roots, it does not seem that English acquired the word blue from the Germanic languages.

The Latin word *flavus* also became the general Romance language word **blavus* which in turn became the Old Spanish *blavo* (yellowish-grey), Welsh *blawr* (grey), and the Frankish word *blao*. It also became the Old French *blau, blo* and *bloe*. Eventually this changed into the Middle French word *bleu* which, because of the Norman invasion, eventually became the Middle English *bla, blead* (meaning blue-grey or dark blue) *bleu* and *blew*, which since the sixteenth century has been spelled as blue.

Many Indo European words seem to have had a word to describe the colour of the sea, meaning grey-green-blue. For example, Irish *glass*, Old English *haewen* (blue-grey), Serbo-Croat *sinj* (grey-blue) Lithuanian *šyvas* and Russian *sivyj* (grey).

The problem is not confined to the Indo-European languages. Modern Cantonese distinguishes between blue and green; however, an older word, *qīng*, is also used to refer to either blue or green, or even (though much less frequently) to black. For example, the Flag of the Republic of China is today still referred to as *qīng tiān, bái rì, mǎn dì hóng* ('Blue Sky, White Sun, Whole Field Red'); however, *qīng cài* is the Cantonese word for 'green vegetable'. Many languages -- for example Kurdish, Kazakh, Pashto, Korean, Vietnamese and some of the languages of China -- do not have separate terms for blue and green, but instead have one term for both. Vietnamese for example does not use separate words for green and blue: both are xanh; blue is specifically described as 'xanh like the sky' and green as 'xanh like the leaves'.

The Japanese word *ao* or *awo* (which uses the same kanji character as the Cantonese *qīng* above) can refer to either blue or green. Modern Japanese also has the word *midori* for green, although this seems to be a modern development since ancient Japanese did not have this distinction: the word *midori* only came into use in the Heian period, and at that time *midori* was considered only as a shade of *ao*. School teaching materials distinguishing green from blue only came into use after the

Second World War, during the US Occupation. Even though most Japanese consider both words to mean green, the word *ao* (blue) is used to describe most vegetation, certain vegetables and traditional turquoise shades. It is often used where English speakers might expect green -- for example the traffic signal for 'go'. However, other green objects -- a car, a sweater -- are generally described as *midori*. Some Japanese people also sometimes use the English word 'green' for certain shades. The Korean word *pureu-da* may mean blue, green or a bluish green. The word is used as blue in the phrase *pureun haneul*, blue sky, or as green in the phrase *pureun sup*, green forest. Distinct words for blue and green can also be used; *paran, paransaek, parang* mean blue, and *chorok, choroksaek* or *noksaek* mean green.

Historically in Celtic languages, like Welsh and Irish Gaelic, there are slightly different colour boundaries. In Irish and Breton Gaelic, *glas* is the word for 'green' and refers particularly to green plants; other shades of green would be referred to as *uaine*. In Middle Irish and Old Irish, *glas* was a blanket term for colours ranging from green to blue and various shades of grey (i.e. the *glas* of a sword, the *glas* of stone, etc). In Modern Irish and in Scots Gaelic *gorm* (as in Cairngorm) is the word for blue. In Welsh the word *glas* refers mainly to blue, but it is also used to refer to shades of sea or grass or it can refer to grey or silver. It is used to describe animate growing things and is usually thought of as green. Inanimate objects may be said to be *glas* but are thought of as blue. In modern Welsh *gwyrdd* is the standard modern word for green, while *llwyd* means grey. Thus:

English	Welsh	
green	gwyrdd	(inanimate, not growing)
green	glas	(animate, growing)
blue	glas	(inanimate, not growing)
grey	glas	
grey	llywd	
brown	llwyd [338]	

Like Welsh, Navajo has only one word for grey and brown, and one word for blue and green, but it distinguishes two kinds of black: the black of

---

338 Geoffrey N. Leech, *Semantics* (Penguin: Harmondsworth, 1984).

darkness or the absence of light, and the colour black of objects such as coal. Also like Welsh, Navajo has the same word for grey and brown, and the same word for blue and green.

In English we generally see shades of colours as simply shades, rather than separate colours. In Russian, however, there is a distinction between *Голубой* (golobuy, light blue) and *Синий* (sinny, dark blue). Greek too distinguishes between azure blue *μπλέ* and dark blue *γαλανός* and these are generally regarded as two separate colours -- rather in the way we think of red and pink as different colours. Italian regards *azzurro* (light blue) as a separate colour: Turkish too distinguishes between *lacivert* (blue) and *mavi* (dark blue, from the Arabic root word Ma'i, meaning like water).

We sometimes refer to blue movies, but blue is not the universal colour of porn. In Italy porn films are *film a luci rosse* -- red. In France and Spain blue (dirty) jokes are green: *en raconter des vertes* and *verdo laga*. In Japan blue movies are pink.[339]

In linguistics, when the cross-over between green and blue is discussed, it is often referred to as *The Grue Problem* or *The Colour Grue*.[340]

Arbitrariness in Language

Just because our language seems to function adequately, that does not mean that we are necessarily any better off than anyone else in the world with a completely different language. What makes perfect sense to us may be totally alien to someone attempting to learn the language. In Welsh the term *gwyn* means white, in German it is *weiss*, in Spanish *blanco*, in Polish *biały*, in Greek it is *λευκός* or *ασπρος*. There is no obvious connection between these words except that they all mean white; and there is no particular reason why these words mean white, instead of others, but they do. Even the connection between these words and the idea of whiteness is not immediately apparent -- none is more suggestive of white than the other words -- but they are socially agreed, historically derived, temporary, handed on by habit and tradition, continually and always overlaid by newer meanings: and they all had to be learned.

The point is that all languages carve up the world and represent meaning in language in different ways and these things do not come

---

339 Notes and Queries, 'Explanations out of the Blue' *The Guardian* (14 Nov 2006), p.22
340 www.Wikipedia, 'The Colour Grue'.

to us naturally, on the air -- we have to learn them. And it is this arbitrariness, across languages and even within one language, which I want to emphasize.

There is a short essay by Jorge Luis Borges, called 'John Wilkins' Analytical Language' (1942) which illustrates the way the human mind divides up the world rather arbitrarily. In this essay Borges quotes from a (possibly non-existent) Chinese encyclopaedia called *The Heavenly Emporium of Benevolent Knowledge*. This encyclopaedia categorizes animals into various kinds:

(a) those that belong to the emperor; (b) embalmed ones; (c) those that are trained; (d) suckling pigs; (e) mermaids; (f) fabulous ones; (g) stray dogs; (h) those that are included in this classification; (i) those that tremble as if they were mad; (j) innumerable ones; (k) those drawn with a very fine camel's-hair brush; (l) etcetera; (m) those that have just broken the flower vase; (n) those that at a distance resemble flies.[341]

What this list tells us is that the mind -- and language as a function of the mind -- has more than one way to slice the pie of daily life. Language faces the universe as a random response to the world as we see it and the puzzle of 'reality'. I hope that when I write that we certainly cannot trust language to tell us accurately about the world, you see what I mean. But then again, I am using the very language I am questioning, so maybe not … But next time we feel tempted to assume that our language gives us an accurate picture of the world, perhaps we should remember Borges' list of animals.

It is clear that we cannot trust written texts -- even the Bible -- to tell us the truth, let alone the whole truth, about themselves, us, our world; we can also see that as writers we must take each text -- perhaps each word -- into our hands and study them as patiently, closely and as carefully as we can for what they tell us about not only themselves and the world they were made in, but also the about unpredictable and fragmentary way writing of all kinds represents our world to us.

---

341 J. L. Borges, *Selected Non-Fictions* (Penguin: Harmondsworth 1999), p.231.

Directed Study

It has been said that a history of words, language and languages is a history of the human mind, a history of human thought and an indicator of creativity. How can these be so? In what ways? Why might this be of interest to a writer?

Why should we worry about what a word is? Should writers worry more or less about words and the definition of words? How and in what ways do you think your relationship to words is different from that of non-writers?

Imagine the world has gone black and white. Try writing a description of a snooker tournament without using any colour words.

What can language do well? What does it have problems with? Try either or both of these two exercises:
- a) Imagine you are a Martian on a visit to planet Earth. You plan to send home a sample of tea which you would like your family to try. Write them instructions on how to make a good cup of tea.
- b) Imagine you have a friend who has just bought their first pair of lace-up shoes. The problem is they don't know how to tie the laces. Write them a letter with a set of instructions.

Look at the words *after, absence, barrier, deception, envy, father, imprisonment, mother, obsessed, rumour, watch, spy.* Let your mind wander around these words and their up creative possibilities. Write down a few of the emotional resonances you feel in each word. Select two or three of the most powerful of these words. Look up these words in a dictionary or a Thesaurus: make a list of the range of meaning for each word. Make a list of the other words you could use instead of the one you chose. You will find some old and obsolete meanings as well as more up-to-date meanings. What are the advantages and disadvantages of using the word you chose, rather than one of the alternatives? Write a short piece of prose about one of these words describing what they triggered for you. Try to show the full range of meanings -- old and new -- that you have discovered.

Can you invent satisfactory terms in English for the following kin-family relationships:
- My step-son's child
- My step-son's adopted child
- My step-son's half-brother and half-sister
- My step-daughter's husband
- My step-daughter's husband's adopted child
- My ex-wife's adopted son
- My ex-husband's step son
- My sister's second husband's child
- My wife's uncle's adopted son
- My partner's adopted son's child

10
THE INNER LIFE OF LANGUAGE: WAR IN WORDS -- WORDS IN WAR

This chapter looks at the kinds of things writers do. In particular it examines how words are used in a time of war, and at the war of meaning that goes on within words. It draws on examples from the Second World, the Vietnam War and the long War on Terror. This chapter develops the idea of meaning by raising the issue of what is 'in' words and the writer's duty to be an 'earwitness' to the fate of words.

Every year I ask Creative Writing students: What do writers do when they write? Usually, as soon as the question is asked, a chasm of uncertainties opens up. What do we mean by *writer*? We all write, so in what way is what a writer writes different from what a non-writer writes? Why? Who says? And so on. To a certain extent the question has faced writers down the ages and it is exactly the kind of open-ended conundrum you might expect in a university. But it is not an idle question, and over the last few years the question has been increasingly focused for me, not by disinterested academic speculation, but by current events.

One of the most important things writers of all political persuasions do is direct us to think about how words are used and what is in words. Dictionaries tell us the meaning of words in the past, at particular moments in time, but writers tell us about the inner life of our language, about what is happening to words now. Because language and words are tied to issues of identity, perception, ambition and ideas of community, writing is much more likely than other art forms to be judged, not only in artistic terms but also in moral and political terms.

The Nobel Prize winning Bulgarian writer, Elias Canetti (1905–94) was very aware that the content of words shifted through time and daily usage: he was aware that just because a word once had a particular content or meaning it did not mean that it would always have that same meaning or content. He said that to notice changes in meaning and to make use of these changes was to be an *earwitness*, and this, he said, was a writer's duty.[342]

Lewis Carroll (1832–98) studied language very carefully: he loved to play with words and was aware of the arbitrary nature of meaning. In *Alice Through the Looking-Glass* (1871), Humpty Dumpty explains to Alice that although we get birthday presents once a year we could get un-birthday presents on the other 364 days of the year. He ends his explanation ends with: 'There's glory for you!'

"I don't know what you mean by 'glory'", Alice said.

Humpty Dumpty smiled contemptuously. "Of course you don't -- till I tell you. I meant 'there's a nice knock-down argument for you!' "

"But 'glory' doesn't mean 'a nice knock-down argument,'" Alice objected.

"When I use a word," Humpty Dumpty said, in rather a scornful tone, "it means just what I choose it to mean -- neither more nor less."

"The question is," said Alice, "Whether you can make words mean so many different things."

"The question is," said Humpty Dumpty, "which is to be master -- that's all."

Alice was too much puzzled to say anything; so after a minute Humpty Dumpty began again: "They've a temper, some of them -- particularly verbs: they're the proudest -- adjectives you can do anything with, but not verbs -- however, I can manage the whole lot of them! Impenetrability! That's what I say!"

"Would you tell me, please," said Alice, "what that means?"

"Now you talk like a reasonable child," said Humpty Dumpty, looking very much pleased. "I meant by 'impenetrability' that we've had enough of this subject, and it would be just as well if you'd mention what you mean to do next, as I suppose you don't mean to stop here all the rest of your life."

"That's a great deal to make one word mean," Alice said in a thoughtful tone.[343]

---

342 E. Canetti, *The Conscience of Words & Earwitness* (Picador: London, 1987).
343 L. Carrol, *The Annotated Alice* (Penguin: Harmondsworth, 1970), pp.267-269.

WRITING THE WORLD

Generally, unlike Humpty Dumpty, writers work with a language which, while it is constantly changing and responding to social pressures, is given. For example, although we now avoid using it, at one time the word *nigger* was in common use. Neither Agatha Christie nor Joseph Conrad saw anything wrong in using the word in their book titles -- *Ten Little Niggers* (1939) and *The Nigger of the 'Narcissus'* (1897). The word also appears in the works of Charles Dickens, G. B. Shaw, D. L. Sayers, Mark Twain, Rider Haggard, D. H. Lawrence, Ernest Hemingway, Carson McCullers and even US President Woodrow Wilson. Enid Blyton's story 'The Three Golliwogs' has characters named Golly, Woggie and Nigger. It would be very difficult to wipe this from the language or delete these books from the literature. It would also be a falsification of the past and the language of the past.

Now, although the British National Party and National Front, KKK, White Supremacists in the southern states of the USA and White Separatists in South Africa still use the word, and Quentin Tarrantino and Spike Lee often have black characters in their films use the word, it has not been socially permissible to use this word for some years and in the US there has been pressure to remove all books containing the word from schools and libraries. Now it is often referred to simply as *the 'n' word*. From being *the* word to describe black people, the taboo on its use is now so strong that even an informed discussion about its origins, history, spelling and changing function can hardly take place. An actor is reported as saying:

> The N-word. I don't use it ... ever ... I don't want *anybody* to use it. If somebody uses that word towards me, I'm going to take issue with it because it's not a definition of me. I don't think it gives anybody any power over me to use that word; in fact, I think if you use that word towards me, you've lost all power. Once you've used that word towards me, I know exactly who you are and I'll crush you. No question, no ifs, buts or maybes ...[344]

And when the actor Michael Richards was recorded abusing a black heckler in the audience with the words: 'you fucking nigger' the furore which followed was as much about the racist epithet as about the problem of trying to report and discuss the incident without repeating

---

344 S. Hattenstone, 'Doing the Right Thing', *The Guardian Weekend* (7 June 2003), p.17.

what had been said.[345] But if we cannot air-brush this word entirely from the present, we certainly cannot make it vanish from the past either. It is important if we want to chart race relations in USA, the history of the anti-slavery movement, the issues of the American Civil War, the history of jazz, blues and rock and roll, the musical achievement of Elvis Presley, population shifts and urban and industrial development in the USA, the history of the KKK, or even slavery and the histories of Bristol and Liverpool.

It is important for writers to follow the shifts in the language since these represent shifts in understanding and social relations. Conrad, Christie, Blyton, McCullers and the others could not avoid the word -- indeed, there was no reason for them to think they should -- and there were few alternative words available to them. None of them could have predicted a shift in sensibility that would make that word unacceptable. And when, in the 1970s, John Lennon said 'Woman is the nigger of the world' he was making use of this change to highlight a different shift in perception.

If words have revealing pasts they also have revealing futures. Although he did not predict the rise of Nazism, Franz Kafka (1883–1924), a German speaking Czech Jew, foresaw one development in Nazi language. In his tale *Metamorphosis* (1912), Kafka describes how one morning a man called Gregor Samsa woke up to find he had been transformed into a giant bug. Kafka describes this bug in the opening line with the word *ungeziefer* (vermin). This very powerful word was to become a favourite Nazi description of the Jews -- along with maggots, bedbugs and *Weltpest* (world plague). It appeared on a great many Nazi propaganda posters and in *Der Stürmer*, the Nazi newspaper: Anne Frank, writing in her diary, noticed that the Nazis referred to *cleaning out* the Jews as if they were *cockroaches.* [346] And this verbal transformation was a necessity since without the transformation of people into vermin there could be no *vernichtung* (extermination). Kafka, it seems, in Gregor Samsa, anticipated the overnight creation of sub-humans in the Nuremberg Race Laws.

Nazi Language hid the consequences of Nazi actions for as long as people wanted it to. Nazi language legitimized genocide by giving a gloss of normality and innocence, by making things appear normal. George Steiner has described the process:

---

345 I. Mayes, 'A word for word account of racist abuse', *The Guardian* (27 November 2006), p.33.
346 A. Frank, *The Diary of Anne Frank* (Longman: London, (1947, 1989), p.72.

The unspeakable being said, over and over, for twelve years. The unthinkable being written down, indexed, filed for reference. The men who poured quicklime down the openings of the sewers in Warsaw to kill the living and stifle the stink of the dead wrote home about it. They spoke of having to *liquidate vermin.* In letters asking for family snapshots or sending season's greetings (…) A language being used to run hell, getting the habits of hell into its syntax. Being used to destroy what there is of man in man and to restore to governance what there is of beast. Gradually, words lost their original meaning and acquired nightmarish definitions. Jude, Pole, Russe came to mean two-legged lice, putrid vermin which good Aryans must squash, as a party manual said, 'like roaches on a dirty wall'. *Endgültige Lösung* (the Final Solution) came to signify the death of six million human beings … And as the circle of vengeance closed in on Germany, this snow drift of lies thickened to a frantic blizzard. Over the radio, between the interruptions caused by air-raid warnings, Goebbels' voice assured the German people that 'titanic secret weapons' were about to be launched. On one of the very last days (…) Hitler came out of his bunker to inspect a row of ashen-faced fifteen-year-old boys recruited for a last-ditch defence of Berlin. The order of the day spoke of 'volunteers' and élite units gathered invincibly around the Führer. The nightmare fizzled out on a shameless lie. The *Herrenvolk* (master race) was solemnly told that Hitler was in the front-line trenches, defending the heart of his capital against the Red beasts. Actually, the buffoon lay dead with his mistress, deep in the safety of his concrete lair.[347]

The Nazi state was administered by ordinary men and women performing routine bureaucratic tasks none of which, in itself, seemed sinister.[348] And so effective was this strategy that Rudolf Höß, commandant at the Auschwitz death camp, a man who sent thousands to their death every day, described himself as merely 'a cog in the wheel of the great extermination machine created by the Third Reich'.[349] This is part of what Hannah Arendt summed up in her phrase 'the banality of evil'.[350] There were plenty of banal shifts of meaning under the Nazis.

347 G. Steiner, 'The Hollow Miracle' (1959), in *Language and Silence* (Penguin: Harmondsworth, 1968), pp.141-42.
348 C. R. Browning, *Ordinary Men* (Penguin: Harmondsworth, 2002).
349 S. Esh, 'Words and their Meanings', *Yad Vashem Studies* 5 (1963), p.153.
350 H. Arendt, *Eichmann in Jerusalem* (Penguin: Harmondsworth, 1963).

For example, on 4 October 1943, Reichsführer-SS Heinrich Himmler addressed a group of SS Major-Generals in an annual leadership gathering in Posen with these words:

> I mean the clearing out of the Jews, the extermination of the Jewish race. It's one of those things it is easy to talk about. *The Jewish race is being exterminated*, says one Party member, *that's quite clear; it's in our programme; elimination of the Jews, and we're doing it, exterminating them.* And then there come 80 million worthy Germans and each one has his decent Jew. Of course, the others are vermin, but this one is an A-1 Jew. Not one of all those who talk this way has witnessed it, not one of them has been through it. Most of you must know what it means when 100 corpses are lying side by side, or 500 or 1,000. To have stuck it out and at the same time -- apart from human weakness -- to have remained decent fellows, that is what has made us hard. This is a page of glory in our history which has never been written and is never to be written...[351]

Himmler may have recognized 'human weakness', even among the SS -- in fact, several of these leaders and a great many of the soldiers in the *Einsatzgruppen* had nervous breakdowns -- but he did so only to sort out the weak from those hard enough to accomplish the task set by the leadership -- namely genocide. But what, we are left wondering, in his mind determined *decency*? What kind of *decency* was it that could not be written about? Was there a special category of *decency* called Nazi decency? What did Himmler think *decency* was? Was his idea of *decency* the same as ours?

Himmler kept a private collection of tables and chairs made from human body parts, which his mistress showed to visitors. He had his own personal copy of *Mein Kampf* covered in human skin and a lampshade made from tattooed human skin. He ordered and watched the execution of 100 Jews in Minsk in August 1941. He ordered and watched the gassing of 300 naked young Jewish women at Sobibor in February 1943. He ordered and watched a prostitute beaten on her naked buttocks when he visited Auschwitz.[352] What did the word *decency* mean to him?

It is rare in Nazi documents to find any reference to killing, death

---

351 www.dsu.nodak.edu/users. A more chilling translation can be found in: 'Eichmann Interrogated', *Granta 6: A Literature for Politics* (Granta: Cambridge, 1983), p.154.
352 G. Sereny, *Albert Speer: His Battle with the Truth* (Vintage: New York, 1995), p.309.

or extermination. Instead we have only references to *final solution, resettlement, evacuation, special treatment, change of residence, labour in the East* -- a host of ambiguity and euphemism. Adolf Eichmann, who kept the minutes of the Wannsee Conference on 20 January 1942 at which the mechanics of the Final Solution were worked out, confessed himself surprised that people spoke there so openly of what was intended. But then, under the direction of SS-Obergruppenführer Reinhard Heydrich (Chief of the Reich Security Service, Deputy Reich Protector of Bohemia and Moravia) who had called and chaired the meeting, Eichmann took the stenographer's verbatim record and turned it into the surviving, sanitized Protocol, where the proposed genocide was totally disguised. (Given Heydrich's reputation for torture and murder in Czechoslovakia we might also wonder about Nazi use of the language in awarding him the title: 'Protector'.) When policeman Avner Less, Eichmann's interrogator in Jerusalem, read the Protocol of the Conference back to him, he had to keep asking Eichmann with increasing frustration about the language: 'What is he suggesting?', 'What does it mean?', 'What is meant?' 'What *does* it all mean?'[353]

The damage worked upon the inner recesses of the German language lived on long after the Nazi military machine had been defeated. Words like *system, battle, gas, concentration, special treatment, pneumonia, liquidate, organic, police action, storm, radical change, privilege, resettlement, relocation, homeland, living space, loyal, fanatic, pure, blood, soil, spontaneous, installation, problem, solution, turning point, will, eternal, cleanse, global, historical, international, exterminate, final* and *total*, among thousands of other words, could never be quite the same again. For example, just after the war German-Jewish philologist Professor Victor Klemperer wrote about Nazism and the word *heroic*:

> I have observed again and again how young people in all innocence, and despite a sincere effort to fill the gaps and eliminate errors in

353 M. Roseman, *The Villa, The Lake, The Meeting* (Penguin: Harmondsworth, 2003); D. Cesarani, *Eichmann: His Life and Crimes* (Vintage: London, 2005); J. von Lang & C. Sibyll (eds.), *Eichmann Interrogated: Transcripts from the Archives of the Israeli Police* (Bodley Head: London, 1982), pp.90-4. The record of the Wannsee meeting may have been doctored by Heydrich and Eichmann, but there have been two attempts to reconstruct it for film: *Die Wannsee-konferenz* (Komplet-Media: München/Grünwald, 1984); and *Conspiracy* (BBC/HBO, 2001). Both films were scripted to run for the exact length of the conference -- 90 minutes.

their neglected education, cling to Nazi thought processes. They don't realise they are doing it; the remnants of linguistic usage from the preceding epoch confuse and seduce them. We spoke about the meaning of culture, of humanitarianism, of democracy and I had the impression that they were beginning to see the light, and that certain things were being straightened out in their willing minds -- and then, it was always just round the corner, someone spoke of some heroic behaviour or other, or of some heroic resistance, or even simply of heroism *per se*. As soon as this concept was even touched upon, everything became blurred, and we were adrift once again in the fog of Nazism. And it wasn't only the young men who had just returned from the field or from captivity, and felt they were not receiving sufficient attention, let alone acclaim, no, even young women who had not seen any military service were thoroughly infatuated with the most dubious notion of heroism.[354]

But the Nazis have no monopoly in this. H. T. Nash, who worked in the US Defence Industry during the Vietnam War, wrote:

Beyond its usual function of facilitating communication, language in Defense, and in the intelligence community in general, helped to obscure the reality of what the work was all about -- to distract attention from the homicidal reality and give a brighter hue to the ominous. Presumably certain words and expressions 'took hold' because civil servants felt comfortable with them. Certain words helped link Defense work with familiar and positive experiences of each individual's past and thereby reinforce the innocuous quality of ongoing projects. Some examples of Defense language can help clarify these observations. Changing the name of the *War Department* to the *Defense Department, Strike Command* to *Readiness Command,* and the Air Force's use of the maxim *Peace is Our Profession* are examples of this. Impressions of the benign were strengthened by the careful construction of acronyms, such as PAL (Permissive Action Link), and electronically controlled DOD (Department of Defense) a system of interconnected locks used to prevent the unauthorised launching of an intercontinental ballistic missile ... As America's involvement in the Vietnam War

---

354 V. Klemperer, *The Language of the Third Reich,* (East Berlin 1946; Continuum: London 2006), p.2; V. Klemperer, *I Shall Bear Witness 1942-45* (Modern Library: London, 2001); V. Klemperer, *To The Bitter End: Diaries 1942-45* (Phoenix: London, 2000); J. W. Young, *Totalitarian Language* (University Press of Virginia: Charlottesville, 1991); M. Towson, *Mother-Tongue and Fatherland* (Manchester University Press: Manchester, 1992).

grew deeper, the Defense vocabulary expanded and displayed an even greater imaginative and anaesthetising flair. Bombing raids became surgical strikes and the forced movement and impounding of Vietnamese citizens were part of America's pacification program -- terms suggesting images of the hospital operating room or a Quaker meeting. The enemy was not killed, but, instead, was taken out, wasted, or blown away as a consequence of executive action or a protective reaction foray. A military ground offensive was termed aggressive defense and spraying an area with machine gun fire was nothing more than reconnaissance by fire ...[355]

Mrs Thatcher also left a linguistic legacy. She thought General Pinochet was a *democrat*, even though he destroyed a legitimately elected democratic government and was responsible for the death of several thousand political opponents. Her understanding of the word choice was similarly her own. Under her the *unemployed* became *job seekers* and *unemployment benefit* became a *job seeker's allowance*. After explaining to voters that 'There is no such thing as society: there is only the individual', Mrs Thatcher's 1984 plan to release patients from mental hospitals into the 'care of the community' simply meant that large numbers of mentally ill people were pushed out of institutions with no arrangements for care or treatment at all.

The playwright John McGrath listed massive shifts in the meaning of dozens of words around this time, including *radical, freedom, caring, community, enterprise, regionalisation, society, standards, devolution* and *aid*, all of which, he said, were brought, over the period of Mrs Thatcher's leadership, to mean the very opposite of what might at one time have been expected of them.[356] For example, Alan Clark, the Conservative historian and Government Minister under Mrs Thatcher, when faced with evidence that he had authorized illegal arms sales to Iraq, could not bring himself to admit that he had lied, but did admit he had been 'economical with the actualité'.

My point is that language in use, the content of words, reflects the totality of its environment. And in these days of *spin* we have words to worry about, too. As a result of 9/11 we have been involved in a

---

355 H. T. Nash, 'The Bureaucratisation of Homicide' in E. P. Thompson & D. Smith, (eds.), *Protest And Survive* (Penguin: Harmondsworth, 1980), pp.70-73.
356 J. McGrath, *Naked Thoughts That Roam About* (Nick Hern Books: London, 2002), pp.179-85.

decade-long 'War on Terror' and a part of this is a war against the *Axis of Evil*. This is a phrase which echoes the war against the Axis powers of Hitler, Mussolini and Hirohito, and it begs rather a lot of questions. Bush presented the war as a *crusade* to defend *civilization* against *dark forces*. As a result, an ill-defined *terror* has been combated in the name of a barely recognizable security, by a very depleted democracy and dubious business deals. Several words in our lexicon have undergone a shift in their meaning during this time. We now have: *targeted elimination* instead of *assassination; regime change* instead of *coup d'etat; liberation* instead of *invasion; reconstruction* instead of *occupation; asymmetrical conflict* instead of *state terrorism.*

As always one side's *freedom fighter, hero, martyr* is the other side's *guerrilla, insurgent, terrorist.* However, in Iraq we were told there was a struggle for *independence, dignity, sovereignty, democracy* and *freedom*, for which Britain and the USA were prepared to go to war. But these did not appear to be the same *independence, dignity, sovereignty, democracy* and *freedom* that Palestinians wanted and for which Britain and the USA are not prepared to go to war.

We now have *collateral damage*, which used to mean damage to property, but now means *civilian casualties*. Collateral means literally by the side, coincidental, but it also means, I was shocked to realize, spare, unimportant, expendable, not needed. In Iraq journalists became *embedded* in the military, and as a result instead of getting killed and maimed by the opposition, were killed and maimed by their allies: *smart bombs* it seems are not so smart and sometimes they even contradict themselves with *friendly fire*. Few British journalists in Iraq won commendations or awards for the independence of their reporting, but several were offered military medals for their embedded efforts.

These changes have to be seen in the general context of a political realignment resulting from the collapse of communism and a rapid shift in the balance of power which brings the radical fundamentalism of US Christianity directly into conflict not only with Muslim fundamentalists, but also with liberal secular values. Language itself is inevitably part of the collateral damage in this clash. With the phrase *New World Order* George Bush Snr drew upon one of Adolf Hitler's favourite phrases. The USA now has a *Department of Homeland Security*, which sounds as if it comes straight out of a Nazi phrase book. And it is disconcerting to realize that the phrase *Fortress Europe*, now used to describe the steady tightening of restrictions on entry to Europe, was first employed by the Nazis -- *Festung Europa* -- to mean a Europe saved from the barbarian hordes by the strong order-bringing power of military organization. Use of these words has already come dangerously close to the sense in which the Nazis employed them.[357] And given the questionable circumstances of G. W. Bush's election to office and his subsequent assault on liberal values and civil liberties in the US, his attempt to *export democracy* to Iraq forces us to wonder what, for Bush Jnr, the word 'democracy' might mean. But, in a war over *weapons of mass destruction* that could not be found, Prime Minister Blair's use of the words *totality* (a word the Nazis made frequent use of), *intelligence, believe, conscience* and *trust* all came to be closely scrutinized. It also is a world where political shifts purposely confuse the words *migrant, refugee* and *asylum seeker,* and where *asylum seeker* is often prefaced by the word *bogus* and the word *economic* is often placed before the word *migrant*.

War on an abstract noun ('Terror') was always going to be tricky. Even so, we have to remind ourselves repeatedly that words are not interchangeable: *occupation* is not *liberation; capitalism* is not *democracy; a beating* is not *abuse; kidnapping* is not *rendition; torture* is not *questioning by experts*. While it may be too early to pick this up in many stories and novels, over the course of the eight-year military occupation of Iraq I noticed articles and opinion pieces from writers as diverse as Dannie Abse, Julian Barnes, Jim Crace, Louis De Bernieres, Margaret Drabble, Antonia Fraser, Nadine Gordimer, David Guterson, David Hare, Thomas Keneally, Francis King, David Lodge, Ian McKewan, Sara Paretsky, Harold Pinter, Will Self, Alan Sillitoe, Studs Terkel, Paul Theroux and D. M. Thomas – some agreeing with the war in Iraq, others not, but all drawing attention to the effects of this war on how we used our language. John Le Carré, for example, wrote:

> With every day that passes in our contemporary world, the exercise of great power becomes a game of virtual reality, with terrible and deliberately under-reported consequences for the wretched of the earth. The vast bulk of western media is so corporatised as to be indistinguishable from the forces it purports to expose.

---

357 V. Klemperer, *The Language of the Third Reich,* (East Berlin 1946; Continuum: London 2006), pp.163, 164, 228.

Instead of telling us what they see and hear journalists in harness to competing armies of the entertainment industry have become torturers' accomplices, mouthing phrases like *collateral damage* when they mean civilians blown to bits, blotting out the screams and sweeping over the traces in their rush to present their nation's heroes in a pleasing light.[358]

For all writers the conscious creation of new work entails the choice of words, and that means dealing with two contradictory impulses. The first is the temptation to use words as they are given, to set down only words which are current, which do not cause problems, which can be easily absorbed, which do not challenge. This is, I think, to see the writer merely as part of the entertainment industry and to accept the idea that the writer can make no meaningful intervention in the world. The second, opposite impulse, is to seek out and make use of words to probe meaning, to make it obvious how words change, are changed, are compromised in daily use, to reveal what is often hidden in words. A writer must always choose between these two possibilities, must always choose between 'servility and insolence'.[359] For a writer to say what they hear, to record what is happening to words, to struggle to represent things accurately in writing, to be an *earwitness*, will always be characterized as an act of treachery, sedition, opposition or aggression by those who do not want these things represented in words, observed, recorded or dragged to light. Writers often see their work as a struggle to understand what is happening to words, to reveal some of the hidden possibilities. My way of thinking about words is the mantra:

Writing tells us what is happening to words
Words tell us what is happening to feelings
Feelings tell us what is happening to people

---

358 . Le Carré, 'Service on the Front Line', *The Guardian* (11 October 2003), pp.34-35.
359 S. Sontag, 'The Aesthetics of Silence' (1967) in *A Susan Sontag Reader* (Penguin: Harmondsworth, 1982), p.190.

Directed Study

In what way is the world of politics linked to the theme of
Representation?

Alexander Solzhenitsyn once remarked that writers are
like an alternative government – particularly threatening to
repressive and authoritarian regimes. What do you think?

What, if any, are your obligations as a citizen and as a writer
to the state? What can the state legitimately require of you as
a writer? What would you consider was sufficient cause for
civil disobedience? For a writer is it ever a case of 'my country
right or wrong'?

Are there times when it is wiser for a writer to keep quiet, or
do you think writers must always speak up? What would you
sign a petition for? What would you actively campaign for?

Do issues like exploitation, colonialism, pollution and global
warming take precedence over a writer's other loyalties? If so
why?

In what ways does language show how we think? Does it
matter if politicians mangle the language? Do you think
writers are somehow opposed to politicians? In what ways?

Orwell in his essay 'Politics and the English Language (1946)
said he thought the English language was 'diseased'. Do you
agree? If so, why and in what ways, and what can you do
about it?

George Orwell thought of writers as natural 'anti-totalitarians'. Do you feel this is a reasonable attitude for all writers? Are honesty and integrity part of a writer's work? Should writers bother themselves with these things? Why? In what way? Do you feel the description of 'anti-totalitarian' fits you and your work in any way or on any level?

Consider your own style. Is there anything in this chapter that might apply to the way you write? In what ways do you think this chapter might link to the development of *your* writing style?

11
KEY ISSUES

I said at the start of this book that it has never been possible to 'just write' because there is much more to writing than simply putting words on paper. I hope by now that I have made my point, or at least managed to describe my own thoughts and feelings on the subject and my own struggle to get to grips with this thing, this bizarre activity, we call 'writing'.

On one level this is a fairly straightforward academic monograph, a teaching text: on another it represents my own puzzlement about writing, my attempts to answer the questions I have about it, about my writing and me writing, my efforts to sketch in the connection of writing to the world, and my struggle to make my thoughts accessible in writing. I have questioned writing as a university teacher, as a practising writer and as a citizen. Perhaps this is the moment to focus on some of the key issues of the book and restate some of those questions:

- In what way is the study of writing an intellectual preparation for anything at all, let alone for public life?
- How is the idea of representation in writing connected to citizenship?
- In what way is writing the original subject of study?
- Writing imitates something, but what?
- Why can't we 'just write'?
- What does it mean to say: 'For writers language is raw creative material'?
- What is 'the intimate connection between how an individual sees the world and then puts their perceptions into writing'?
- How is representation connected to the idea of the alphabet and writing?
- How is writing connected to the idea of a university?

WRITING THE WORLD

By now I think it is possible to see that these apparently innocent, perhaps even 'academic', questions actually have quite demanding and complex possibilities within them for the writer... So let's see about pursuing some answers:

Knowledge
Can you list some of things you have learned about writing and representation?
Can you list the different ways in which you now see the act of writing?
What do you think writers do?
How does your thinking differ now from how you thought before you started to consider this topic?
What do you think writing can accurately depict?
In what ways are your feelings about writing different now?
*

Comprehension
Can you discuss how these things have affected your thinking about writing?
Can you give an example of how your thinking has changed?
Can you think of a book or a writer whose work illustrates the kind of point you want to make about how you see writing?
Can you think of a book or a writer who has had a positive influence on you and say how they influenced you?
Can you give an example where a writer's sense of language has shaped how you see an event or has changed the way you understand the world?
What do you think about the act of writing now?
*

Application
What effect do you think this topic has had on your development as a writer?
Why and how does this particular   example affect the way you think about writing and the way you write now?
Can you discuss a particular writer or book that had a positive influence on you?
Can you think of a writer or book that did the opposite?
Can you describe your feelings about how this topic has changed your thinking about the way you write?
What themes do you need to tackle at the moment and in what ways has this topic changed the ways you might approach them?
*

Analysis
What do you think it means, to be a writer?
How does this example compare with the work of any other writer you know?
What are the things you most admire about this writer as a person and as a writer?
What is it that you least admire about this book or writer?
Can you say how your sense of yourself as a writer has changed?
What is the most significant change in your thinking as a result of this topic?
*

Conclusion
What makes a person want to write -- what makes you want to write?
Can anybody write or do writers have a particular relationship to words and language?
Do you think it is possible to say what it is that writers do when they write, or what readers are looking for when they read?
What themes interest you as a writer and how have they been affected by the topic of representation in writing?
What, as a writer, would you say is your responsibility to writing and representation in the future?
Can you imagine how any change in your thinking on this topic might affect your writing over the next few years?

12
TIMESCALE

This timescale locates the development of speech and the technology of writing in human history, and links them to other significant developments. It concentrates on Europe, the Mediterranean and the Middle East. The timescale is tentative and many of the dates are approximate or conjectural.

13,700,000,000,000BC	Astronomers using the Hubble telescope suggest this is when the Universe was born in the 'Big Bang'
500,000,000,000BC	Geologists suggest planet Earth was formed around this time
70,000,000BC	The Sea of Tethys, between Europe and the gigantic continent of Gondwana (Africa and Arabia), begins to narrow
47,000,000BC	The earliest fossil primates appear
45,000,000BC	The continental plate of Africa (with Arabia still attached) begins to impact on the continental plate of Europe; where the African plate is forced under the European plate, the Alps and the Mediterranean islands begin to form
23,000,000BC	*Dryopithecines* (early apes) appear in East Africa, India, Turkey, the Balkans, Hungary and the Far East

20-15,000,000BC	The eastern end of the sea of Tethys is closed off by a collision between Gondwana (Africa and Arabia) and Eurasia; at about the same time the north western coast of Africa comes into contact with the southern tip of Spain, forming the Mediterranean
7,000,000BC	Ape and human lines of descent separate. *Sahalanthropus Tchadensis*, earliest ape-human ancestor, discovered in Chad
6,000,000BC	In Kenya *Ororin Tugenensis*, possible human ancestor, abandons trees
3,200,000BC	Some apes start walking upright
1,800,000BC	*Homo erectus*, the first upright ape, about 1 meter tall, appears: probably used basic words and gestures, the first meat-eating ape appears
1,500,000BC	*Homo-erectus* loses body hair
524-478,000BC	*Homo erectus* begins to migrate and settle in the Caucasus, Orce and Atapuerca in Spain, Isernia in Italy, Ubeidya in Israel, Dmansi in Georgia, Schoningen, Steinheim, Miesenheim and Mauer in Germany, Boxgrove, Clacton and Swanscombe in Britain, also in Romania, Sicily, Spain, Greece and Hungary
265,000BC	End of the Günz Glaciation, start of an interglacial warm period
c. **255,000BC**	**Start of the Early Stone Age**
230-30,000BC	In Europe *Homo erectus* evolves into *Homo sapiens neanderthalensis*
200,000BC	End of the interglacial, start of the Mindel Glaciation: in East Africa a new and different version of *Homo sapiens* emerges -- *Homo sapiens sapiens* and begins to migrate northwards

175,000BC	End of the Mindel Glaciation, start of an interglacial warm period
160,000BC	*Homo sapiens sapiens* living in Morocco and Ethiopia
130,000BC	End of interglacial, start of Riss Glaciation
100,000BC	End of Riss Glaciation, start of a warm interglacial period
70,000BC	The signs of Neanderthal habitation appear at Creswell Crags (north of Derby) -- this is the earliest trace of humans in what was to become the UK
65,000BC	End of interglacial period, start of Würm Glaciation
50-30,000BC	A thaw in the Würm Glaciation
39-37,000BC	*Homo sapiens sapiens* migrates towards Europe during interglacial period
32-29,000BC	*Homo sapiens sapiens* migrates into Europe via Arabia, the Caucasus, Anatolia and the Ukraine during the second interglacial period: cave art and engraved bones begin to appear in settlements in France and Spain; the new settlers are called *Cro-Magnon*, after the village in France where their remains were first discovered
30,000BC	Warm period ends and Würm Glaciation resumes, wild barley harvested in Syria, Palestine and Mesopotamia
29,000BC	'Red Lady' of Paviland -- the first modern human to be found in Britain -- is buried on the Gower Peninsula in South Wales
22,000BC	Würm Glaciation starts to thaw, glaciers begin to retreat

16-12,500BC	The dry tundra stretching across Britain, Ireland, the North Sea, Holland, Belgium, German and northern Poland begins to transform into rich grasslands supporting large animals, while most of southern Europe -- the Iberian Peninsula, France, Italy and the Balkans -- becomes an open woodland mainly of conifers
13-10,000BC	Cave decorations are made at Creswell Crags; transition from Neanderthal to Cro-Magnon occupation begins; in the Fertile Crescent sheep are domesticated, barley and wheat are cultivated
9700-8000BC	The end of the Würm Glaciation: glaciers retreat, sea levels rise filling the Mediterranean: settlers arrive in Ireland via a land-bridge from Scotland. Farming spreads to the Balkans. Total human population of Britain estimated at 1000-3000[1]
8000-6000BC	Signs, seals and clay tokens used for accounting appear in Middle East
8500-7650BC	Early pits and wooden structures begin to appear near the site that will eventually become Stonehenge
7000-3000BC	Early *Indo-European* settlers appear on the Eurasian steppe, in the Ukraine, Anatolia and the northern Caspian; total human population of Britain estimated at 2500-5000[2]
6800BC	**End of the Early Stone Age, start of the Late Stone Age**

[1] C. Smith, *Late Stone Age Hunters of the British Isles* (Taylor & Frances: London, 1992); F. Pryor, *Britain BC* (Harper: London, 2004), pp.32, 37, 158-60, 413-4.
[2] *Ibid.*

7500-6000BC	After a brief period of intense cold the climate suddenly warms again and the glaciers retreat quickly. Rising water from melting glaciers affects the Mediterranean and causes sea-water to break through the land-bridge at the Bosporus: flooding at about 50 cubic km per day begins to form the Black Sea. The grasslands of northern Europe are slowly replaced by woodland spreading northwards
6500-5200BC	Earliest European farming sites in Turkey, Greece, Cyprus and Crete; farming reaches Britain; rising sea levels cut off Ireland and Britain from the continent
6300-6000BC	Evidence of forest clearance at Shippey Hill in Cambridge and Broome Hill in Norfolk, and in Northumberland, and of substantial settlement at Skara Brae in Orkney
c. 5000BC	Ireland and Britain become separated from each other by the rising sea levels
5000-3000BC	Written plaque at Gradesnica in Bulgaria and three pictographs on clay tablets from Turdas near Cluj in Romania
5000BC	Sumerians begin to develop cuneiform; total human population of Britain estimated at 2750-5500[*1]
5000-2500BC	Indo-European language begins to break up into dialects
5200-4000BC	Farming sites in the Balkans, Danube Basin, Germany, Hungary, Romania, Italy, France, Britain and Austria

---

[*1] C. Smith, *Late Stone Age Hunters of the British Isles* (Taylor & Frances: London, 1992); F. Pryor, *Britain BC* (Harper: London, 2004), pp.32, 37, 158-60, 413-4.

4050BC	The archaeological record begins to differ significantly from earlier cultures: farming and settled development begin to spread into the British Isles: connected to this megaliths, stone circles, stone burial chambers appear in Portugal, Brittany, Denmark, Ireland, Wales and England
4000BC	At Dereivka, south of Kiev on the river Dniepr, domestication of the horse; in Romania and Bulgaria a kind of writing -- conventional signs -- on tablets and seals
c. 3700BC	Massive defensive earthworks are built throughout Britain
3500–3200BC	Mesopotamian cuneiform begins to develop.
3000BC	New Stone Age peoples build passage graves at Dowth, Knowth and Newgrange in Ireland
3100BC	In the towns of Ugarit, and Byblos in Lebanon, in Palestine and the Sinai peninsula a simplified system of <u>twenty-four</u> signs begins to emerge from hieroglyphs
c. **3000BC**	**End of the Stone Age, start of the Bronze Age**
c. 3000–2400BC	Egyptian hieroglyphics. Indus Valley script
2950BC	First phase of construction begins at Stonehenge
2870BC	First settlements at Troy
2800BC	Minoans settle on Crete: development of Linear A script
2500BC	Second phase of construction at Stonehenge; Indus valley civilization flourishes
2400–1600BC	Third (final) phase of construction at Stonehenge
c. 2200BC	The Sumerian *Epic of Gilgamesh* is composed orally

2000–1600BC	Construction of Arbor Low 'the Stonehenge of the North' in Derbyshire
2000–1000BC	Indo-Europeans in the Caspian and Ukraine displaced by the arrival of another people (probably Turkic) from Asia, and are pushed into Romania, the Balkans, along the Mediterranean shores and south into Anatolia. The first Greek settlements appear in Greece and Anatolia: this is the start of Mycenaean Greek history
c. 2000–1650BC	Ancient Cretan hieroglyphs
2000BC	Alphabet begins to develop in Mesopotamia with local variations in Iran, Iraq, Syria, Palestine and Lebanon: the Phoenician alphabet emerges in twenty-two wedge-shaped signs made in clay, discovered at Ugarit
1860–1500BC	Phaistos Disc is made in Cyprus; standing stones of Stonehenge are erected
1800–80BC	The early alphabet spreads to Phoenician settlements and colonies around the Mediterranean, and then to Greece, where it is adapted to Greek language needs
1792–1750BC	There is an attempt to produce a standardized version of the Sumerian *Gilgamesh*
c. 1750–1450BC	Minoan Linear A script developed on Crete. Aryans arrive in Pakistan and India
1625–1500BC	The volcano island of Thera (Santorini) erupts, a massive tidal wave hits the northern coast of Crete, starting the decline of Minoan civilization, also causing poor harvests throughout Europe for several years
c. 1500–1200BC	Mycenean Greek Linear B script developed. The oral hymns of the *Rigveda* composed. Chinese script develops

1450BC	Mycenaean Greeks begin to settle on Crete, replacing Minoan culture and replacing Linear A script with their own Linear B script
1400–1000BC	A Babylonian version of *Gilgamesh* develops
1333–1323	Lifetime of Tutankhamen
1250BC	Destruction of Troy
1230BC	Exodus of Israelites from Egypt and start of '40 years in the wilderness'
c. **1200BC**	**End of the Bronze Age, Start of the Iron Age**
1159–20BC	The eruption of the Icelandic volcano Hekla III causes climatic changes in Europe, which in turn cause huge population shifts across Europe, particularly southwards through the Danube into the Balkan region. As a result Dorian Greeks push into the Balkans from the north, displacing Mycenaean Greeks towards the east coast and Ionian Islands -- Mycenaean Greek culture appears to collapse or to at least starts a 'Dark Age': at the same time the empire of the Hittites in Anatolia is displaced south into Syria and Canaan and then pushed further south to clash with the Egyptians, who call the various invaders of this period -- Hittites and others from Europe, the north and peoples from Asia -- 'The Sea People'. Rameses III eventually defeats the Sea People, but not before all the old empires and the map of the ancient world have been changed completely
1000BC	*The Song of Songs, Proverbs* and *Ecclesiastes* are thought to date from oral compositions around this time
960BC	Solomon builds temple in Jerusalem
800BC	Phoenicians found city of Cadiz
776BC	First Olympic games

950-750BC	Greek culture begins to emerge from the 'Dark Age'; Phoenician alphabet adopted and adapted in Greece
750BC	Phoenicians found city of Carthage; the earliest examples of the new Greek alphabet appear scratched on vases and painted onto clay plaques
753BC	City of Rome founded
669–627BC	*Gilgamesh*, composed orally *c.* 2200BC, is written down in a standardised version in Assyria during the reign of King Assurbanipal
600-500BC	Celts begin to arrive in Britain and Ireland from the continent; Greeks found city of Marseilles
605BC	Rise of Babylonian power: first wave of Jewish deportation to Babylon
597BC	Nebuchadnezzar of Babylon besieges and conquers Jerusalem, second wave of deportation to Babylon from Judah
586BC	Babylonians destroy the Jerusalem temple and town walls and in the third wave of exile, send Jewish priests, military leaders, craftsmen and metal workers to Babylon; *Book of Lamentations* developed during exile in Babylon
c. 740-550BC	Oral compositions *The Iliad* and *The Odyssey*, both referring to Mycenaean Greece of *c.* 1250BC, are set down in writing.
539BC	Cyrus, Persian conqueror of Babylon, allows Jews to return to Jerusalem: collection of early Hebrew texts begins
509BC	Foundation of Roman Republic

445BC	Herodotus reads his *History* to the Council of Athens
400BC	Ireland invaded again by tribes moving up from Spain; barbarians begin to settle in France, Germany, Austria, Hungary, Czechoslovakia, Romania, Yugoslavia and Italy
390BC	Celtic tribes invade Rome
350BC	Celtic tribes begin to invade Ireland and settle, displacing earlier inhabitants
340BC	Aristotle's *Ethics*
246BC	Start of the Roman Empire
214BC	Great Wall of China built
206BC	Romans conquer Spain
180BC	In Alexandria Aristarchus edits the works of Homer
149BC	Rome destroyed Carthage
120BC	Rome begins conquest of the Celts in Gaul
c. 100BC	Gaels arrive in Ireland from the area of modern France and Belgium
65–49BC	Caesar invades and conquers Celtic Gaul
55–7BC	The first Roman invasion of Britain
42BC	Rhodes School of Rhetoric destroyed by Romans
31BC	Octavian becomes first Roman Emperor and takes the name Caesar Augustus
6–4BC	Birth of Jesus Christ
c. **AD 1**	**End of the Iron Age, start of the Modern Era**
43	Second Roman invasion of Britain, starting at Richborough, Kent
60	Romans invade Anglesey and massacre the Druids and the local inhabitants

70	Roman Emperor Vespasian's troops put down a Jewish rebellion in Palestine, set fire to the Jewish temple and demolish Jerusalem
c. 75–100	Last known use of cuneiform
378	Germanic Visigoths defeat the Roman Armies
406	Barbarian hordes -- a tribal confederation of Germanic Suevi, Vandals and Alans -- the cross the frozen river Rhine
409	Rome begins to withdraw troops from Britain to defend itself
410	Barbarian Visigoths under Alaric sack Rome and then move on to settle in Aquitaine; Rome withdraws its last troops from Britain; the 'Dark Ages' start
475	Romulus Augustus the last Roman Emperor is deposed by the barbarian leader Odoacer -- thus ending the Western Roman Empire
480–500	Slav tribes expand westwards from the Ukraine reaching Denmark, Germany, Italy and Yugoslavia; Germanic Alans, Vandals, Suevi, Alemans, Franks and Ostrogoths invade Italy and set up barbarian states on former Roman territory.
c. 503	The 'last battle' between Romano-Welsh King Arthur and Germanic invaders from Continental Europe
597	Pope Maurice sends Augustine to preach Christianity to the English; he lands in Kent
c. 600	Welsh and Irish texts based on earlier oral compositions begin to appear: Irish monks introduce spaces between words in manuscripts, but this is not adopted elsewhere until the twelfth century

610–632	Prophet Mohammed experiences visions
632-52	Verses of the Koran written down and collected
731	The Venerable Bede writes *Ecclesiastical History of the English People*
c. 775	Offa's Dyke constructed to contain the Welsh
793-5	First recorded Viking attack on Britain at Lindisfarne; first recorded Viking attack on Ireland at Lambay, near Dublin
829/30	The earliest written references to King Arthur in Welsh
870-78	Monks abandon Lindisfarne: Great Danish Army arrives in England -- English army overwhelmed
c. 1000	*Beowulf*, composed orally c. 793, becomes a written text; the *Lebor Gabála Érenn* (Book of Invasions of Ireland) is written down based on much earlier oral traditions
1014	Vikings defeated at the battle of Clontarf by forces of Brian Boru
c. 1150	Moors, informed of the paper-making process by Chinese prisoners taken in Samarkand, set up a paper mill in Spain
1066-70	Normans invade Britain. Viking raids continue
1086	Normans compile the *Domesday Book* of valuable property and land, showing a population of about 4,000,000 in England[1]
c. 1138	Geoffrey of Monmouth writes his *History of the Kings of Britain*
1100-75	Irish *Táin Bó Cualnge* (Cattle Raid at Cooley) based on earlier oral compositions, is written down

[1] F. Pryor, *Britain BC* (Harper: London, 2004), p.414.

1228	Welsh Prince Llewelyn ap Gruffudd killed: Edward I conquers Wales
1250	Llyfr Du Caerfyrddin (Black Book of Carmarthen) is compiled containing some of the earliest Welsh language poetry composed in the ninth and tenth centuries
c. 1300	The hymns of the *Rigveda*, based on earlier oral compositions, are written down. Papermaking process spreads into France, Italy and Germany
1300–1325	Welsh *Llyfr Gwyn Rhydderch* (White Book of Rhydderch) compiled
1375–1425	Welsh *Llyfr Coch Hergest* (The Red Book of Hergest) compiled
c. 1386	Geoffrey Chaucer begins to write *The Canterbury Tales*
1450–55	Johannes Gutenberg perfects movable type for printing and publishes the Gutenberg Bible
1476	William Caxton sets up the first movable type printing press in Westminster, London and publishes Chaucer's *Canterbury Tales*
1495	Paper produced in England
1526	William Tyndale's translation of *The New Testament* into English
1564	Birth of William Shakespeare
1604	Richard Cawdrey publishes *A Table Alphabeticall* -- the first dictionary of the English language
1755	Samuel Johnson's *Dictionary* published
1813	Thomas Young identifies an Indo-European language group

1822	The 'Red lady of Paviland' (the first Cro-Magnon fossil) is discovered
1829	The first typewriter is invented by William Austin Burt
1835–51	Henry Rawlinson begins to translate cuneiform texts
1856	First discovery of Neanderthal human remains in a cave above the river Dussel near Wuppertal, Germany
1868	The typewriter is manufactured by a US engineer called Christopher Latham Sholes, and put into factory production in 1873 by the Remington Arms Company
1870–1900	Heinrich Schliemann excavates Mycenae, Tiryns and Hissarlik (Troy). Sir Harold Evans excavates Knossos on Crete
1900	The first Nobel Prize for Literature is awarded to French writer Sully Prudhomme
1928	The first *Oxford English Dictionary on Historical Principles* is published
1930	Milman Parry proposes a theory of oral composition for Homer's poems
1966	ISBN numbers are introduced in the UK
1970	Archaeologist Marija Gimbutas identifies the 'kurgan culture' of the Ukraine as the earliest evidence of the people who were to become the Indo-Europeans. The first commercial electric typewriters become available
1971	Launch of Project Gutenberg, the first digital library
1982	The first home computers become commercially available

2004	Cave drawings and decorations dating from *c.* 13,000 BC are found at Creswell Crags, near Derby, along with evidence of both Neanderthal and Cro-Magnon settlement
2006	Launch of the Sony E-book Reader in USA, the following year Amazon launches the Kindle with a wireless internet connection, followed in 2012 by the Kindle Fire.

13
FURTHER READING

Almost all new writing starts with reading and proceeds by further reading. That is also the case with thinking about writing. Items marked with an asterisk * can be found on The Guardian Online Archive.

General background on representation

J. Berger, *Ways of Seeing*

E. H. Carr, *What is History?*

M. Gray, *A Dictionary of Literary Terms*

E. Hobsbawm & T. Ranger (eds.), *The Invention of Tradition*

G. Hoskins & G. Schopflin (eds.), *Myths & Nationhood*

Representation theory and history

Aristotle, *Poetics*

E. Auerbach, *Mimesis: The Representation of Reality in Western Literature*

R. Barthes, *Elements of Semiology*

C. J. Brodsky, *The Imposition of Form: Studies in Narrative Representation and Knowledge*

J. B. Carrol (ed.), *Language, Thought and Reality: Selected Writings of Benjamin Lee Whorf*

C. Caudwell, *Illusion and Reality*

J. Derrida, *Of Grammatology*

J. Goody & I. Watt, 'The Consequences of Literacy' in: P. P. Giglioli, *Language in Social Context*

P. de Mann, *Aesthetic Ideology*

M. Krieger, (ed.), *The Aims of Representation: Subject, Text, History*

Plato, *The Republic*

M. Potolsky, *Mimesis*

R. Williams, *The Long Revolution*

L. Wittgenstein, *Philosophical Remarks*

www.wikipedia.org/wiki/Representation_(arts)

Representation, misrepresentation and fraud

M. Atwood, *Strange Things: The Malevolent North in Canadian Literature*

B. Eskan, *A Life in Pieces: the Making and Unmaking of Wilkomirski*

T. Borowski, *This Way for Gas, Ladies and Gentlemen Please*

P. Carey, *My Life as a Fake*

R. Ealestone, *Postmodernism and Holocaust Denial*

K. L. Feder, Frauds, *Myths and Mysteries: Science & Pseudoscience in Archaeology*

Grey Owl, *Three Complete Works*

D. D. Gottenplan, *The Holocaust on Trial*

N. Groom, *The Forger's Shadow: How Forgery Changed the Course of Literature*

M. Haywood, *The Ern Malley Affair*

M. Katsoulis, *Telling Tales: A History of Literary Hoaxes*

E. Lappin, 'The Man with Two Heads', *Granta* no.66

P. Levi, *The Drowned & The Saved*

P. Levi, *If this is a Man*

P. Levi, *The Periodic Table*

D. Lipstadt, *Denying the Holocaust*

S. Maechler, *The Wilkomirski Affair: A Study in Biographical Truth*

Penguin Books, *The Irving Judgement*

B. Schlink, *The Reader*

E. von Alpen, *Caught by History: Holocaust Effects in Contemporary Art, Literature and Theory*

B. Wilkomirski, *Fragments: Memoirs of a Childhood 1939-48*

*Terry Eagleton, 'Faking it: the Art of Literary Forgery', *The Guardian*, 6 June 2002

*Rachel Cusk, 'Author, Author', *The Guardian* (30 January 2010)

*I. Gassert, 'The Brothers of Invention', *The Observer*, 14 April 2002

*Fiachra Gibbons & Stephen Moss, 'Fragments of Fraud', *The Guardian*, 15 October 1999

*Anna Karpf, 'Child of the Shoah', *The Guardian*, 11 Feb 1998

*H. Lane, 'Two Funerals and a Book Deal', *The Observer*, 13 Dec 2000

*Robert McCrum, 'The World of Books', *The Observer*, 16 Jan 2001

*J. Mullan, 'A Short History of Literary Hoaxes', *The Guardian*, 6 September 2003

*A. Munslow, 'Facts to Fight Over', *The Guardian*, 6 Feb 2001

Representation and English

M. Bragg, *The Adventure of English 500AD to 2000*

B. Bryson, *Mother Tongue: The English Language*

G. Chantrell (ed.), *The Oxford Dictionary of Word Histories*

D. Crystal, *The Stories of English*

D. Crystal, *The Cambridge Encyclopaedia of the English Language*

W. R. O'Donnell & L.Todd, *Variety in Contemporary English*

B. Foster, *The Changing English Language*

E. Partridge, *Origins: A Short Etymological Dictionary of Modern English*

S. Potter, *Our Language*

The Oxford Dictionary of Word Histories

R. Williams, *Keywords*

J. Willinsky, *Empire of Words: The Reign of the OED*

www.oed.com The Oxford English Dictionary website – good for word histories.

Representation and language

J. Ayto, *Dictionary of Word Origins*

L. Bauer & P. Trudgill (eds.), *Language Myths*

A. Burgess, *Language Made Plain*

J. Butterfield, *Damp Squid: The English Language Laid Bare*

W. Empson, *Seven Types of Ambiguity*

J. Green (ed.), *Cassell Dictionary of Slang*

E. Gowers, *The Complete Plain Words*

G. Hughes, *Swearing*

J. MacDonald, *Dictionary of Obscenity & Taboo*

E. Partridge, *Dictionary of Slang and Unconventional English*

L. Todd, *Pidgins and Creoles*

www.netlIngo.com A website devoted to new words and phrases.

Representation and the human mind

E. W. Barber, *The Mummies of Ürümchi*

G. Bibby, *Four Thousand Years Ago*

J. Bronowski, *The Ascent of Man*

B. Comrie (ed.), *The Major Languages of Eastern Europe*

G. Deutscher, *The Unfolding of Language*

G. Deutscher, *Through the Language Glass: How Words Colour Your World*

S. R. Fischer, *A History of Language*

C. Gosden, *Prehistory: A Very Short Introduction*

S. S. Hall, 'The Other Humans: Neanderthals Revealed', *National Geographic* (October 2008), pp.36-59.

J. Jaynes, *The Origin of Consciousness in the Breakdown of the Bicameral Mind*

A. Karpf, *The Human Voice: The Story of a Remarkable Talent*

P. Lieberman, *On the Origins of Language: An Introduction to the Evolution of Human Speech*

D. Lewis-Williams & D. Pearce, *Inside the Neolithic Mind*

J. P. Mallory, *In Search of the Indo-Europeans*

S. Mithen, *The Prehistory of the Mind*

S. Oppenheimer, *The Origins of the British*

N. Ostler, *Empires of the Word: A Language History of the World*

S. Pinker, *The Language Instinct: The New Science of Language and Mind*

C. Renfrew, *Archaeology and Language: The Puzzle of Indo-European Origins*

C. Renfrew, *Prehistory: The Making of the Human Mind*

D. Spender, *Man Made Language*

B. Wood, *Human Evolution: A Very Short Introduction*

www.handprint.com/LS/ANC.

This website was designed for younger students, but it is still very useful.
www.mnh.si.edu/anthro/humanorigins.

Smithsonian Institute Human Origins Programme
www.gsu.edu/~wwwlrc/biograpies/kanzi.

This website is about the Bonobo chimp called Kanzi and her daughter, Panbanisha, and their understanding of language
www.unfoldingoflanguage.com.

A valuable series of web links to online articles on related subjects

www.becominghuman.org.
Arizona State University Institute of Human Origins
www.talkorigins.org
A summary of major fossil discoveries
www.ucm.es/paleo/ata/portada.
Details of discoveries at Atapuerca in Spain
www.neanderthal.de.
A German site with details of discoveries near Düsseldorf
www.bbc.co.uk/radio4/history/inourtime.
Melvyn Bragg's 'Human Origins', from the series In Our Time.
(16 February 2006)
www.bbc.co.uk/ahistoryoftheworld/objects/early writing tablet.
A chance to learn about early writing in Mesopotamia.
www.bbc.co.uk/ahistoryoftheworld/objects/flood tablet.
A look at one of the earliest examples of literature in the world –
a Mesopotamian tablet detailing a pre-Biblical version of 'The Flood'

A. Roberts & G. McGavin, Prehistoric Autopsy: Neanderthal, BBC2 22 October 2012. Available on Catch-up TV, also available on:
www.bbc.co.uk/programmes/p00xfdmw and
www.tv-links.eu/tv-shows/Prehistoric-Autopsy_33187/.

Cave art and writing

N. Aujoulat, *The Splendour of Lascaux*
P. G. Bahn, *Journey Through the Ice Age*
S. Cole, *The Prehistory of East Africa*
J. Cook, *Ice Age Art: Arrival of the Modern Mind*
A. Lamming, *Lascaux: Paintings and Engravings*
C. B. M. McBurney, *The Stone Age of Northern Africa*
P. A. Saura Ramos, *The Cave of Altamira*

Representation and the alphabet

J. Chadwick, *The Decipherment of Linear B*

J. Drucker, *The Alphabetic Labyrinth*

S. R. Fischer, *A History of Writing*

D. Harden, *The Phoenicians* (particularly Chapter 8)

R. Harris, *The Origin of Writing* (particularly chapter 4)

J. F. Healey, *Reading the Past: Early Alphabets*

G. Jean, Writing: *The Story of Alphabets and Scripts*

A. Robinson, *Lost Languages*

A. Robinson, *The Story of Writing*

A. Robinson, *Writing and Script: A Very Short Introduction*

D. Sachs, *The Alphabet*

www.bbc.co.uk/radio4/history/inourtime
Melvyn Bragg's 'The Alphabet' from the series In Our Time
(first broadcast 18 December 2003). Available as a podcast.

www.bbc.co.uk/local and www.bbc.co.uk/ahistoryoftheworld.
Several examples of ancient writing can be found as part of the BBC
/ British Museum series A History of the World in 100 Objects. This
project can be accessed at and images can be uploaded at these two
websites. Available as a podcast.

www.bbc.co.uk/programmes/writtenworld
Melvyn Bragg's five-part radio series on the development of
writing and the technology of writing through the ages; the podcast
archive also contains substantial visual material to accompany the
discussion. Available as a podcast.

Representation and the transition from oral to written culture

Beowulf
The Bible
The Koran
Homer, *The Iliad*
Homer, *The Odyssey*
Julius Caesar, *The Conquest of Gaul*
Rig Veda
Tacitus, *Germania*
Táin Bó Cúalnge (The Táin)
The Mabinogion
The Epic of Gilgamesh

M. Cook, *The Koran: A Very Short Introduction*
J. M. Foley, *How to Read an Oral Poem*
T. H. Lim, *The Dead Sea Scrolls: A Very Short Introduction*
A. B. Lord, *The Singer of Tales* (This book comes with a CD of musical and visual clips)
M. McLuhan, *The Medium is the Massage: An Inventory of Effects,*
W. J. Ong, *Orality and Literacy*
J. Riches, The Bible: A Very Short Introduction

www.bbc.co.uk/radio4/history/inourtime.
   Melvyn Bragg's radio programme In Our Time on 'The Odyssey'.
   First broadcast on 9 September 2004. Available as a podcast.

www.bbc.co.uk/radio4/history/inourtime.
   Melvyn Bragg's radio programme In Our Time on 'The Druids'.
   First broadcast on 20 September 2012. Available as a podcast.

Representation and the literary canon
H. Bloom, *The Western Canon*

INDEX

Lightning Source UK Ltd.
Milton Keynes UK
UKOW04f1522180714

235355UK00001B/1/P